The Business of Theatrical DESIGN

James L. Moody ASLD

ALLWORTH PRESS
NEW YORK

07 06 05 04 03 02   5 4 3 2 1

Published by Allworth Press
An imprint of Allworth Communications, Inc.
10 East 23rd Street, New York, NY 10010

Cover and interior design by Mary Belibasakis
Cover photograph by James L. Moody

Page composition/typography by Rachel Reiss

ISBN: 1-58115-248-5

Library of Congress Cataloging-in-Publication Data

Moody, James L.
The business of theatrical design / by James L. Moody.
p. cm.
Includes bibliographical references and index.
ISBN 1-58115-248-5
1. Theaters—Stage-setting and scenery—Vocational guidance—United
States. 2. Costume—Vocational guidance—United States. 3. Stage
lighting—Vocational guidance—United States. 4. Performing
arts—Accounting. 5. Performing arts—Finance. I. Title.

PN2086 .M66 2002
792'.025'023—dc21
2002013999

Printed in Canada

ACKNOWLEDGMENTS

The author wishes to thank the following organizations and people for the use of selected materials in the cover photograph: The Great American Market, Joseph Tawil, president; The Sacramento Theatre Company, Peggy Shannon, artistic director; United Scenic Artists Local USA-829, Beverly Miller, president; and Mr. Robert Frye, scenic artist.

For the support and encouragement of so many of my colleagues, thank you. A special thanks to Dawn Hollingsworth, managing partner of Visual Terrain Inc., who, armed with her Pepperdine M.B.A. degree, has greatly enhanced the growth, efficiency, and profitability of the firm with fiscal responsibility. To my other partners, Jeff Ravitz and Lisa Passamonte-Green, for their contributions and support. To the staff, particularly Jeremy Windle, who has had the misfortune to be around to help me with two books, and Matt Levesque and Erin Powell, who read the early manuscripts and made invaluable comments. Also, I must thank Francis Mempin, our office manager and computer guy, who tries to keep me out of computer hell!

Outside of the firm, Paul Dexter, Mike Zinman, Charles Berliner, Liz Stillwell, D. Martyn Bookwalter, and Craig Wolf all provided thoughtful comments and suggestions, particularly on the future of design. And to my old friend and longtime mentor, Joe Tawil, for listening to my rants concerning what is bad about the business... and what is so very good.

DEDICATION

To all the colleges and universities where I have spoken in an attempt to awaken the system to the need for young designers to realize that they are about to enter the business world. To all the publishers who have printed my articles and interviews related to this subject. To the people who have sat through my rants at conferences and seminars. To all the students I have mentored over the years. To my business partners, staff, and friends who gave comments on and assistance with this manuscript. And finally to my companion, Trudie, whose love, encouragement, unwavering support, and youthfulness I cherish most of all.

CONTENTS

INTRODUCTION

The definition of *theatrical* is more broadly interpreted today than it used to be. I would be remiss not to include venues such as concerts, theme parks, television, film, corporate productions, retail display, party planning, architecture, nightclubs, cruise ships, landscape lighting, home decorating, commercial businesses, themed restaurants, fashion design, boutiques, security, location-based entertainment, public art, and more, to which students graduating from traditional theatrical design programs can now apply their creative talents. With this rapid expansion comes a need to explore what the business of being a theatrical designer means in today's worldwide, open marketplace.

It is easy to say to someone, I am a theatrical designer. But under what circumstance is this statement being made? Are we talking about a traditional theatre, or is the person standing in front of a rock group's manager, or in the employment office of a theme park? That answer is harder to define than it has ever been in the history of theatre. If we only think back forty years, lighting was not even counted as one of the specialty fields of design study. The major areas of design specialization in theatre design now are:

* Costume Designer
* Scenic Designer
* Lighting Designer
* Sound Designer

This book will also be of great value to others working in the theatre or related entertainment specialties such as:

* Makeup Artist
* Property Designer
* Special Effects Designer/Builder
* Stage Manager/Production Manager

I include the last four positions, even though they are not normally considered part of "design" study, because in today's market of nontraditional fields, a broad range of opportunities may easily contain diverse (and often unwritten) elements as part of the job description. We can no longer narrowly define positions based on the theatre system that was in place forty or even twenty years ago. Anyone who clings to that ancient system will be left in the dust. The fireworks from the new millennium are just a precursor to an explosion in new career paths and almost limitless opportunities.

There are only seven major titles in entertainment I am not specifically addressing: producer, director, choreographer, actor, writer, composer, and musician. Others whom I have not specifically listed will find value in the main topic this book raises: the business we call theatre.

We live in a time when traditional college, regional, and professional theatres, as well as support of the arts in general, have undergone an upheaval never imagined two decades ago. Government and institutional financial support that was once counted on to underwrite millions of dollars in shortfall from lagging ticket revenues for theatre companies, museums, school arts programs, and others, has been slashed. Questioning the value of these programs due to the objections of a highly vocal minority, motivated by the ideology of the religious right, our national government and institutional contributors have reduced, and in some cases eliminated, funding. This has had a direct impact on show budgets, design staff, rental, and construction budgets. The theatre community has been forced to become proactive in securing funding from private donors or face huge cutbacks in their programs.

Every once in a great while I run across a quote, such as the one that follows, that serves to reaffirm my resolve to bring a sound business sense to the world of design. In a recent article entitled "Design and the Bottom Line," in the November 2001 issue of *American Theatre,* Marjorie Bradley Kellogg wrote:

> *Some comforting news for worried designers toiling in the fields of the not-for-profit theatre. It is not your fault. You are not supposed to be able to make a living working in the not-for-profit theatre.... By 2000, most of the respondents have given up even hoping to make a living from designing shows. Now they simply accept that if they wish to go on doing what they love, they'll have to look elsewhere for a livable income. (34)*

Even sadder is word from the late 2001 United Scenic Artists-LORT (League of Regional Theatres) contract negotiations, where it came to light that management salaries at some of the smallest not-for-profit theatres were the same as those paid in equivalently sized commercial ventures. Yet the same not-for-profit managers contended they couldn't afford to pay the designers parity with their commercial competitors. Another revelation was that telemarketers at one not-for-profit theatre represented at the negotiations were paid more for selling tickets to the show than was the set designer.

What does all this mean to the student moving out into the professional world? What does it mean to the young professional? Does it mean anything different to the established designer? Yes. It means that we are all thrust into a market that is expanding and not easily defined. Unfortunately, the traditional trade unions have not negotiated collective bargaining agreements in many of these satellite markets. They seem to have their hands full trying to deal with their more traditional foes. But they have not turned a blind eye to these new markets. Trade unions have provided contracts and protection support for their members and continue to push for health and welfare benefits on a show-by-show basis, even when a collective bargaining agreement has not been reached (see chapter 12).

The good news in all this is that we have an explosive marketplace in which to ply our talents. It is a daunting and somewhat scary task to send out resumes and portfolios to all these new potential clients when there is no grand list available. But we should be thankful that we have a greater number of possibilities and opportunities to choose from than ever before to showcase our design abilities. Now we can investigate employment opportunities further afield, even if we want to stay in the traditional structure of the theatre, to avoid that waiter job while we wait for that Broadway producer to come knocking on our door!

I would liken our traditional dilemma to that of an actor who wants to "act" in theatre, yet must spend a far larger percentage of his time doing commercials, films, and television—if he's lucky. Otherwise, it is back to waiting tables or selling insurance between acting gigs. So, although aspiring actors often languish in menial jobs while awaiting that big break, designers can now use their theatre skills for great financial rewards. These rewards will most likely earn them more income than they would receive from theatre, thus allowing those who choose to pursue theatre design to support their "habit."

In the larger picture the idea is to create such demand for your talent that it will afford you a decent living. One old adage still rings true: *It takes work to get work.* When you are outside the circle of people who have the ability to offer you work, you are quickly forgotten. And I can hear some people saying, correctly, that if I work outside of the theatre community then I will be forgotten. My reply is this: We are such a mobile society today, and most designers move about the country from coast to coast already, so if you are afraid to admit that you are doing other work, don't tell your theatre cronies—that is, until you start making more than you ever dreamed of, and then you'll want to shout it to the heavens! Learning to market to new potential clients is absolutely essential. But make no mistake: marketing doesn't end with getting one job. You must constantly search out new clients. The reality is that most designers outlast their client base. That is to say, the client who is sometimes your most loyal and steady may join another production company that has other loyalties, move out of the country, or even change professions altogether. Designers must constantly prepare themselves for when the current show, production company, or best contacts evaporate. Where is your *next* meal ticket coming from? You will need to be on the lookout for new contacts and new opportunities at all times, particularly when there is a lot of work. Because the day will come when suddenly there is a big, unexpected hole in your schedule, yet the bills must still be paid.

Every time you walk into a production meeting, you must sell (market) your ideas to the rest of the team. Never delude yourself into thinking that the best, most creative ideas are just naturally the ones that will get used. You need to sell your concepts and know how to "read" the others in the group. You need to know how to negotiate with your coworkers as well as a producer.

The career paths for designers have been complicated, not only by the new, wider, and very fertile fields now open to them, but also by the need to figure out how to take the best advantage, both financially and artistically, of those opportunities. In the pages that follow I hope to expand your understanding of how we, as trained theatrical designers and other specialists, can and must arm ourselves with the knowledge that is necessary to be successful in today's expanded marketplace. I have quoted from quite a number of books that are not in most designers' libraries—but they had better be added quickly. For those of you who have pushed open the door a little to look into the business world, I trust I am restating what is now obvious.

In order to contend with the onslaught of competition—the people who undercut the market by taking lowball fees, the employers who do not live up to their agreements, the expanded market opportunities—we must gather the best weapons available. And that means that we must understand the principles of business. We must become marketing specialists who can open the doors to this highly diverse market. We must institute sound financial planning and understand our legal obligations. There must be no question; if we want to protect our economic well-being and see that our careers move forward, we must face the fact that theatrical design is a business.

Lastly, I want to openly admit that I am very biased. My thirty-plus years of professional life have been as a lighting designer/director/consultant, as well as a director of photography, so it may appear that my references, stories, and advisers all lean toward lighting. But you must know that virtually every time the word "lighting" appears, you can substitute the word "scenic" or "costume" or "sound" or "production/stage manager." If this bothers anyone, I'm truly sorry. But the fact remains: lighting is the specific field that has led the technological explosion into the modern era of theatre design. From the first use of computers and advanced electronics interfaced directly into a production, lighting has almost single-handedly pushed and shoved theatre into the twenty-first century. So the practitioners of that craft are, in large measure, ahead of the other crafts in embracing the challenge of the broader definition of *entertainment design*.

Also peppering the text are my own stories, which I hope will personalize the struggle inherent in creating a lifestyle and building a career in the business. I have also repeated some subtopics, generally with additional information, where I felt it would be worthwhile and make it easier for the reader to get the full sense of a major topic.

And to those who find that I left things out or dwelled too much on certain points, I can only say, give me feedback so the next edition is even more helpful. This is new ground for all of us. We are learning more every day about how to fit into this profitable and expanding world of entertainment. Use all the resources available—books, articles, lectures, conferences, business seminars—as well as obtaining advice from an attorney and CPA. And don't discount the effort the trade unions are making on your behalf; they have a tough job in the current economic climate. All these things together will give you the ability to meet the challenge of being a *business*.

CHAPTER 1
What Kind of Business Am I?

When the business world defines "doing business," it usually means that two or more parties, individuals, or companies have created a relationship in which one party does something the other party wants in exchange for the second party doing something for the first party. All this is memorialized in a contract, which is a legal document, verbal or written, that defines the relationship between two parties. In layman's terms, a contract essentially means, *I will give you something if you do something for me.* Furthermore, the way two parties arrive at this endgame is that somehow they become aware of each other and learn what each could do for the benefit of the other. That phase of business is called marketing.

When a theatrical designer says that he is not a businessperson but a creative person, I have to control a laugh. The simple interaction of two people, each of whom has something and is willing to exchange it for something needed, is basic to human survival. Once humans decided to divide the tasks of food gathering and preparation we entered into a "business relationship" with another person or group. I have two birds and you need a bird. I am willing to give you one of my birds if you are willing to keep my fire going until I return from hunting. How is that different from what we do every day to survive? We take money, after we earn it or are given it, and trade it for a bird. We can then look at and listen to it sing or put it in a pot and cook it!

Our services as designers that are given to another individual, such as a show producer, fit this simple analogy. I have chosen to try and earn money by being a theatrical designer. Who wants my theatrical design services? What will you pay me for that service so I can buy food and shelter? All of these, admittedly highly simplistic, examples do not take away from the fact that we are conducting business almost every hour of every day of our lives. So why does it come as such a shock to newly minted designers that they must use business models and tactics to obtain gainful employment?

The advantages of forming a business of your own include:

* Being your own boss
* Controlling your own finances
* Earning more than as an employee (possibly)

* Tax benefits
* Business deductions

The joy, or fear, of being able to control which project you pursue is a key element in all of this. If you don't care what you work on, perhaps you should move on to being an employee. In that case, you better hope the company keeps you on for thirty-plus years and then hands you a gold watch. But let's be realistic: That is not going to happen to many of us even when we have given years of loyal service. It is just not in the master plan of employers.

You will earn from 20 to 40 percent more as an independent contracting designer because the employer saves on employee taxes, insurance, and retirement plan benefits. But this larger (some would say inflated) fee should not be viewed as "free money."

Some things that you may consider to be drawbacks of forming your own business are:

* No steady income
* No employer-provided benefits
* Risk of not being paid
* Liability for business debts
* More complex tax filings

I believe, on balance, that the first list is far superior, and I trust that the rest of this book will support my premise.

Service Business

Now let us move on to the question posed by the title of this chapter. What kind of business am I? As theatrical designers, we are in what is broadly defined as a "service business." Service people include retail salespersons, waiters, accountants, architects, housepainters, dry cleaners, doctors, police officers, firefighters, lawyers, and others. Although a few may look down on some of these "service" jobs, we cannot deny that they are skilled, trained members of the workforce. Are we, as theatrical designers, not highly skilled and trained, too? I trust we all agree on the answer.

Some of the above categories of service people are termed "professionals" and others are called "tradespeople." In general, the distinction is derived from the level of education necessary to gain entry into the field. Where do we, as theatrical design professionals, fit in this hierarchy? Most theatrical designers have attended high school and at least a four-year college program. Many have gone on for a two- or, most likely today, a three-year postgraduate M.F.A.

program at a university. A few will bypass the formal classroom for on-the-job training. In either case, most will put in time assisting an established designer before being truly called a professional. On the whole, we are on a par with accountants and architects in terms of level of education. Thus, we can truly say we are service professionals.

It has been estimated by *Fortune 500* that 80 percent of the workforce is employed in nonmanufacturing jobs. If you don't manufacture or build something, then the only other broad category of work is the "selling" of a service, product, or skill. As people with creative skills, we should market those skills to as wide a market as we can. That places us in the category of "service" businesses. By admitting that we are in a service business we have the right to sell those services to the highest bidder or the one willing to pay our (or the union's, which serves as the collective bargaining agent for many areas of theatrical work) fees and salaries.

As service providers we are marketing an intangible. When we shake hands with the person who has just hired us to design something, we don't hand him a box containing nice new shiny widgets. What we are selling is the perceived belief on the part of the buyer that we can deliver the contractual service at some later point in time. To get to this point takes research, marketing, salesmanship, and business knowledge.

The fact that we must conduct the work we do in a businesslike manner is a revelation, both to many people within academic circles and to their students as they leave those hallowed halls. But this state of affairs is changing, even if we only admit intellectually that theatrical designers do not create work in a vacuum. Many designers, however, find it very difficult to actually say that *theatrical design is a business.*

Does this mean that you must run out and rent a store, hang a sign, hire employees, place newspaper ads, and sponsor little league teams? Maybe! But before you close this book right now, consider that when we admit that what we do makes us a business, we are 65 percent of the way to becoming a true professional, because business is largely based on perceived worth. It follows, then, that the remaining 35 percent of the journey is split between the physical property (desk, computer, etc.) and legal obligations (licenses, tax filings, etc.) that must be amassed and created due to our status as a business.

Profit-Making Business

Are we a profit or not-for-profit business? Seems like an easy question to answer, doesn't it? We are all aware of charities, such as the Red Cross or our church, that qualify as not-for-profit businesses, but what does that mean? It means that they may not show a profit at the end of the year for tax purposes. Does that mean that the employees are not paid? Does that mean that they cannot own expensive equipment and property? The answer is "no" to both questions. So, who draws the line and makes the determination as to which businesses qualify for nonprofit status? The Internal Revenue Service (IRS) makes that determination based on the forms you or your CPA or tax attorney file with the state or city for your business license or the Articles of Incorporation that establish the business (see chapter 6). The IRS then determines the sections of the tax code applicable to the type of business and reviews your filings based on those criteria.

Well, since I think of myself as doing a community service by designing for a not-for-profit theatre or dance company, why aren't I able to take advantage of their status? Because the laws and regulations are designed to encourage profit and thus create revenue to run governmental agencies. A charity avoids many taxation issues. But since the government needs revenue to pay for its agencies and services, it makes every attempt to bring in as much tax revenue as possible and thus restricts those who wish to avoid paying their fair share.

When you get into chapter 6, a picture of how this works should emerge. Right now, understand that as a for-profit business, you can seek protection from some taxes or mitigate the amount due by taking legal advantage of tax breaks in the codes via allowable deductions to your business, many of which are not available to the private citizen.

Lastly, I want to make it very clear that you must personally verify the advice and statements I pass along when legal obligations are discussed. Not only am I not a trained, licensed attorney, but the laws and regulations change so quickly that you must always have the most up-to-date information at hand to make a sound business decision. I intend to base some parts of this book on personal experiences from thirty-two years of being a professional theatrical designer. I strongly hold the belief that sound business practices must be a factor in our design careers. Throughout this book, I hope to give you reasons to join me in bringing a more professional status to our crafts.

CHAPTER 2
Office, Home, or Studio

A physical location with an address is necessary to begin a business. The IRS uses the term "principle place of business," about which I will say more later. Now, that address may be as simple as a post office box that could cost $15 a month, or it can be at your residential address where you are already paying rent or living free off your parents. But for most people, an office denotes at least a room in a commercial building. Office space can go for from $0.60 to $10.00 or more per square foot. A small 8 x 10 office is not terribly expensive, and there are businesses that specialize in catering to the small startup business that needs a short-term rental. They do get a premium for being flexible, but often the offices, at least here in Los Angeles, come with some furnishings, Internet lines, and occasionally even provide a conference room that you can schedule and pay for by the hour. Often a business service center is located in the building to provide copying, faxing, parcel pickup services, presentation graphics design, and other services for additional charges. This method of renting or leasing office space does have great advantages: a short-term commitment, business services already on site, and a businesslike environment. A standard office with a long-term lease of three to five years is less expensive per square foot because the owner is willing to offer a discount to secure a longer relationship. Every time an owner must advertise space for rent, a few months rent is lost, which cuts into profits. But either way, the reality is that most offices are at least two rooms and average $500 to $1,000 a month.

You're right if you guessed that office rent is the largest single monthly expense that a designer can face. Therefore, you will want to come up with some creative ways to maximize your space both for designing and for storing catalogs, show files, research, and the business records you need for taxes. No matter where the space is, it needs to be quiet enough to work and at least offer the ability to control your environment to make private calls, keep your records secure, and store materials.

Oddly enough, where your office is geographically doesn't always seem to matter. There are highly successful designers living in small towns away from urban centers who do very, very well. And there are designers living in high-priced, very small apartments in New York who barely making ends meet. Why choose one over the other? How do you decide what is best for your career?

Geographic Location

First, you should establish what needs your surroundings must satisfy. Do you have a family and need to find a home that is in a neighborhood with good schools? Does your spouse or partner also work, and does his or her job dictate the general area? Do you need to be physically in the same town as or live close to your primary client? In other words, if you are targeting a specific area of entertainment such as film, your location choices will be limited, because film companies tend to cluster around the studios—although they are no longer in Hollywood alone; studio facilities have sprung up in San Francisco, Phoenix, Chicago, Orlando, New York, New Jersey, Toronto, and many other places. Themed or location-based entertainment producers tend to be clustered around Los Angeles, New York, and Orlando. Are you going to teach, in which case the position you land will dictate your primary residence? Are you addicted to a sport such as sailing or horseback riding or skiing that beckons you to a certain geographical area of the country?

Selecting your location can be a major factor in the direction of your career. But it is not an absolute determinant. Many people have chosen unconventional living over ease of access to clients. I drive seventy-five miles to and from my office and further when I see clients at the studios. But I choose to live aboard my sailboat at a marina and spend the rest of my time in a secluded area up the coast from Los Angeles with my companion, who hates Los Angeles. We also take three to four trips to my condo in the little town of Telluride, Colorado, each year. I work with a television technical director who lives in northern California and commutes to Los Angeles several days each week. Other coworkers, including camerapeople, directors, and theatre people, live in Las Vegas and commute to Los Angeles. Certainly such arrangements are nothing new to New Yorkers, who often choose to live upstate or in Vermont or Connecticut.

My point is that we need to make these choices for ourselves, not to please some producer we hope to get work with eventually. Living close to our work location is not as necessary as it was for the last generation. It is rare for all the members of a family to occupy the same house as their grandparents anymore. We live where we choose (a choice made by most working professionals), or we follow the work—and there's nothing different about that for designers. But somehow, I don't think many of us really understand why we live where we do. It sort of happens by accident, and then one day we wake up and say, why am I living here? So, make it a conscious choice.

Balance in Your Life

Something I have grown to feel very strongly about is that our lives outside our work must be discussed early on in the process of determining where we live.

My family said I was a workaholic in my early years, so I have been seeking some balance between my professional career and my outside interests for the past twenty years. In 1980, I moved aboard a sailboat up the coast from Los Angeles toward Santa Barbara, California, to get away from the 24/7 life of the business. This balance is not easily achieved, and I admit I didn't always follow my plan. Then, one day, you wake up and a year has gone by, during which you didn't do something you pledged to do. Psychologists and family counselors tell us that it is more important than ever that we create a social balance that isn't involved with our careers. With the pressure of business and the insecurity we all feel from time to time, family, friends, and hobbies may be the things that keep us from falling apart.

I am heartened by the way my own son has limited his travel and work schedule to ensure time with his four young children, something I did not do for him and his sister. I now regret that I missed the joy, laughter, and tears of their young lives. But when I was starting out, all I could see was the cloud that hid the peak I was clawing my way towards. It cost me my marriage, a lot of money in child support, and 50 percent of my business (that's California law). So, what I worked so hard to earn was taken away from me, as was my family. Is it worth it?

Someone is bound to say that that's easy for me to say now that I've got an established career. And yes, the early years of struggling to gain acceptance involved hard work, long hours, and much travel. Time, even when home, was often taken up with folding and addressing letters to potential clients and reading trade publications to find new projects, all of which took away from the quality time I should have spent with my family. Many young professionals delude themselves into believing they are doing it for their families. No, we're not; we're doing it for our own egos. We can never go back and use the money we earn to recover what we missed. So just think about it if you are considering getting married, and think even harder if you want a family early on in your career. Take the advice as you will, but I feel obligated to give it. There can be balance between a great career and time for personal activities, family, and friends. In the end, no job, no project, ends up being more important. Determine your priorities before anything else, or just when your career starts to move, so might you—right out the door of your house and onto the courthouse steps.

Cost of Living

Couple the above with a realistic delineation of the costs associated with your choice of lifestyle. If you live in a major metropolitan area, for example, your rent will be higher, but in many cites public transportation can be used to offset automobile expenses. Some cities are hubs for airlines; therefore, fares are lower when flying to and from an out-of-town job or meeting. Weather is another factor to consider. A colder climate will require seasonal clothing purchases that are unnecessary in a warmer climate, and heating and fuel bills can mount quickly in colder climates. Also, consider the consequences of being delayed due to weather-related conditions and possibly missing an important meeting.

In the end, the location you choose will be a big factor in what type of design work you can expect to attract. This is an issue that not only affects you, but also has a huge impact on your family and friends. It can affect your social and cultural life, as well. Are arts facilities, sporting events you like to attend, and continuing educational opportunities available in the area? Are there support facilities close by, such as set or costume construction houses, rental houses, storage facilities, and material centers that you need to make your design business successful? I suggest you make a chart that contains headings such as: Activities, Schools, Transportation, Weather, Big Town/Little Town, House or Apartment; pick a few locations, and see how the chart fills in. Another chart should be constructed that covers the costs of: Housing, Utilities, Auto Expenses, and Insurance. I'd also suggest making a third, as a Wish List for all the things you want in your personal life. Setting these goals can also be used to spur you on to set your fees high enough to meet your wish list, and as a watermark to achieve a way of looking at your financial needs. And even if your needs are simple, you feel footloose with no ties, and travel and adventure await you—hold on, things will change!

Cost of Doing Business

Once you have fixed on one or two locations to live, then it is time to make another list. This one should contain the going market price per square foot for office space in that area. Local tax rates, city business licenses, insurance rates, and average utility costs should also be on that chart, as well as a provision for an assistant, even if part-time. Then add in the cost of local telephone service, long distance charges, fax line, Internet access, and possibly a message service. Another list is made up of the physical equipment needed in your office. Such things as a telephone, fax machine, copier, computer, file cabinets, desk, chairs, bookshelves, drafting board, or plan table must be priced. These expenses may be necessary, even in a home office, so make the list now, even if you have initially chosen to work out of your home. It is certainly an eye-opener when you add up the initial expense of starting a business, but don't let it scare you. All these things are lumped together in what is called the *cost of doing business*.

However, the initial out-of-pocket expense for these items can be reduced by leasing some equipment, purchasing used furniture, combining a fax/copier machine, and not upgrading for the latest bells and whistles for your computer just yet (assuming you have one left over from college). Purchases on credit cards are not a good idea, as interest rates can run as high as 23.98 percent or more. Check out the office supply chains; some will carry purchase contracts at much better rates. And then there is the Bank of Mom and Dad. Don't be shy; they just plunked down $40,000 to $100,000 to get you through school, so another $10,000 may be possible (cross your fingers). In speaking with some other small business owners around my area, I have tried to come up with an average initial investment in office equipment and furnishings. At best, the number is $4,000 and can run to $20,000 for all new equipment.

Then you will also need money to pay the first month's rent, a security deposit with the phone and utility companies and landlord, plus cash to tide you over for at least three to six months. The estimate here is, at the low end, $2,000 to $5,000, and, at the high end, $6,000 to $10,000 a month to stay in business. A little daunting, but it is possible.

Credentials

An adverb that is often tacked onto titles is "licensed" or "certified"—as in "licensed broker" or "certified public accountant" (CPA). As theatrical designers are we allowed to add anything to our names? Yes. We have certification programs by industry professional organizations, such as the National Council on Qualifications for the Lighting Professional, which entitles people to add **LC** (Lighting Certification) after their names. Of course, in film and television there is the **ASC** (American Society of Cinematographers) suffix you see with the credits of a select group of directors of photography. Others will use the letters of industry specialty organizations, such as **ASLD** (American Society of Lighting Directors) or **CSA** (Costume Society of America). Or a suffix could be used to signify membership in a union, such as **USA** (United Scenic Artists), indicating that a person has passed testing and experience standards to be admitted as a member. Finally, using one's academic credentials, such as M.F.A. or Ph.D., is still the conventional standby for teachers.

I have seen many other designations used to further delineate a person's status in his or her profession. I for one feel this is a positive trend. It brings a visible indicator of professional standing and connection to the person using it. Currently I am using ASLD after my name, because I belong to many groups and unions, and I find that ASLD more completely embraces the diverse design work I do.

Since I am the CEO of a California corporation, I could use those letters and it would be considered very proper in the business world. You can also consider titles such as "Marketing Manager," "Sound Consultant," or "Principal Designer." For a long time I used "Director of Photography," because I was very proud of the fact that I had qualified with the Production Experience Roster in Hollywood, even through I was theatre trained and not a film school graduate. But what does any of this do to further a prospective client's impression of you? This begs the question, Is this just ego talking? We will explore that issue more in chapter 7. Letters after your name are taken as an indication that you have reached a position of status in your profession. Entertainment has often been called an "exploitation media," so why should we not use the technique for whatever benefit we can?

Business Stationery

One of the tasks that you must complete early on in your career is to design simple business stationery and a card. What you do not need to do is pay someone to create a fancy, funny, or whimsical logo. Keep the stationery in the style of a law or accounting firm: clean and easy to read. My firm has a logo, but we are a diverse group, and anyway, we can afford it! There are several business books and computer programs that will give you sample forms and even let you create one on your own computer. With today's printers and copying machines you can forgo the expensive print shop and simply merge your preformatted letterhead, invoice, or resume right from your computer when you need it. The business card is a little trickier and probably needs to be done professionally to get good paper stock and maybe a touch of color. But don't go overboard. I will guarantee that before your first year is out you will want to make changes to all these as you find a clearer focus in your marketing and get feedback from friends and clients.

Realize as well that the business community has standards, and when you send a letter or present your card it is making a specific impression that is equal to your personal appearance—something we will discuss in chapter 9.

Home Office

The next possibility, working out of your residence, may sound the easiest, but it has many pitfalls. Does this method have automatic savings? Only possibly. Many cities impose very strict rules about home offices. Consider that your residence must have one room of full-time devoted office space to give you the "IRS sanctioned" deduction. Some community developments stipulate in their CC and Rs (Covenants, Conditions, and Restrictions) that no home-based business shall be run from the condo or home property. So check your lease or sales contract to make sure you will be able to work out of your home. However, as a single designer with only a part-time or occasional assistant, you more than likely will not be in violation of the rule against businesses on the property. But it is much safer to check the rules and ask the salesperson for clarification.

Access to the room you are setting up as your office or design studio may require a separate entrance, one that is not used normally by family to gain entry to the home, under a strict reading of the IRS regulations. Also, no other activity may transpire in that room—that is, there can be no ironing board or playpen. Sounds ridiculous, I know, but the IRS takes a very hard line on this issue.

In 1993, the U.S. Supreme Court handed down a ruling regarding the Tax Reform Act of 1976. It involved defining the word "principal," as used in *principal place of business*. The Court defined it broadly, not only as regards a commercial office property but also a home office. This opened the door for cities to tax the location as personal property, as well as demand business taxes and licenses on home-based businesses.

Many cities restrict business activity in residential areas, although they often overlook it unless a neighbor complains. If your neighbors feel that your clients or employees make too much noise or cause parking problems, the police and the city council can get involved. If they determine that there is excessive parking on public streets they can fine you and close the business. And if you register your business as being at a residential location, some cities add a special tax to cover the increased road use. A couple of years ago, the City of Los Angeles tried to collect such a tax, but the Writers Guild threw up a big cry and got the new law repealed . . . for members of the WGA, but not for anyone else. Chapter 6, "Financial and Legal Considerations," will detail more obligations.

A factor that cannot be placed on a chart is the emotional one. Can you work in the environment of your residence? Are there too many distractions from children, neighbors, traffic, and television? Can you make and receive business without distractions? Can you leave out your paints, swatch books, and samples? And the bigger question is, do you have room enough to spread out your research, drawings, patterns, or models?

One factor that is not often considered but can be significant in some areas of the design business, particularly for architectural and corporate clients, is that these clients do not consider a home office a "real" business and will not contract with you. Another factor that these same people will bring up is the legal status of your business. Do you have the proper insurance to protect them in case of a lawsuit? We'll go into this in chapter 5, "Business Liability and Insurance."

The Studio

Lastly, we turn to the studio concept, in which a designer or a group of designers share the expenses of an office and related services. This is often modeled on law practices, architectural offices, and some medical co-ops. Generally, the members agree to be responsible for a fixed monthly fee or a percentage of the actual expenses. One member becomes the holder of the lease and responsible for the office debts. There should be a written understanding that this person will make a profit from the fees charged to the other designers in compensation for her added responsibility and liability. Another approach is where the designers are part-owners in a partnership or have stock in the corporation. Each party is responsible for the costs associated with running the business, yet they each retain a major percentage of the fees that they earn individually.

In any of these situations, others can join and share expenses. This is one reason partnerships are formed. But usually it is because two or more can work together on the same projects, such as a production manager and a stage manager or several scenic designers and a construction partner. Of course, this means that the physical space will be larger and the expenses will increase. But often sharing expenses will decrease each partner's contribution, making it less than it would cost if each were working alone. Besides, it is great to have other people to bounce ideas off and sometimes trade or share projects.

Flexibility

Test the waters; don't dive into the deep end right away. But you must also understand that being flexible means you can't make long-term commitments either. The bigger apartment you leased for five years so you could have room to work is huge now that you've joined a firm or taken a staff position and don't use it anymore, but the rent is still the same.

I have tried all of the possibilities discussed at one time or another in my career, and even worked out of my home. Back then I had a separate, small guesthouse out back to ease the pressure on my family. Yet the kids still ran in and out, wanting to show me everything from their drawings to clumps of dirt, so the distraction factor certainly came into play. I did learn to stop work about 3:30 when the kids got home from school, and then I went back to work after their bedtimes as often as I could. But if you are on a deadline, this is a real problem, because they just do not understand why you can't play.

Moving into my first office was a pretty big move. I applied for an SBA (Small Business Administration) loan for $150,000 to start a concert lighting rental business. With a five-thousand-square-foot warehouse and five offices, I soon had a couple dozen employees to worry about. When I sold the equipment years later, I downsized to a nice Victorian-style office building and one employee. I only had four rooms, but the space was stylish enough to attract some very big corporate clients. That worked until I took over my first of three long-term television series, *Entertainment Tonight*, at Paramount Studios in Hollywood. The office was thirty miles away and halfway between the boat and the studio. I found I was running back and forth several times a day. So when the lease was up, I moved into a small condo building near Universal Studios, where I also had clients. It had a loft I could use for an office and a second bedroom for files and storage. It was much nearer the studio and worked well for five years.

But I was getting more work than I could handle, and a friend suggested I get together with fellow concert designer Jeff Ravitz. We decided to start a partnership and took offices in Hollywood near the studio. We had a sixty-foot-long room into which we put temporary dividers. We worked out of that for about two years before we moved several blocks away to a small house that had been a film editing company. It had six rooms and worked well. We actually wanted to stay, but the building went on the market and we felt the property was too small for the additional room we now needed. In the meantime Dawn Hollingsworth had joined us and the staff had doubled, so we moved to the San Fernando Valley nearer where most of the staff and two of the partners wanted to live.

We found a 2,700-square-foot office-warehouse complex that we could design and build out. We paid cash for the remodeling in exchange for a break on the lease. Now we have four offices, a conference room, a lunch- and break-room, and a large "bull pen" that has five cubicles, a library, and a very large plan table. Although we have increased in size, adding our fourth partner last year, we feel that the space is right for the moment. We designed it to be flexible, and so far everything has fit. But you cannot predict the future, and we are already thinking ahead to the end of the lease in a year. Shall we stay, or buy our own building? Are we headed for the trap of growing too big, and then seeing no way of downsizing when it is called for due to a long slack period? That is an important issue, and one we must carefully weigh if we are to maintain a healthy economic picture well into the future.

I have told you all this to illustrate that you can grow, cut back, grow and grow, and still cut back. In several books that describe the failure rate of architect offices, the reason most often cited is their inability to react expediently to a down market, and therefore not lay off unneeded staff quickly enough. The high overhead burden sinks them. It is a big responsibility and expense simply to hire and train staff, but it is much harder to let someone go. The truth is that many commercial design and architectural firms get into cash flow problems because they cannot bear to let someone go when the work slows down, believing that all the training and loyalty they feel toward the person outweigh the consequences. Nothing could be further from the truth. The continued existence of the firm hangs in the balance. With no income to cover salaries, a vicious circle begins of borrowing money or not paying all the bills. If the company is formed as a sole proprietorship or partnership, nonpayment of bills can become collectable directly out of your and/or your partner's personal accounts, even jointly held accounts you might have with a spouse. Some judgments could go so far as to result in legal action that could cost you your home. Chapter 5 will deal with these issues.

The lesson is clear: Keep your office space and staff matched to your average workload. It is better to be bursting at the seams for a short period than to have room to play tennis eight months out of the year. Unfortunately, keeping people on your staff simply out of loyalty is a very bad business decision. You not only sink yourself but you also sink them, because they still end up unemployed.

CHAPTER 3
Staff and Design Associates

Staff, whether associates or assistants, full-time or part-time, can be the greatest factor in turning a hit-or-miss, project-to-project, hand-to-mouth existence into a sustainable business with assets and attainable long-term goals. It will be easier to string projects together with overlap if you have help. Your staff will also help lend the appearance of a firm that can handle larger projects. Producers want to feel that the work they entrust to you can be handled. They have people to assist them, and if they see that you do, too, it is a sign of a going concern—not a one-person show that could turn around and walk away tomorrow. Seeing that you have staff also helps your clients feel that they are getting more for their money.

Design Assistants

Every designer will at one time or another have the need for the services of someone in an assistant or associate capacity. Even a production manager will need assistance from time to time. In some cases, the assistant may be provided by the client, or the cost may come out of your fee. Many theatre designers try to call for an assistant of their choice in their contract, with a stipulation that the assistant's salary will be paid by the producer. This protects the designer from having to create an employee/employer relationship and the tax and liability ramifications it brings with it. The recently completed agreement between the LORT (League of Regional Theatres) producers and United Scenic Artist (USA) union does contain specific language about payment for assistants on "Tony eligible" shows. For many years, Broadway shows have had this issue covered in their agreement between the League of American Theatres, Producers Inc., and USA. The significance of the LORT agreement is that for the first time, theatres and production company owners acknowledge assistants as true employees who will be paid by the theatre, a payroll service, or some other legal entity, and not the designer.

While the unions would like to see everyone determined to be an employee and not an independent contractor, Congress has determined that certain workers are automatically considered to be employees for purposes of Social Security, Medicare, and federal unemployment taxes. This is so even if the person meets the IRS test for independent contractors. *Statutory employees* have a dual status. They are employees for certain purposes and independent contractors for others. The hiring producer pays half of the contractor/employee's Social Security and Medicare payments, as well as appropriate federal unemployment taxes. However, the statutory employee remains an independent contractor when it comes to any pension plans of the employer, and does not participate in such benefits. While the latest LORT agreement is very new, a number of issues and ways of handling the paperwork of exactly who will be the employer of record for assistants and designers are still being worked out. The interpretation is that they are not independent contractors when they work under the contract between USA and the producer or theatre.

But the state may still qualify that same person as an independent contractor under state law for the purpose of paying workers' compensation and unemployment compensation insurance.

The producer files a W-2 form and checks a special box (15) that indicates that the Social Security and unemployment tax is withheld. He must file this form with both the IRS and the Social Security Administration. Thus, the legal status of the assistant and liability issues for the designer are eliminated when you work under many of the USA contracts. Without the USA contract to protect you, the producer will try and make a "cash" payment: he simply will write a check in the full amount of your fee. Then, at the end of the year, if the amount is over $300, he will file a 1099 form with the IRS. That puts the IRS on notice that you were paid and no taxes were withheld. If you made quarterly estimated tax payments to cover this income, great. Otherwise, the IRS can assess penalties because they didn't get their *blood money* in time.

Here is something that we must come to grips with: an assistant can and often does make more than the designer over the course of a year. First, because assistants are usually paid on an hourly basis, and as Marjorie Bradley Kellogg showed in her article "Design and the Bottom Line" in *American Theatre* magazine, when broken down on an hourly basis, designers' fees often come out well under the minimum wage, and assistants can't be paid that low! Plus, assistants can work on many more projects a year by moving from one designer to another without waiting. The downtime the designer faces once booked for a show cuts into the continuing cash flow. In addition, assistants do not have to worry about marketing.

Sometimes, however, it is to the advantage of the designer to have "control" of the assistant or associate, rather than ceding that authority to the producer. Why? Simply so that there is an obligation on the part of the assistant or associate to work for the good of the designer and not make unfavorable reports to the producer about what you said or didn't do. Loyalty is very, very important. Just remember that assistants won't feel much loyalty to someone who yells at them or pays them late or abuses them in other ways. Don't do this to your assistant.

Staff

Designers whose work keeps them on the road, especially internationally, may feel the need for someone to stay at their office to keep things running, following through with such things as sending plans, doing research, depositing checks, and paying bills. For some designers, a spouse or life partner may handle these duties. But most partners are already occupied with their own work, or simply do not want to take on these chores.

When you decide to employ someone, even part-time, a red flag should go up. Am I acting in a legal manner that meets the IRS, state compensation fund, insurance, and liability laws? Am I just paying a small sum, usually under $600, which need not be reported to the IRS? Is the status of the person a subcontractor or, the more proper term, independent contractor? Many people think the two terms are the same, but a subcontractor may only do a small portion of the work under the supervision of the person "contracted" by another to complete a defined body of work for a fee. While a subcontractor may in fact be an independent contractor in his or her own right, there are times when an independent contractor "subcontracts" his or her services to another contractor. This is fully discussed in Chapter 6. How do I know if the person meets the very narrow definition of an independent contractor? If I choose to employ the person on a permanent basis, what am I legally responsible to provide, in financial compensation, insurance, and medical coverage?

On the other hand, it isn't wise to hire an assistant right before boarding the plane to Germany; it could turn out those references weren't exactly correct, but you didn't have time to check. Did you leave the new assistant alone with your checkbook? I know a true assistant horror story from a friend. He not only got a bill for the assistant's overtime that she piled up on the project he left her to watch over, but when he returned, she promptly handed in her resignation. Then she went directly to the client, even though the assistant had not kept in contact with him, and convinced the client that the problems were her former boss's fault and took the account.

In any event, taking on an employee is one of the hardest things you will do. Finding the perfect person, training her, making sure she is doing her job when you are away, and lastly, bringing in additional fees to cover her salary, can cause you some sleepless nights—all this with the knowledge that one day she will leave and become "the competition." It is best to discuss your options and responsibilities with a certified public accountant and a tax attorney. Each state has its own labor laws, and the federal regulations must also be studied.

Interns

The employment of interns is very misunderstood, because there is much misinformation about how they can be utilized. Some interns are taken advantage of and, you could say, even abused. Should they work hard and be subjected to long hours, because, yes, that's part of the real life of theatrical design? We see this all the time on shows that deal with doctors interning or lawyers clerking for judges; why shouldn't design interns put in as much time?

Some government agencies and unions interpret the law to say that an intern must be in an accredited educational program and shall not supplant a full salaried worker. While it has been debated in courts by unions and state unemployment agencies, the widest held definition is that the intern's position must be for a specific, short-term period. In other words, you can't hire an intern for $50 a week to do a job that would ordinarily be handled by an employee whom by industry standards would be paid much more. Even big studios have had their hands slapped for doing this. One studio actually advertised for an internship in the trade papers, saying the position could lead to a full-time position, but the real intent was to fill a full, salaried position that already existed.

How interns are used, and the laws circumvented by summer stock theatres that rely on the cheap (often free) labor of young "interns," is up to some speculation. Many laws are open to broad interpretation, and in this case long-standing community support for a not-for-profit summer theatre may override any threat of prosecution.

Trying to find "qualified" interns can be the next problem. I am amazed that quite a few colleges do not encourage or even allow their students to leave campus or get credit for an internship. They explain this policy by saying they have a limited number of senior design students, and they do not want them going away just when they become "valuable" to the program. In translation, this means that they are very reliable, trained, unpaid labor for the school. On the other hand, some schools encourage intern programs to the extreme, providing school-owned housing in Hollywood for students to live in while away from campus, and even send a teacher to accompany them to provide added educational experiences and supervision.

A good way to find interns is to advertise at USITT (United States Institute for Theatre Technology) or other educational conferences. My firm's Web site has a section devoted to explaining how to apply for an internship, the qualifications that we are looking for, as well as how much time we require. We have our younger staff associate designers talk to potential interns to answer their questions. They also help our managing partner choose a new intern. There are also several Web sites and magazines that list internship openings. *ArtSEARCH* is one such publication, produced monthly on paper, as well as on the Internet (*www.tcg.org*). It can be subscribed to either way by contacting the publisher, Theatre Communications Inc., which also publishes *American Theatre* magazine. Also available to provide assistance is Theatre-Jobs.Com. but it is only on the Web at *www.theaterjobs.com* or by contacting the company at 749 LeMay Avenue (PBM) A3 251, Fort Collins, Colorado 80525, (970) 204-4144.

I am a big supporter of internship programs, which I feel can be beneficial to both the company and the student. Gauged by the response of former interns and the fact that we later hired several interns as full-time employees following their graduation from design programs, I feel that our program is very successful on both fronts. Internships are a good way for a student to get first-hand experience in the real world before they decide on a specific career path, as well as a way for the employer to check out potential new hires. But I would also caution against misuse of the program. Many employers have been caught and fined for underhanded tactics. Interns *can* be a very cost-effective way of getting help, but it works both ways. You must remember, they are still in training and don't necessarily know what to do. Time must be spent educating them about your work and the methods and systems you use. Don't expect them to walk in and take over. And don't forget: they are not there to get you coffee and pick up your laundry; even if that does save you time, it isn't fair to them.

Hiring

When it comes to staffing, consider the first position as one that requires multi-tasking. Maybe a draftsperson with general computer skills who can also function as office manager when you are away would be your first choice. Your choice could be an "assistant" directly out of school who is looking to hook up with a name designer, but try and look past that to the broader need you face. The often mundane tasks of sending information to potential clients, collecting checks, making bank deposits, and sending out invoices for services based on direct billable expenses on a project can be very time-consuming and boring for an ambitious assistant.

In the information age we live in, the cell phone has become an essential tool for the designer moving along the information highway. A full-coverage, nationwide service plan will allow you to keep in touch with clients so that office workers are no longer relegated to telephone operator, a time-consuming task that requires that they sit by the phone the whole business day. Now they are free to do outside research, drop by clients to get progress updates, pass information on to you, and have time to draft. Often clients do not even need to know where you are because of the way the service works. Thus, they can think you are hard at work on their project even when you are out of town putting out a fire on another project. Phone tag is a thing of the past. Instant contact makes the client feel you are on top of her needs.

Ultimately, the decision to employ someone must be based both on actual need and financial resources that are firm enough to ensure continued operation. It does no good for you to set up a studio or office and then close it within a year. It hurts your reputation as a businessperson, even if you consider yourself a "designer" first and foremost. It says to the clients that you cannot handle your own affairs—and that may mean you should not be entrusted with their projects.

CHAPTER 4
Accounting for Small Business

I know exactly what you are thinking. The right side of your brain is screaming, I'm not going to understand this! Well, get over it. Some things are good for us, like eating our vegetables. And the fact is that, at least on a very basic level, this is a topic that we very much need to understand. Some artists, actors, and designers have lost what little money they were able to put away due to the misbehavior of unscrupulous people, some using the term *business manager*.

Many years ago there was no certification or licensing process or agency watchdog to keep such managers honest. I know, because I was a victim of one early on in my career. I was not alone; taken along with me were a couple of directors and other actors. We were taken because we all thought our manager was taking care of our money, paying the bills, and investing, but ultimately we realized he had used our money to line his own pockets. This all happened because we were lazy. Yes, lazy when it came to keeping a close eye on what was being done. So, that awakened me to the fact that I was the only one who could protect me. Although I didn't rush out to become a CPA, I did start to read accounting and business books so that I would have a basic understanding of the principles. That way, I could interview accountants and, if I hired them, comfortably follow their discussion concerning what was happening with my money. It saves time—time I was paying for at an expensive hourly rate—and it gave me peace of mind.

Business Manager

A *business manager* can be a very key person in guiding your finances. Under the right circumstances, employing the services of an honest manager is a possible avenue for designers who need someone to pay their bills and handle their finances. You can have someone work in your office in this position, but most of us will never be able to afford one on a full-time basis. Normally, they are hired on a consultant basis, much the same as your CPA or attorney would be to advise you on business matters. The business manager may or may not be a certified public accountant. She may or may not be a licensed attorney, either. Therefore, use caution in applying her advice without further consultation with the appropriate professional. You will find that some CPAs and attorneys do hang out a shingle calling themselves business managers, but they will likely charge a much higher rate for their services, and will often not take on young designers who do not have extensive credits and six-figure incomes.

Since business managers are often intimately involved with clients, more so than accountants or CPAs, you would think they would have an even higher duty to protect their clients. Unfortunately, I was not the last person to be deceived by one. Just last year, a scandal broke about such a person taking a group of Hollywood's "A" list actors for millions of dollars. So, be very careful when choosing a business manager, and make sure yours is reputable and able to provide the type of advice you need.

In New York and California business managers are specifically legally prohibited from engaging in activities that amount to being an agent for their clients—that is, to actively seek work, which is the job of an *agent*.

Certified Public Accountant

You must plunk down some money and go see a CPA very early on in your career. A certified public accountant will have the most up-to-date information on the tax code, forms, and filing deadlines. CPAs will know what you will be required to present for municipal, state, and federal taxes and can advise you on business deductions. They will help you determine which category your business should be filed under with the different agencies.

The difference between an accountant and a certified public accountant has been blurred in recent years. Several lawsuits have contended that someone calling him- or herself an accountant is not distinguishable in the general public's eye from a CPA. But there are distinctions; a CPA has passed exams with his state to obtain a license issued by a state board of accountancy. CPAs are also required to take and pass an eight-hour refresher course every six years to keep their license. Although training is the key, they probably also belong to the AICPA (American Institute of Certified Public Accountants) and sign a Code of Ethics. These certification and licensing processes attest to the educational background and training of CPAs. Signing the code not only makes a statement of the moral obligation of CPAs, but is also a visual reminder that their job is to protect their clients. They also bear legal responsibility for the forms they file with government agencies and stockholders. Intentionally falsifying documents will land them in court just as it will you, but the greater fault is theirs, since they are professionals who should know the rules.

There are many gray areas in the tax codes, and a CPA will discuss interpretation of the code and advise you on your options and liabilities. You are allowed to take advantage of benefits that would not be readily apparent to an individual trying to read the tax codes. But you are responsible for providing accurate data to the CPA for him to use to compile the forms. And you, and only you, are ultimately responsible for the accuracy of the facts presented on the forms. So, if you withhold material facts or present incomplete data, you could pay a big fat fine, as well as back taxes, potentially well beyond your means to repay. Finding the taxman at your doorstep isn't necessarily a sign of your wrongdoing, but having a CPA by your side to explain what was done is always wise. If it is discovered that the CPA made a computational error, the IRS will often forgive the penalties—but not the tax that is still owed, plus interest. Since late penalties on taxes can be very stiff, this still amounts to a big break.

I skipped over the term *bookkeeper.* Frankly, anyone can say she is a bookkeeper. Yes, she may hand you a resume that shows she has worked in the accounting field for years, but handling a small, creative service-based business takes particular understanding. And just because the bookkeeper you are interviewing says she worked for General Electric or Mobile Oil Corporation for twenty years does not attest to her understanding of the tax code and what your liability might be. A bookkeeper should not be giving tax advice.

If you feel you can't afford a CPA, then an "enrolled agent" is acceptable for tax preparation only. Enrolled agents have passed a difficult IRS test or they have worked directly for the IRS for at least five years. They often work for a company such as H & R Block, Inc. Companies like these are storefront operations that specialize in personal tax filings. But check: They often have special business services divisions that are fully accredited and capable of servicing your business needs.

Will the IRS forgive penalties if one of these firms prepared your taxes? That is a case-by-case decision made by the IRS auditor. If the IRS feels you purposely hid material facts from the person who prepared the forms, you will pay. If it was a computational error on the part of the preparer, sometimes the tax preparation firm will pay the penalties. Check the agreement you signed for the service to see what the preparer is obligated to do in an audit situation.

You can contact the AICPA for the background of any member CPA to see his or her business history. If it's a firm, one of 1,300 member firms that audit U.S. Security and Exchange Commission corporations, the AICPA will provide very detailed information. But you and I probably cannot afford such large firms.

Computer Programs

Most of us are educated enough to get the hang of basic accounting by reading a book such as *The McGraw-Hill 36-Hour Accounting Course* by Robert Dixon and Harold Arnett, but there are also a number of computer programs on CD such as Peachtree Accounting 2002 and Quicken Basic matched with Quicken Turbo Tax business programs.

The one our firm uses, MYOB Accounting Edge, version 2.0, from MYOB Technology Ltd., literally walks you through with prompts that make it fairly simple to make the entries the accountant will need later for reviewing your finances and preparing your taxes. Since there are several good programs in wide use, check with your accountant to see which she is using; it will make it easier and quicker for her to download your information.

In these systems, you simply enter your *transaction* into your bank register. That could be a check you wrote for rent or a deposit into your checking or savings account; it could be a direct payment of a utility bill over the Internet, a fee you invoiced to a client, or a purchase you made on your credit card. Some even allow you to download your online banking information and import it into this system for easy account reconciliation. No more wondering if you have deducted those bank charges; you will have an up-to-the-minute balance to work with. If you have payroll, these programs can make all the appropriate entries, even calculate union fees, employer expenses, and accruals such as vacation and sick leave, along with tax deductions. A time billing program lets you bill for your consulting the way an attorney does, by the clock, so there is no question from the client as to what amount of time you put into the project. If you have assistants or associates working for you, you don't have to look over their shoulders; simply check their time sheets to see how much effort was put into the project from an *activity log*.

These programs can also produce reports. And they can print forms including invoices, bills, checks, and mailing labels, all to make your involvement with accounting as painless as possible. But the final word has to come from an accountant or CPA. They should review your entries on a regular basis. How often such review is needed is determined by how skilled you are at operating one of these programs, but a year-end review is a must.

Specialized Business

A very specialized business involving the kind of services a designer or production manager provides will not be something many CPAs have experience in handling. With the possible exception of those in Los Angeles, Chicago, and New York, I doubt there are many CPAs who have worked with theatrical designers. But not to panic. First, get recommendations from other designers. Check trade publications and your fellow union members to see if a name keeps coming up. A word of caution here: if it is a large firm that handles major entertainment clients, you probably want to steer clear, as you will truly be the little fish in a big ocean. You'll get passed down to an entry-level person and not get the personal attention that you really need; plus, you will be paying for their fancy office. But there are people out there, at least in the major entertainment centers of the country, who will know enough about creative people's business that they can learn your particular needs very quickly. And when you can't find someone with entertainment experience, look for someone who handles professional consultants and architects, or maybe even an actor or singer.

If all else fails, get out the phone book and start making calls. If possible engage the CPA in conversation right then. If the person "sounds" like he is interested in your business and, more importantly, gives you some indication that he understands something about what you do, set up a meeting. Yes, you may be told that this meeting is not free! But an active, good CPA's time is worth something. Even if you do not ultimately decide to go with the person, at least you have gotten a one-hour basic accounting lesson out of it. Move on and try again; it may take a while to connect with a person who you feel is trustworthy enough to take a personal interest in helping you toward a solid financial future.

This is the "business" in our business that cannot be shortchanged. The ramifications arising out of sloppy books and records will never go away. You could end up paying fines and penalties for years, which could keep you in a hand-to-mouth financial mode. And that's not what any of us want, is it?

What we are really talking about is learning a highly specialized language that spells out a system of recording and analyzing your economic picture. Effectively communicating this information is the key to the success of any business, be it a large or a one-person operation. Others besides the IRS rely on the accuracy of this information. Banks in particular need financial statements and records that show the soundness of your finances if they are to lend you money for office equipment, a line of credit, or a new car.

Are you ready for Accounting 101? Well, neither was I, really. I don't pretend to be a trained accountant. I do know, however, from many personal experiences, the pitfalls of not having good accountants and of keeping sloppy records. But that is a book all its own. I believe strongly in an artist/designer knowing the basics of accounting. When you are talking to your accountant you can save time and money (you are paying hourly for the lesson, after all) by collecting the records she asks for in advance. I can't emphasize this enough.

What follows are the most basic accounting topics with simple explanations and examples that should get you on the track to understanding the principles of accounting. But the moment you finish this book you must go out and purchase a basic accounting book, such as *Accounting Principles I*, by Elizabeth

A. Minbiole, from a company students know all too well (Cliff's Notes Inc.), any basic college accounting text, or, better yet, one of the computer programs discussed earlier, which will guide you through without the academics!

Some Principles of Accounting

Although I will not try to fully cover this weighty topic, I have selected portions of the subject that nonbookkeepers and nonaccountants should understand to protect themselves. Accountants use what are termed *generally accepted accounting principles* (GAAP). These are guides that have been evolved over the years by the accounting profession and the Securities and Exchange Commission.

Basically, these principles have a foundation based on some underlying assumptions. In short, these assumptions set forth guidelines for doing business. First, it is assumed that the records for a company will be kept separate from any other books, and the records may not include any personal assets or liabilities of the owner(s) (this is where you hear the term *comingling of funds* thrown about). It is also assumed that the records only contain quantifiable transactions in a stable currency such as the U.S. dollar. A full disclosure principle is used so that the well-being of the company is not disguised as lawsuits pending against it. A time-period assumption must be factored in when major purchases of equipment are anticipated, so that a false or misleading picture of the company's liabilities is not given.

Accrual versus Cash-Based Accounting

This is the big issue that must be resolved before statements can be prepared. Cash-based accounting shows no receivables or payables. Transactions are recorded as either actual received income or paid expenses as they happen. This system makes it much easier for a person new to business to understand why he can't take more money out of the business.

The *Accrual* system cannot be used by an individual; only businesses can use this accounting method. Under this system, revenue is recognized in the period in which it is actually *earned,* as in when the service was performed. Whether the payment in cash or check is received before, during, or after the period of the contact has no bearing on the timing of the revenue recognition. The aim of accrual accounting is twofold:

a) To record and report in any given period the revenue earned during the period.

b) To report the expenses that properly are to be matched against the reported income.

Therefore, the overall effort is to show earnings performance for the period. This amount may have little or no relationship to the amount of net cash for the period.

There are too many intangibles in the accrual method, and it doesn't reflect the reality of how much cash you have available on a day-to-day basis. Some accountants will allow you to keep accrual books and then convert them to cash at the end of the year if there is an advantage for the company. This addresses what the taxable income picture looks like as you approach the end of the year, so start reviewing your books with your CPA early.

Calendar Year versus Fiscal Year

Speaking of the end of the year, for a business, it does not necessarily mean December 31. In place of the calendar year, businesses are also allowed to choose a *fiscal year*, which closes at the end of any month they choose. It is still a twelve-month reporting cycle for filings and taxes, but some tax attorneys will build a strong case for its use. This gets tricky. I have used a fiscal year with a couple of my companies, but I never felt I understood the real need for it. It just seemed like a game the accountants and attorneys were playing. Did it have an economic advantage? Possibly, but I never understood if it did.

Principles

In the accounting world everything is based on principles. Several that you should understand are *revenue recognition* and three others that are tied to how that revenue is viewed by accountants. *Revenue recognition* is the principle that revenue is recognized as such only when the product is received or the service has been performed. For example, if you receive a retainer (an advance) against your design fee, the money, even though it is in your pocket, is not recognized until the service has been performed or the product delivered.

* *Matching principle* asserts that the costs of doing business should be recorded in the same period as the income they helped generate.

* *Cost principle* says that if you purchase an asset that increases in value while you own it, you do not reevaluate its worth for financial reporting purposes. In fact, you cannot keep switching the value without raising the eyebrows of the IRS. Such maneuvers start to sound like the overreporting of assets by large corporations that has been exposed recently.

* *Going concern* is a principle indicating that you pass your assets and liabilities along, assuming there will be no need for a quick liquidation; they

are thus classified as short-term (current) and long-term (not payable or debt due for more than a year).

Accountants also act on the principle that you have provided honest, accurate information to use in preparing the statements and tax forms.

Now that we have a quick overview of what accountants use to guide them on their journey of discovery about your financial position, let's take a look at the two basic statements they will provide so that you can understand the financial health of your business.

Financial Statements

The most common accounting reports are called *financial statements*. Although the format changes for different types of businesses, we'll look at the *sole proprietorship,* which is the legal business formation you will probably enter into first. This is a legally formed business owned by only one person, namely you. There will be a number of statements your CPA may propose she prepare. I find that the *statement of owner's equity* and the *cash flow statement* are not particularly useful to a single-owner business. But a corporation or partnership will need at least the statement of owner's equity once each year when the books are "closed."

Two other forms that are key to a business's understanding its financial status are the *income statement* and the *balance sheet.* These statements are for a specific period of time, sometimes a month, a quarter, or at least a year. When you are starting out you may be tempted not to pay an accountant to do a monthly statement to save a little money. That's a bad idea, because it is on a monthly basis that you need to pay the closest attention and work on your understanding of this whole process.

Income Statement

This is the first form prepared. It lists revenues and expenses and presents figures to show the company's net income for the period of time stated. *Net income* is the money beyond the total expenses for the period. *Net loss*, therefore, is when the income has not met the expenses for the period. What specific items will generally appear in this statement are shown below. However, due to the nature of our business, your accountant may suggest additional line items to present a clearer picture of your financial status. Some of these are only required for tax computation needs and may seem useless to you. Others I ask for to assist me in seeing where I am spending my money, even if that area does not have tax ramifications.

THE J.P. MILLIAN COMPANY

INCOME STATEMENT
FOR THE MONTH ENDED MARCH 31, 2001

REVENUES	
DESIGN FEES	$2,500.00
EXPENSES	
RENT	$800.00
INSURANCE	65.00
TRANSPORTATION	212.93
TELEPHONE	104.45
OFFICE SUPPLIES	63.74
UTILITIES	28.40
BANK CHARGES	7.00
TOTAL EXPENSES	$1,281.52
NET INCOME	$1,218.48
NET INCOME	$1,218.48
WITHDRAWALS	(1,000.00)
J. MILLIAN, CAPITAL, MARCH 31	$5,318.48*

Balance Sheet

The *balance sheet* is what accountants call a **financial statement.** This is the statement that proves the accounting equation:

Assets = Liabilities + Owner's Equity

Again, this statement is made at the same time as the income statement hown above and reflects each asset, each liability, and the owner's equity in the company at that moment. It is like gathering your allowance as a kid and stacking it up as a pile of coins, then taking away the money you need to spend for a school notebook and putting it in a separate pile. What is left is what you have to spend on candy!

What most accountants will tell you is that there are so many ways to come up with the value of an item to make the actual usable figure a little suspect. For the professional accountant, the balance statement is only a minor part of any true analysis of the company's financial position. But, for the beginning owner, it is helpful to see the money you have, the money you have put into "stuff" to make your design studio operate (computer, desk, etc.), and a line that represents the cash you are likely to have available to pay for food and clothing.

---

* Refer to the balance sheet on page 36.

THE J.P. MILLIAN COMPANY	
BALANCE SHEET MARCH 31, 2001	
ASSETS	
CURRENT ASSETS	
CASH	$134.45
ACCOUNTS RECEIVABLE	3,750.00
SUPPLIES	303.00
PREPAID INSURANCE	600.00
TOTAL CURRENT ASSETS	4,787.45
EQUIPMENT AND PROPERTY	
EQUIPMENT (COMPUTER)	$2,600.00
LESS ACCUMULATED DEPRECIATION (200.00)	2,400.00
TOTAL ASSETS	$7,187.45
LIABILITIES AND OWNER'S EQUITY	
CURRENT LIABILITIES	
ACCOUNTS PAYABLE	$788.97
ASSISTANT'S WAGES	300.00
TOTAL CURRENT LIABILITIES	1,088.97
LONG-TERM LIABILITIES	
BANK LOAN (COMPUTER)	780.00
TOTAL LIABILITIES	780.00
OWNER'S EQUITY	
J. MILLIAN, CAPITAL	5,318.48[*]
TOTAL LIABILITIES AND OWNER'S EQUITY	$7,187.45

Other Terms

The field of accounting has many terms and principles that are well beyond what we, as designers, need to have a working understanding of for our day-to-day business needs. However, there are several terms that you must at least recognize.

Assets

Assets are things that are of value to the company. They can be either tangible or intangible. Tangible assets are usually broken down into three categories: (1) current assets, such as cash, securities, bank deposits (checking and savings in the name of the company), and prepaid expenses (an airline ticket you pur-

---

* Refer to the income statement on page 35.

chased for a trip next month); (2) accounts receivable (invoiced or contract fees due from clients); and (3) inventory (fabrics, lamps, color media and patterns, platforms, drapery, etc.). Intangible assets don't generally have physical substance. A patent or copyright falls into this category. Or, for you designers who want to have a small business on the side, something like a franchise for a product line, such as two-way radio systems or a specific brand of color media, would also be intangible assets.

Accounts receivable are another form of liquid assets. When someone wants to know what your *liquid assets* are, they are asking for the amount of cash you can get your hands on in a reasonable amount of time. (By the way, if you need quick cash, you can ask the client to pay in advance or sooner than agreed upon—but be prepared to offer a discount.)

By the way, cash is defined as not only the physical dollars and coins in your lockbox (or under your mattress) but also money-market accounts and certificates of deposits with maturities under ninety days. Cash (bank balances are easiest), certificates of deposits, and money-market funds can be withdrawn early with some penalty. To get money out of stocks and inventory is much trickier and should not be counted on for fast conversion to cash.

Liabilities

Liabilities are the company's debts and obligations owed to other parties. These could include credit card bills, employees' wages, subcontractor fees, or goods purchased for a project, such as patterns or fabric, that are to be billed back to the client. Principal and interest on the bank loan for a computer or a company automobile also fall into this category.

Owner's Equity

Owner's equity is not very important unless there are partners or some type of corporation has been formed. If either is the case, then this issue of owner's equity and how it was derived will definitely be of interest to the attorney representing each partner or shareholder. To a sole proprietor, owner's equity simply shows how much you may be able to realize in cash if you close the business. Selling a business or shares gets into a whole other level of finance and is best discussed with a CPA and an attorney.

Double-Entry Bookkeeping

This system of bookkeeping has been around for a long time. Its principle is that every transaction is recorded as a debit or credit to one or more accounts and at the same time is recorded as the opposite, a credit or debit, to one or more accounts. This means that the accountant can look at the totals of each side of the ledger, and they should always be equal. An increase in income is a credit entry, and an increase in cash is a debit entry.

This may sound a little confusing, I know, which is why the new breed of bookkeeping programs mentioned earlier is so helpful. You will know where to put these entries after you answer simple prompts.

General Journal

When we write an invoice for our services, our assistant's time, for an invoice sent to recover expenses incurred on the project, or to track the receipt for the office supplies just purchased, we need to record these transactions in one place. This is called the general journal or simply the journal. Most journals have five columns: Date, Account Title/Description, Posting Reference, Debit, and Credit. Many designers have learned to keep this journal up to date and pass it on to their accountant for posting in the general ledger on a monthly basis.

To record a journal entry you first put down the date of the transaction. Then list the account affected by the transaction, such as cash if you paid cash for the office supplies. It is best to put in a short description, such as "office supplies." Skip the next column for now; it will be checked off when the transaction is "posted" to the General Ledger later by the bookkeeper/accountant. Then if the transaction was money spent, record the amount in the Debit column; if it was a check received from an invoice for your design services, record it under the Credit column. It is pretty simple. The hardest part is deciding what account to assign the transaction, so a call to the bookkeeper-accountant may be in order. At worst, write a note to yourself to explain the transaction to the bookkeeper the next time you speak to him, or deliver the journal for him to do the posting.

General Ledger

Now the bookkeeper/accountant takes the journal and does the posting to the general ledger. This is another point where I say, refer to another reference book on accounting or take a class! Understanding this process is why accountants and CPAs get paid to do what they do. I am certain very few of you would want to tackle this part of Accounting 101. Suffice it to say that this is where they enter the transactions you put into the journal and place them into their appropriate accounts. It is the book they will use to put together the statements and tax forms for you. It is a document that should be kept secure, and it can be opened for inspection by legal authority under certain circumstances or some-

J.P. MILLIAN COMPANY

DATE	ACCOUNT TITLE & DESCRIPTION	REF	DEBIT	CREDIT
2001				
March 1	Office Supplies			$127.45
	Cash Received		$127.45	
March 3	Income # 234		$2,500.00	
	Invoice #234 paid		$2,500.00	
March 6	Computer purchase		$8,500.00	
	March payment			$180.00
	Note balance			$8,320.00

times upon request of your lending institution (with your permission). Here again, the accounting programs will automatically assign your credits and debits to the proper side of the ledger.

Depreciation

This is another area best left to the accountant. In this phase, the accountant takes the general ledger and adjusts the line item that has depreciation. Depreciation is defined in *The McGraw-Hill 36-Hour Accounting Course* as "the exhaustion of the useful service potential of an asset through the combined effects of utilization, wear and tear, aging, and obsolescence" (131). There are, specified in the tax codes, ways for you to devalue a large piece of equipment so that you do not pay inventory tax or other taxes on property at the rate based on the cost of the item when it was new. What needs to be predetermined is how many years that item will have a useful or service life. Then employ one of the many depreciation patterns, such as straight-line, wavy-line, decreasing-line, composite, or group depreciation schedules. What do those terms mean? Read an accounting book, or better yet, ask your CPA to explain and advise you on which is the best pattern for the item you own.

In general, though, you deduct the estimated salvage value and then divide the remainder by five or ten years (or whatever you assume the usable life of the item is for your use). But keep in mind that the IRS has standards, and your accountant can tell you which depreciation schedules the IRS will normally allow. (Keep in mind, however, that they always reserve the right to change their minds after reviewing your methods and procedures.) That item then has a depreciated value and is the amount you are then going to deduct from your books each year to offset the reduced value of the item.

Trial Balance
Both before and after entering the adjustments to the books, the accountant will do a trial balance to make sure the books are in "balance" and in proper order. Accountants often use a work sheet; however, this is not required and is an optional step in the process. It should be considered an informal document not to be used as part of the final statements that can be viewed by you or shown for other business reasons.

Closing Entries
When you hear people talk about "closing the books," what they are referring to is that the accountant or bookkeeper has made all the adjustments and reconciled the bank accounts, and the information as of that date is to be used for the preparation of statements. This can be done on a monthly, quarterly, or yearly basis, depending on your discussion with your accountant. Remember that the more often your accountant does this, the more time is spent on your books—and that translates into more expense for you. But pay heed: a few dollars saved can cost you hundreds or thousands of dollars later. Discuss this issue with both your accountant and attorney for good measure.

The Rest of Accounting 101
There is much more to be learned about how accounting works and what it means to you as a designer, but for our purposes, if you simply understand the elements I have discussed, you will have a great advantage over your competitors. Getting started on a sound financial footing while you are young will make life so much easier when times are hard. Banks and loan brokers look at your history, and if they see a well-run business that has just fallen on hard times, they are more likely to grant credit. Also, an understanding early on of how finance works will most likely convince you that starting to save early in your career is a very wise thing to do.

We are in a business that may seem recession-proof, but history has punched many holes in that old wives' tale. I have spoken at length to many designers, production managers, and stage managers who have been very successful financially. Yet none would hesitate to tell a story or two of how they got caught cash poor at the most inopportune moment. Please, start a savings account and a conservative investment strategy; don't wait twenty years.

There are hundreds of books and seminars you can attend that purport to give you advice on investing and handling your money. Always approach an investment opportunity—especially a "can't fail" offer—with caution. Remember the old adage—if it sounds too good to be true, it probably is. But do look to securing your future, because no one else will. If you plan on working for the same company your whole career, forget it; 99.7 percent of the time that will not happen in this age of billion-dollar companies merging or going under. Even the old tried-and-true position of being a college professor with coveted tenure is no longer sacrosanct.

Lastly, I cannot stress enough that, as designers, we will probably never truly understand the world of finance and accounting because our brains are just not tuned that way. But please, seek assistance and guidance from creditable professionals whenever you feel the need to invest or make financial decisions. No one will take care of your money as well as you; look at the many bad examples of sports figures and musicians who are broke now.

Choosing a Bank

When it comes time to opening your business accounts, choose a bank that handles commercial transactions. These are often smaller banks, or a local branch of a bigger bank that have "business centers," as they are often called. Get to know the people by name and likewise make sure they know you on sight. Spend some time talking to the loan officer and business accounts manager, explaining the type of work you do, as well as what amounts and kinds of transactions you want them to handle, especially if you travel overseas often or receive bank transfers between financial institutions. When you then run into an overdraft situation or a client bounces a check, your bank contacts are more likely to make a courtesy call so you can correct the problem before it goes on your records. Now, they are under no legal responsibility to do this, but I have found that once a personal relationship has been established, a bank is much more likely to help, though only to the legal extent they can.

More Reading

Normally I would not do what I'm about to do, but at the risk of appearing to butter up my publisher, Tad Crawford, president of Allworth Communications, I am willing to take a chance this time. One of the reasons I wrote this book is because I have long held the belief that we in the creative community, and specifically the entertainment industry, have not received a fair shake when it comes to classes, books, and seminars that deal with our financial well-being. I was shown a book that Crawford had published called *The Business of Being an*

Artist by Daniel Grant. It was exactly what I believed we needed in our field. Although its main subject is fine artists and their search for ways to exhibit and sell their works, I think many of you may learn something from reading it, too. And lastly, Crawford, the author of several books himself, has written a novel that I am sure should be read by every designer, stage manager, and actor. It is called *The Money Mentor: A Tale of Finding Financial Freedom*, and is the story of a girl with financial troubles. It is an entertaining yet very effective tale that shows how everybody can reduce their debt and gain financial security. Happy reading!

CHAPTER 5
Business Liability and Insurance

If you have read the last chapter, the first thing that will probably come to mind when you hear the word *liabilities* is in regard to financial statements. But liabilities are not just the numbers in a ledger but something that you, as the company owner, are obligated to eventually clear from your books. This can be done in several ways: by paying money for the item, trading something such as services for it, or using a rebate certificate that will equal the amount due, plus many other ways of balancing the liability = debt formula. The practical understanding of liabilities can best be put into these words: *you have received something, and now you owe something.* This is as true about receiving a fee for services that you will now perform as it is if you agreed to defer a payment for a purchase in the future, such as on a credit card: Until you provide the service or pay the bill, there is a liability on your books. For example, when you tell your assistant that she will not be paid until you actually receive your fee, that amount is a liability until it is paid.

The problem that designers have with numbers on ledgers is that they mean very little to us. They aren't real. Things like profit and loss are just terms for accountants to use. What we care about is whether or not we can buy that new design book or replenish our tempera paints. But, here it comes . . . just because there is money in your business account, don't spend it! Check the liability column. What do you need to pay by the end of the month? Will the bills need to be paid out of what is in the account today, or will another check come in before the rent is due? And are you absolutely positive the check is in the mail? We must get a handle on where our money is going, both immediately for items we purchase with cash, as well as on the big items that will be due later.

Credit Reporting

When we don't pay a small credit card bill, even as little as $10, by the due date, that information goes into a monster pipeline and is sent to every credit reporting agency in the country. So, it was just a stupid ten bucks! Maybe it was a credit card you had while you were a student. Don't they realize students are always broke or waiting for their parents to send money? Everyone in school is in debt! But you have to realize that the credit reporting companies stay in business by telling member businesses bad things about you, not the good things! Just remember that having no credit history at all is an even bigger problem.

So you say, okay, I will never get a personal credit card, I'll never open a charge account in my name, and I'll only pay with cash—that way I won't ever have debt. Therefore they will have nothing bad to report. Wrong. That in itself makes for a bad report! If you go to lease an office the landlord will run a credit check. If the report comes back showing no credit history, you will probably not get the lease. Why? Because the landlord has no assurance as to your ability to pay an obligation over a long period of time. There is a saying often attributed to bankers: you need to be in debt to get a loan. Businesses rely on the fact that you have met your obligations in the past. So, your past personal credit history will be a big factor in starting your own business even if you have the cash to purchase the furniture, computers, and all the tangible items. The phone company and the office leasing agency, and anyone else that extends you credit wants a credit report showing that you have paid obligations over a long period of time.

Your credit suffers most easily from those unexpected late notices. In your carefree life as an artist, you may have had no time for the mundane world of finance. But you better change that tune, and quickly. The modern world revolves around *credit ratings*. And just because the bill is due on your business rather than your personal accounts does not necessarily insulate your personal credit rating. They are very intertwined. Once you show your ownership in a business on a credit application at Sears, that late notice goes into this monstrous network of interlinked computers that spread your personal and business financial history throughout the credit-reporting world.

If you see that you will not have money in the company account to pay a bill on time, contact the creditor immediately. Do not wait until the due date has passed. A call with an assurance of payment by a reasonable date is often enough to get them to hold off reporting the late payment to a credit agency. Now, don't try this too often or you will be doing nothing more than crying wolf.

Current and Long-Term Liabilities

Mortgages are liabilities, as are automobile loans. Liabilities fall into two categories, *current* or *short-term*, which are due within a year, and *long-term*, which will be paid over a number of years. Paying the rent monthly is a current liability, as are annual payments, such as property taxes. Long-term liabilities are mortgages on your house or condo, and your car payments, which are probably contracted for more than a year. Credit card debts are considered current or short-term debts.

We need to have an understanding of accounting, because the liabilities we add to the company reflect on us personally. Having a business will open some credit opportunities that you may not be able to get under your own personal credit. When the business is formed as some type of corporation, for example, there are more avenues open to a business for credit than an individual. But be warned: Just because it is a business, don't be surprised if the bank asks you to sign a personal guarantee for the loan, even though it is specifically a business item, such as a big drafting plotter.

So, you may ask, why bother with a formal business if you are still personally liable for the debts of the company? There are many reasons, some intangible, some that take time to build. Among the intangibles is the perceived view of clients that you are organized and dedicated to fulfilling their needs, and that you are responsible, have insurance and established business accounts, and will be around to finish the project and beyond.

Although this is not directly related, I also find the ability to "hide" behind a business name a plus. Have you ever gone into a meeting and been asked to make a commitment immediately? Will you do a project for XX dollars? Why? Because "they" (that mystical group you can never pin down) want someone else, but if you agree to the fee they are offering right now then they can get them to go with you. Car salespeople use this tactic. They get you all excited about that bright, shiny new car and then tell you they can only hold that special, low, low price *if* you buy it right now! No pressure.

The fact that you gave the guy a business card with a name other than your own allows you to say, if it were up to me personally, I'd jump at the chance to work with this great group. But, I don't have the authority to cut my rate. I'll go back to the office and really fight for it. I'll get right back to you, okay? What you have done is blunted and possibly even reversed the tactic. You have come back excited and shown you want to do the project—the only thing is, you are not the boss, you'll have to check first. What this does is give you a moment in the parking lot to take a deep breath and really consider the implications. Will the fee cover your minimum expenses? Will you be giving up other projects, and is that worth it? Is this the direction in which you want your career to go? Do you believe they are going to live up to the hype they have just handed you? Taking a moment to reflect, without pressure, is something I have always needed. Because I'm the type of person who is always ready for a new challenge, I jump at every project without thinking clearly what impact it will have on my other obligations. Ninety-nine percent of the time it works out, but why not have that moment to reflect? So, don't put your own name in the company name or list your title as "owner."

How Are We Liable?

Meeting with an attorney before or shortly after you start your business is a must. First you want to get to know someone you can trust before the day comes when there is "panic" and you need to get a contract reviewed quickly. That is not the time to explain your business. Yes, you probably will be charged a couple hundred dollars for this get-acquainted, informational meeting, but it is money well spent. After you outline your work and, if you are a member of USA, show him the form contracts and agreements you will be working with, she will have a sense of what service will be needed. Then any other legal help you may want, such as forming a corporation or checking your office lease, is much quicker. The attorney can describe all the ramifications from your incurring contractual obligations and debts, especially debts that you cannot pay. Can you say *bankruptcy*?

The facts are that it is no longer as easy as it once was to simply declare bankruptcy and start over without repayment of your debts. Those regulations were tightened just recently due to pressure from lending institutions. And as I have already pointed out, many business debts can also bring personal responsibility for repayment when the business closes. Remember as well that a partner who, without your direct knowledge, incurs a debt against the business, has also obliged you as a party to the agreement. In most circumstances it is the same as if you had written the check yourself, unless you have a written agreement that says a partner is not allowed to place the firm in a contractual or debt situation without a co-signature. Even then you will probably have to fight it out in court. Although the powers that be no longer put you in debtor's prison or take your firstborn child, the depths to which banks and loan institutions will go to collect from anyone even remotely connected with the obligation are legendary. So, avoid the problem in the first place. Put in the partnership agreement or the articles of incorporation limits on the amount a partner or shareholder can obligate the company.

What Can We Do to Protect Ourselves?

I cannot emphasize enough that even when you are first getting started, even if you do not think you will be incurring large liabilities, take every precaution to ensure that you keep your personal and business record clean. The easiest way for me to do this is to keep a day-by-day list of bills with their dates in order of date due (with a notation on when the *late fees* kick in). I keep a list updated in the notebook I carry with me. When I'm at a late rehearsal or on a plane, I can quickly check due dates and make notes about payments. One reminder, even if you pay the late fee, that does not stop merchants from reporting you to a credit-reporting agency. And believe me, they will not accept the fact that you were in tech hell or flying back from Spain and just didn't have time or simply forgot. Better yet, before you leave or start into tech, check your list and pay all bills that will become due while you are too pressed to think about business.

Protect yourself from bad debts by making sure that before you commit to a payment plan, you are sure you can meet the obligation. A good rule of thumb is that your debts should not add up to more than one-quarter of your long-term projected profit. That is usually the money you can expect to take out of the company to pay personal bills. That leaves half for housing and one-quarter for food, clothing, and out-of-pocket expenses. Remember to discount your disposable income by 33 to 45 percent for taxes (talk to your CPA about possible deductions and your tax bracket). If you are confident that you can draw $3,000 a month ($36,000 a year) from the business to pay your personal bills, you actually have something close to the following:

PERSONAL INCOME BUDGET			
DRAW, MONTHLY	$3,000.00		
ESTIMATED TAXES (35%)		($1,050.00)	
DISPOSABLE INCOME, NET			$1,950.00
RENT AND UTILITIES, PHONE		($975.00)	
CREDIT PAYMENTS		($487.50)	
FOOD, CLOTHING, POCKET		($487.50)	
BALANCE			$0.00

What I am leaving out of this equation are two very important items, so don't consider yourself home free. First, those unexpected expenses, such as that DVD player you can't live without, or the holiday presents you simply must purchase, or the unexpected flight home when a family member is sick. Second, *savings*. Did I say it loud enough? SAVINGS!

Business managers will tell you that you should have savings equal at least to one year's income to tide you over a slow period. So, if you didn't get a big cash present from Uncle Phil for graduation that you can sock away, you had better build a savings plan into the above budget. How much? Professional planners say it should be at least one-eighth of your disposable income. For the budget above, that would be $243.75 a month. People come up with different ways to save. I have friends who take any check they receive and put final figures of amounts under $100 into savings. Some people give themselves a weekly cash allowance, and anything remaining at the end of the week goes into savings. Whatever you can devise that will let you give up some money without prying it from your clenched and bleeding fingers is okay. I have been told that if you stick with a plan when you start your career, you could be looking at a fund of over $1 million in thirty years. So, save something, anything.

Client's Liability for Payment

Well, we may be able to protect ourselves against going into debt, but can we protect ourselves against what other people do? No, not a chance—forget it! Getting clients to pay on time is a problem for small businesses, especially if you have already completed the work, or they do not agree to payment after the fact. What you can do, in most cases, is not much. You cannot put a lien on a lighting plot. Although you can put a lien on the costumes or the set, I doubt you are really prepared to back up a truck and take it away. Our problem is that we do not have people to do collections, nor do we want to. And even if you feel you will lose a client if you call and bug them about your money, you really have to think about whether it's worth it to have such a client. If the answer is no, then bug them; stand on their doorstep if you have to. Some will only react to strong, but legal, tactics. Surprisingly, they may respect you for taking the action. If you go into a project knowing you will have a hard time collecting, then you just better not do it.

Another way to go is when not-for-profit clients say they don't have much money for designers and certainly can't meet your fee. Tell them you'll do it as charity, for nothing, rather than take a cut in your fee. However, you can deduct materials you use, such as expendable items or rentals or purchases you make for a benefit show. The idea of saying you'll do the work as *charity* is not meant in the legal sense, only as a way of making them feel you are a professional and only work for appropriate wages. Since they do not seem to be able to afford your professional service, you might agree to do it for nothing, rather than lower your standards. Sometimes it is better to work for nothing than to let it be known you will work for substandard fees. But, of course, you will want your out-of-pocket expenses covered. Those expenses often amount to more than the client wanted to pay in the first place, so you may well make out better than you would getting a small fee.

Because we are considered creative people, many producers think designers will just roll up in a ball and go away because they are the ones in control. But that does not have to be true. Using your lawyer to send a letter indicating possible legal action is often enough to get a discussion started on a payment plan. And there are the small-claims courts, which will be discussed in chapter 14. Sometimes the cost of pursuing the client is just too great, and we need to take the loss and move on—always with some knowledge of what went wrong and what we learned from it, so we don't repeat the misjudgment again.

Business Liability

This is the "other" liability we face, both personally and as a business. Our actions, as well as our nonactions, have consequences. Our design business may make a mistake that costs our clients time and money, so they may come to us to recoup those funds, either by withholding part of our fee or asking us to pay for certain claims made against them. Or we could be cited in a lawsuit as a party to some negligent action. Maybe a set wall fell over on a show you designed, and someone is injured who was walking through the stage. Do you think the theatre will be the only one sued? Guess again. Lawyers will file against the theatre management, the theatre owners, the producer, the production company, the person who dropped the flat (if they can find him; if not, they list a hundred "John Does") and *you*. You may not have even been in the building at the time; it doesn't matter. You did the design that said to put the set piece there, didn't you? Did you personally give the carpenter instruction on how to put the wall up? You didn't? How careless of you! Never mind that the guy has twenty-six years of experience as a union stagehand.

You get the idea. We must protect ourselves in every possible way, and even in ways we cannot conceive of sitting here. Is it a crapshoot? You bet, but one in which it is possible to protect ourselves with proper insurance.

Insurance

The amount and kinds of coverage that are required, let alone advisable, for businesses can pile up quickly. Being well insured does not just protect you alone. Some policies are required, and you must keep them in force or be personally liable for any costs of judgments against the company, and be open to criminal penalties to boot. If we define *insurance,* it is understood to mean that a legal relationship between two parties exists in which one party agrees to pay a set amount of money in exchange for protection from a financially devastating loss.

Workers' Compensation

Most states mandate that a *workers' compensation insurance* policy be in place even if you do not have full-time employees. The reasoning is that businesses have a legal responsibility to their employees to make the workplace safe and to protect themselves from lawsuits resulting from workplace accidents, as well as to provide medical care and compensation for lost income to workers injured in a workplace accident. Each state has laws governing the amount and duration of lost income benefits, as well as medical and rehabilitation services. Owners of a business can choose to be covered by this policy or not, but if not, they must be specifically excluded. The issue is cost. Since the premiums are calculated based on the actual salaries paid, adding the owner's salary (assuming you pay yourself or your partners a set salary and not a "draw" against profits), which is most likely the largest one, will raise the cost of the premiums greatly. So, you need to choose carefully. Do you feel you will be putting yourself in a situation where harm can come to you? If the answer is yes, think seriously about this coverage for yourself.

Public Liability

Another standard policy is public liability insurance that protects you in case of a lawsuit for damage or injury in connection with the business. This is often cited as the "old lady who slips on the sidewalk" case. For the insurer to pay a claim on this policy, however, is not automatic. Insurers will investigate to make sure you took reasonable precautions to prevent injury and damage to property and persons. If you, as the owner, are found to be negligent, then they will not pay the claim. But there really is a need to carry this insurance and, in fact, it is probably a legal requirement in many states and towns if you have a business license. Such a policy will need to specifically list the landlord, if you are leasing, as additionally insured so that they will be indemnified if any action is taken against you that they might be listed as being a party to as well.

Business Insurance

This is a general category, which offers policies that combine protection from all major property and liability risks in one package. Although a package can be the best price break that a small or medium sized business can get, it does not traditionally include professional liability, auto insurance, workers' compensation, or health and disability insurance. But each component can be issued separately. They include:

* Property insurance for buildings and contents.
* Business interruption insurance, which covers the loss of income resulting from a fire or other catastrophe that disrupts the operation.
* Liability protection for the business, which covers the legal responsibility for the harm caused to others.

But business insurance can cover much more, as well. Let's say you decide to make a few extra dollars by renting the intercom system and billing the producer with a fair markup. The company you rent or lease the equipment from will want to be insured under an *additionally insured* clause in your policy. This is usually done for free or just a small charge by your insurance agent. Don't confuse this with another term, *named insured,* which occurs when the other party is added to your policy and *all* the protections are extended to that party, not just for the events connected to the specific equipment leased or rented for a short period. If the equipment injures someone and the company is sued because it owns the equipment, the owners don't want the cost taken against their policy, so you must take on the obligation. If you lease or rent equipment, off copiers, or full touring lighting systems, the owner will ask to be added to your policy as additionally insured and will be issued a certificate of insurance by your carrier. This legally shows them as a party to your policy, but for specific items and limits. Then if your business catches fire, not only is your personal property covered but also the physical property you leased or rented. The insurance companies have another term called a "binder." That is what is issued to cover the time between when you pay the policy premium and the arrival of the policy, usually good for thirty days. A "co-insured" places another party as equal to you in ownership of the policy and will divide any proceeds from a claim, unless some limiting language is in the policy.

Professional Liability

This is a policy different from business insurance. It protects you against financial loss from lawsuits filed against you by your clients. Since professionals are expected to have extensive technical knowledge or training in their area of expertise, they are also expected to perform those services according to the standards of conduct in their profession. If you fail to use the degree of skill expected, you can be held responsible for any harm you cause to another person or business.

Errors and Omissions Liability

I have placed this liability under a separate heading, even though it is a component of professional liability insurance, because it is a specific part of the above, not the whole. This is the type of insurance architects need so that when plans leave out the twenty-seventh floor of the building, for example, it is considered an "error," not criminal disregard. But because the building materials were budgeted and the workers hired on the basis of the submitted plans, someone has to pay the extra costs. This insurance protects the architect from digging into his or her own pockets. A lawyer would also have this insurance for when a brief is missing six pages that are critical to the case because the copy machine ate them. The omission isn't caught and the case is lost because of the missing evidence.

The key word here is *inadvertently;* such actions will not be covered if they are deemed to have occurred due to lack of skill or sloppy workmanship.

Does this apply to designers? Absolutely. Does it apply to production managers? Probably. What if, as the production manager or road manager, you are asked to prepare a budget for a large touring show? It goes out to bid and contracts are signed by the producer. Then it is discovered that you missed sending four pages of required equipment that were not included in the winning bid. Who pays for the additional equipment? You may not, but I am sure you will not work for that producer again.

I believe that designers should have this policy, especially if they are going to work in the themed and commercial areas. But talk to an insurance professional, outline your work, and get an opinion. Now, I know it will be easy for you to say you don't have any money anyway, so what can they do? Well, a lot. Again, you need to go over this with professionals for their advice. Although this is not a traditional insurance for theatre practitioners, it is an area of growing concern for our financial well-being.

Key Employee Life

The unexpected loss of your main assistant, associate, or partner is a major blow to a small business. You probably do not have the staff to just move the projects they were working on to someone else. And, quite possibly, the client will not want to just accept a new person whom he doesn't know. So there is a very good chance the business will lose income, which could be of an amount that cannot be sustained by the business. Losses caused by the death of a key employee are insurable. The cost of these policies varies greatly based on a scale consisting of the age, health, and role of the employee in the operation. The insurer will also factor in any hobbies considered dangerous. The policy is normally owned by the company and pays the benefits to the company, not to the person's heirs. *Life insurance* can also be paid for by the company as part of a benefits package to the employee but has no special attachment to the business.

Commercial Auto

As a business owner, you need the same kinds of insurance coverage for the car you use in your business as you do for a car used for personal travel. In fact, many of us use the same vehicle for both business and pleasure. If the vehicle is owned by the business (a perk you should look into after you have formed a legal entity,) make sure the name of the business appears on the policy as the "principal insured" rather than your own name. Although the coverage is generally the same as your personal auto policy, there are some technical aspects that differ. If you have a personal liability policy on your car, there is probably an exclusion for business-related liability written into it that would deny payment if it is proven you were using the auto at the time of the accident for business purposes. Check with your insurance broker.

Home Businesses

If you are running a business from your home, you may not have enough insurance to protect your business equipment. A typical homeowner's policy provides only $2,500 coverage for business equipment, which is usually not enough to cover all of your business property. You may also want coverage for liability and lost income. Insurance companies are not all the same when it comes to home business coverage, so you will need to shop around to find one that understands your needs. Regardless of the type of policy you choose, if you're a professional working out of your home, you probably need professional liability insurance.

Homeowner's Policy Endorsement

You may be able to add a simple endorsement to your existing homeowner's policy to double your standard coverage for business equipment such as computers. A homeowner's liability endorsement will cover a client who drops by or a deliveryman who gets hurt on your property. These endorsements are normally only available to businesses such as those of writers, who have only a few visitors. A designer probably would qualify, but check with an insurance professional.

In-Home Business Policy

This provides more comprehensive coverage for business equipment and liability than a homeowner's policy endorsement. These policies vary greatly depending on the business and the insurer. But they have the benefit of normally reimbursing you for the loss of important papers and records, accounts receivable, and off-site business property. Some will even pay business interruption (income loss) in the event your home is so badly damaged that it can't be used for a while. Some policies provide for a small number of full-time employees to be paid, generally up to three.

In short, you and your partners or shareholders need to discuss the different types of insurance with an agent and talk about what needs to be written to cover the business. Insurance is probably the second biggest expense a small business faces after rent, so it is tempting to cut it short. But if ever a large claim is made against the business, the money spent on premiums might just be a minor amount in comparison to the judgment. One out of five small businesses are sued each year. A word of caution: most policies have limits that will be paid either on a single claim or over the life of the policy, so it is possible that not all the judgment would be covered. Again, check very carefully and consider the options available.

Lastly, the Insurance Information Institute, at *www.iii.org,* has very helpful information on the facts about and uses of the different insurance plans. You can also get booklets from your insurance agent.

CHAPTER 6
Financial and Legal Considerations

Another thing that brings terror to the hearts of many designers is to hear that the IRS is calling! The Internal Revenue Service enjoys a "bully" reputation. They have been accused for years of unevenly applying the tax codes and, in some cases, making them up as they go. However, Congress is hesitant to act to reform the system. It is true that the federal tax codes are very complicated and are subject to many interpretations. That is why tax lawyers are very wealthy. But believe me, you can survive an audit.

Over the years, I have had to face the IRS more than once, and most times came out feeling that the agent tried to be very fair even if I had taken a chance and pushed the "gray" area a little. Now we are not talking federal tax evasion here, just questionable choices from the list of "you can do it this way or do it that way" and maybe get *red flagged* and questioned on something you took as a deduction. A **red flag** is a term used by IRS agents to indicate that their computer program has shown an excessive percentage or dollar amount in a category on a tax filing. Most tax preparers know where these red flags are and will caution clients when entering these areas. It does not mean you have cheated, only that the area is one they watch for excessive deductions. Remember, your CPA "advises" you and then does what you tell her. CPAs do open themselves to legal responsibility if they knowingly violate the tax laws. They can be prosecuted and lose their license. So, no reputable CPA is going to put themselves in such a situation. As long as your papers fully document your business transactions and you have not tried to hide large amounts of profits or written off personal items, you should have little to worry about from the IRS.

Knowing what forms you need, and at what point you will need to file them with the IRS and your state taxing authority, is something that must be discussed and planned far in advance with your CPA and/or tax attorney. A tax attorney is someone who has a special law degree, an LL.M. or a tax specialization certificate from a state bar association. Keeping good records is your responsibility, but making sure you know what is legally deductible so you can track the expenses is why you want a CPA. What tax code section you will follow will depend on what legal form you decide to use to structure your business. Again, discussion with these professionals *before* you form the company is a very wise move.

I am sure some of you are saying, but I don't need to form a business. I work for a college and just do a little designing on the side. Or, I have a staff stage management position with an LORT theatre company, why do I need to go through all this paperwork, hire accountants and lawyers, and assume a big expense just to say I'm the J.P. Millian Company for my off-season work?

The world of theatre and the broader spectrum of entertainment design have exploded in the past ten years. Once comfortable college professors are now on the prowl for outside design work for two very important reasons. First, their departments look upon outside design work as meeting the old criteria of "publishing" when it comes to the arts. And you "publish or perish," as the old saying goes around the ivy halls. Second, pure economics; professors want their families to have the things a little extra income brings. The situation holds equally well for "staff" designers who can pick up extra design or management gigs on the off-season. Corporate shows pay production managers and stage managers very, very well! So, do we have an understanding? It is not even a question that there will be times in your theatrical life in which work will come about that doesn't fall under the legal definition of an employer-employee relationship. Prepare for it now!

Bearing this in mind, do not assume you are obligated to run out, rent an office, hire a secretary, print stationery, and join a country club. The really important step to take is recognizing that you are in fact a business and then proceeding with your career on a businesslike basis. This means you accept the responsibility of dealing with the public, clients, and government professionally. Understanding your position where it concerns the legal system, tax, and liability issues will be your first and most pressing learning curve. Next comes facing the frustration that comes when your accountant tells you at the end of the year that you didn't make any money. But remember that such a verdict is not an absolute; she is speaking in the business-sense of the term, not the coins and bills you have in your pocket. So, as I said in chapter 4, learn some Accounting 101.

What we need to do now is build a solid foundation for your business, both in the economic and legal sense, as well as in your comprehension of how it can work for you. You need to build a better life, both in your dealings with clients and your financial security.

Paperwork for Starting a Business

You have decided to engage in work as an independent designer for a production. Whether your potential client has already said that this will not be a staff position and you will not be added to his payroll or not, you decide to be your own boss and control your own finances. Being a business does not preclude you from working a salaried job at any time. On the contrary, there are ways to have your cake and eat it, too.

d.b.a.—Doing Business As

You must do a *d.b.a.* (doing business as) or, as it is legally called, a *fictitious name* filing. This is true for a sole proprietorship, partnership, or even a corporation. And it must be renewed every five years. The notice is published in a local newspaper for four days and then copied by the newspaper and sent to the city or county clerk's office, where it is kept on file. The cost varies depending on the newspaper it is printed in. Another note of warning: filing a d.b.a. does not protect you from someone else filing the same fictitious name in another city. Such protection requires getting into *trademark* registration of your business name and/or logo; a discussion of this issue is something you need to speak to an attorney about. Trademark registration is not cheap and probably is not worth the expense, but you should get some information if you are worried about it.

Federal Employer I.D. Number

Next on the list is the *federal employer I.D. number,* or EIN. If your business is not a sole proprietorship, you need to obtain IRS form W-9, *Request for Taxpayer Identification Number.* Even if you are not reselling items and only collecting fees for your services, the EIN number is essential. (If you are a sole proprietor you can use your personal Social Security number.) First, most banks will not open a business account without an EIN number. Second, although it may be an anomaly that only holds true here in Hollywood, most studios will not pay any person as a business without that number. If your business does not have a number yet, the employer must pay you as an employee using your Social Security number when it files its tax forms with the state and federal governments. Then you are an individual, and withholding taxes must be deducted from the salary or fee. This brings us to the independent contractor issue, which will be addressed later in this chapter.

What's the problem with getting taxes taken out right away? Don't you need to pay them later anyway, you ask? In fact, many places will do just about anything not to call you an employee and go through all the paperwork with the IRS . . . even pay you more. They also do not want the liability if you get injured or do damage or cause injury to others. And they do not want the expense of doing all the paperwork required when you are an employee. There are a lot of forms and filings of taxes—local, state, and federal, plus workers' compensation insurance payments, and possibly union vacation, health, and retirement plan payments that need to be calculated and paid before you get your check.

Business License

Next you will want to get a business license from your city or county clerk's office. They will usually be happy to help with the paperwork. The fee you will pay is based on the category in which they place your business. Normally it will be "professional services." In addition, if you want to rent or sell equipment or supplies on the side, then other categories will be added as appropriate. Only a few states, including Alaska and Washington, require all businesses to obtain a general business license. You can contact the Small Business Administration at 409 3rd Street SW, Washington, D.C. 20416, (800) 827-5722 for a list of state resources and requirements, as well as on most city and state Internet sites.

If you do decide that renting or selling equipment is a nice way of bringing in extra income, you will need to go to your state's tax board and get a resale number. This is so you can collect sales tax on items sold, which is currently 7.25 to 8 percent in California, depending on the county you are doing business in. A resale number also allows you to purchase the items you are going to sell without paying tax to the person you bought them from. When you the resell it, however, you must collect the tax and pay it to some governmental agency, usually called a state franchise tax board.

Business Entities

Even if you choose to work alone, these are not the only business forms you must consider. Although the sole proprietorship is the simplest in terms of paperwork and tax forms, it does not shield you from being personally responsible for taxes due against the company, for lawsuits, or for liability. Even if you go to the expense and trouble to form your business into a corporation, you may not be shielded from lawsuits. When lawyers manage to get behind the business entity and slap suits on the actual owners, it is often called "piercing the corporate vale" of the company. Just because the law says a business is an entity and has a legal status in our society, doesn't mean that we can always hide behind it.

Who owns a company and to what extent he or she is responsible for debts and taxes, as well as how liable for legal actions taken against the company, is entirely based on the form the company takes in the public eye. Of course, we always hope that our ownership rights bring us profit and security, but "plan for the worst and hope for the best" is a sound motto. The fact is, you may end up being liable for debt and taxes no matter how your company is set up, with some very important exceptions—which need lengthy explanation, by an attorney. Nevertheless, there are still many positive reasons for forming a company, so take advantage of the protection a legal entity can provide for you.

Sole Proprietorship

The simplest legal formation of a business is called a *sole proprietorship.* Only a few formalities are required. And as I said, some municipalities will require you to obtain a business license. Most states require you to do a filing with them if you are doing business under an assumed name instead of your own. Even adding... *and Associates* to your given name is enough to trigger more paperwork.

One of the perceived advantages of forming a sole proprietorship is that the owner can take money out of the business and not pay taxes other than as personal income. The form of taxation here is referred to as *self-employed* taxing. However, there are disadvantages in this, as well. First, you are not automatically covered by workers' compensation insurance, unless you make yourself an employee of your own company (that means you must pay yourself a salary and deduct taxes as a normal employee would). Either way, you will get Social Security benefits because, as a self-employed person, you pay both halves of the tax—employer and employee. FICA, Medicare, and Social Security are normally paid half by the employer and half by the employee. Since you are, in essence, both halves, the taxing entities must get their money—but workers' compensation is different. Owners cannot be covered unless they are also employees, which means getting a regular salary with deductions withheld. Self-employed people normally take out a private insurance policy to cover injuries and other needs (see chapter 5).

It would be wise to keep in close contact with a CPA, as the federal government is tinkering with the Social Security system; you are well advised to look to your own resources for a comfortable retirement, not the dole. Those things are now up to you to arrange. Again, these changes can be viewed as a good thing. You just need to be aware of the options available to you.

A sole proprietor is personally and fully liable for the debts of the company. If the business fails, its creditors can go after the owner's non-business income and assets, such as a car, savings, or home.

Take note that many states allow you to "homestead" your primary residence. Most of us would say our home is our most valuable asset. Homestead laws protect our homes from claims of creditors, but vary greatly from state to state. Under these laws, each state declares that a certain amount of equity (value) of the homestead is protected against particular types of creditors. The problem is that what you might consider a "home" may not qualify under this statute—an example of this is a "live-aboard" boater (a boat is not "real estate"). However, all homestead laws provide that the exemption applies to real estate that is your primary residence and that you own and occupy. But you must look to each state for what they consider your homestead. The bottom line is that the applicable laws as defined in each state may only protect between $10,000 and $60,000 of the equity, not the physical home itself. So you may well still be out on the street, but with some cash in your pocket eventually. If you live in Florida or Texas, those states protect an unlimited value on the property. In whatever state you live, protection is not automatic. You must file for this exemption. Some states require the form to be given to you during escrow; ask your real estate agent how it is done in your state. Some states even have a time limit required for state residence for the statute to apply. The big red flag here is that not all creditors are covered. Therefore the homeowner must be very clear on what his or her state does protect concerning debt collection. The IRS and other federal agencies can take the property no matter what state you live in. However, some states, such as Florida, do protect real estate from private judgments; witness some Enron executives in 2002 still building multimillion-dollar estates while under indictment for fraud.

Then again, if you do not form a sole proprietorship and you get into debt, the same things can happen, so there isn't really much of a downside to forming a sole proprietorship, as far as I am concerned. To me, there are many more positives to forming even this simplest of legal entities.

Partnership

A partnership simply adds one or more persons to the ownership list of the company and can be done initially or any time after the sole proprietorship is formed. The big danger here is that each partner has full power to contract debts on behalf of the partnership. In addition, the wrongful acts of one partner will expose the other partner or partners to equal liability. Each and every partner is responsible for the debts incurred by the other partners. Remember, however, that partnerships do not need to last forever. It may be advantageous to form a partnership solely to meet the demands of a big project, then go your separate ways after the project is completed.

If you are thinking about forming a partnership, it is best to clearly establish each partner's participation. What percentage will each partner hold in the company? Will one of the partners be inactive, such as a silent partner who is only providing capital, while you are the designer responsible for the project's creative input? There are two forms of partnership: *general* and *limited*. The general form means that all parties are essentially equal in their day-to-day participation in the business. However, they can each own uneven percentages of the business. Here also a d.b.a. filing is in order. A limited partnership requires filing of documents evidencing the partnership and the specific relationship between the partners. This is usually a partnership where one or more partners do the day-to-day work of running the firm and the other partners are essential investors hoping to gain profit from the other's work. If you do agree to take on a partner, be very sure you have worked out a detailed business plan with your accountant and a *partnership agreement* with the partner(s). In many cases, people have gotten out of marriages more easily than they have a partnership gone bad.

You must consider worst-case scenarios when crafting this document. Most attorneys will have sample agreements that they can use to help guide you through the process. There are also software programs on CD-ROM that have any number of legal forms and agreements to choose from, but always consult with an attorney before signing anything.

Go through all the "What ifs" you can possibly think of for things that could go wrong. It will be a long list. The potential partners should not take this process personally; you must approach this in a businesslike manner. After you have done a draft, try the "What ifs" out to see if they are all covered. *What if* a partner's husband sues for divorce; will she have to sell her shares to meet the court's demands? *What if* a partner dies and his wife, who has no design background, decides she wants to join the business? Can she do that? No; if a partner dies, the partnership is automatically dissolved. This changes, however, when the stock is owned in a corporation. After all, as the widow, she probably has legal title to the husband's shares in the firm as an asset from the marriage. Each shareholder owns a percentage of the stock in the company. So, the partner, as a person, is not at issue; it is who retains ownership of the stock certificates themselves.

How about the situation where a partner declares personal bankruptcy? Have you the funds to buy him out, or will the whole company be sold to satisfy his debts? This can happen even though they were his personal debts and were not the obligations of the company.

When a partner dies, does it mean that everything must be sold at a fire sale? No; partners often take out insurance on each other, generally to provide money to pay the deceased partner's heirs, but even to cover the possibility of a partner becoming incapable of working full-time due to illness or injury. The insurance can help cover costs of hiring others to pick up the burden, as well as pay for medical bills. In a corporation, the share ownership passes to the heirs unless specific language is included in the partnership agreement forcing a sale.

Partnership/Shareholder Agreement

I see this as a very important document that protects and insures me, as a partner, against others' actions taken without my knowledge or consent. Although not required by state and federal law, it is the agreement you should make if anyone else shares ownership with you in the business. In it, you spell out what each partner is responsible for in the day-to-day activities of the business, what compensation plan will be used, and who has authority to sign checks. It can even put limits on an individual's ability to sign a large check. All this should be spelled out clearly in this document.

Whatever you do, do not think that friendship will resolve these issues later on. You are entering into a business with another or several other people who have their own dreams, goals, and agendas. Make sure up front that you all have goals that are mutually advantageous for all parties in the document. You are forming a business, and it is best to know where everyone stands before you get in bed together. It may seem like you are starting the marriage on a sour note—and believe me, a business partnership is a marriage—but ultimately, all partners will realize the benefits of having resolved issues up front. Then, when there is a problem, which there will be eventually, you will have already crafted very specific actions to be taken to resolve them. Even if that means a partner or stockholder leaves, the mechanism is in place to deal with that specific issue, which will save you a long legal action that could be very costly. One big issue should be worked out prior to the death of a partner. The agreement should obligate the estate to sell the shares to the corporation as laid out in a pre-agreed-upon formula. Thus, the estate receives money quickly, yet the partners do not find themselves with an unwanted shareholder who is not a productive, working partner. The partnership agreement for our firm, which covers four principals who are also the stockholders, is over seventeen pages long.

More Complex Entities

While many of you should start with a sole proprietorship or partnership, a few will have built a practice that has grown beyond hand-to-mouth income to step up to a more complex business arrangement. It is never too early to start discussing this with an attorney or your CPA.

Corporations

To form a corporation is a much bigger step and should be thoroughly discussed with an attorney. However, the advantages usually outweigh the initial costs when more than one person will be actively working for the benefit of the company. But even one person, in most forms of corporation, can be a corporation, and there are advantages to this.

First, some large production companies and studios will not pay an invoice (gross amount without taxes) for services, as a matter of policy, to an individual or a d.b.a. business, mainly because of liability exposure. That exposure relates to whether the IRS would agree that you are an independent contractor. It is possible that after the producer pays you your full fee, the IRS could come back and disallow it. This could cost the producer a lot of money and a 20 percent fine. However, it is less likely to happen if you are a legally incorporated company. And speaking of liability, a corporation provides protection to the shareholders from lawsuits and liability, too. How much protection is afforded is debatable. Unfortunately, in recent years, it has not proven to be an ironclad wall against personal responsibility of the owner for judgments against the company. But it depends on the type of corporation formed, and since there are some sixteen specific types, an attorney must help you decide what affords the best protection for your circumstances.

As for the second point—taxes—stockholder/partners are in some respects doubly taxed, so avoiding taxes is not the major reason for forming a corporation. From a practical standpoint, money can be kept in the company's accounts and not distributed to the shareholders as *dividends,* it is true. But if dividends are paid, they are taxed as income to the partner or stockholder. It is better to vote "bonus" payments to partners and even employees, as that works out at a better tax rate. Remember, the profit shown on the books at the end of the financial year is taxed at the corporate rate. The government, believe it or not, wants companies to keep money so that they can grow, create more jobs, and eventually pay even more taxes. At least that's the theory.

The state will do a search to make sure the name you have chosen to call your corporation is not already taken (this is only for your state; the name could be on file in another state). A form called the *articles of incorporation* must be filed with the secretary of state in the state you form the corporation. This form lays out the specifics of what business the owners wish to engage in. It lists how much stock will be issued and other legal necessities that a lawyer should go over with you. There are computer programs that have the outlines and forms, but a face-to-face meeting with a knowledgeable attorney is preferable. If everything is in order and the filing fees are paid, the secretary of state will issue a *charter* or *certificate of incorporation.* This will cost between several hundred dollars and as much as one thousand dollars, depending on the state. Also, shop around for which state to incorporate in. Some give tax incentives to corporations formed in their states. That is why a check you receive from a big studio or network is often drawn on a small bank in New Jersey or Nevada. California and New York have stricter corporate laws. But if you do have a business presence, such as an office in another state, you will have to file forms there also and may be taxed in addition by that state. In essence you can be double taxed if you are not careful. Need I say again, check with your tax adviser.

The corporation will need to pay withholding taxes, employer FICA, and Social Security on wages for you, even if you are a shareholder. This is unavoidable if you also act as an executive for the firm. So, if you take a regular salary for services you provide to the corporation, you actually become an employee of the corporation.

Subchapter S

For businesses with fewer than thirty-five individual shareholders, you can elect to be governed under a section in the Internal Revenue Code called an *S Election*. Mainly this allows the corporation to take advantage of a taxation issue. The corporation in essence allows the IRS to tax its shareholders as if they were a partnership. This means that the corporation is not a taxable entity. However, the advantages of being this type of corporation in other areas, such as liability, are still in place.

C Corporations

Other corporations, such as *C Corporations*, are treated as a separate legal entity. The business pays taxes on its profits, not the shareholders personally. What the shareholders do pay in taxes are funds they take from the corporation in *dividends*, which must be shown on their personal income tax. The corporation pays other taxes on money it wishes to hold for future expenses, purchases, and long-term investing.

Limited Liability Company

A limited liability company is a relatively new business form that is seeing a lot of use, particularly in motion picture companies but most notoriously in Arthur Andersen, LLC. Through this legal form, the owners' liability is limited to their personal investment, and they enjoy the tax status of a partnership. California recently became one of the last states (Massachusetts is the remaining holdout) to change the California Corporations Code such that a one-person LLC is now allowed. Sole proprietorships can convert their existing businesses into an LLC if they choose. An LLC is not a taxable entity. Ordinarily, the LLC itself does not pay taxes. Rather, all profits and losses pass through to the owner's individual income tax return. The protection afforded them from personal lawsuits arising out of the activities of the company seem to outweigh the higher tax on the profit, at least for a growing number of people. It is currently the most popular business form, and some experts feel it will attract more business than sole proprietorships and traditional corporations in the years to come.

Independent Contractor

Whether you are an individual or a company under any of the forms above, the issue of who is and who is not an *independent contractor* has become a very hot issue in the entertainment industry. This is not just between you and a potential client, but between you and anyone who works under you, such as a carpenter, seamstress, or master electrician, all of whom you may wish to pay a flat fee for their services. The fact is that an independent contractor can save an employer a bundle in payroll taxes, health insurance costs, workers' compensation premiums, and overtime pay, which all add up to around 20 to 30 percent of the payroll. But the rules on who qualifies are complicated.

A recent publication will help clarify this confusing area. *Hiring Independent Contractors: The Employer's Legal Guide*, by attorney Stephen Fishman, does not deal specifically with entertainment cases, but it does give very good legal definitions and examples to follow.

But here's a big warning. You must understand that as an independent contractor you will receive a tax form called a 1099 from the producer at the end of the year, not a W-2 form, which is for someone who is an actual employee and has had tax deducted from his or her pay. If you are paid on a 1099, you are considered an independent contractor and therefore probably not covered by the producer for workers' compensation insurance, especially if you are paid through your corporation. If you are injured on the job the producer you have contracted with has no responsibility. You would need to file suit for damages if you feel the employer was negligent. As an independent contractor you have assumed full responsibility not only for your taxes, but in many cases, complete liability.

How often has a friend who helped you out on a job said to you, I will send you an invoice, and I don't want any taxes withheld? You and your friend probably assume that he is not an employee and, likewise, that others you hire under similar circumstances are not employees of yours either. Wrong, wrong, and let's throw in another one for good measure . . . wrong!

The Employer Resource Institute Inc. gives a very good checklist for employers to follow concerning the hiring of outside workers. (They can be contacted at P.O. Box 378, Tiburon, California 94920-0378, or on their Web site, *www.employeradvise.com*.) The institute points out that to mistakenly classify an employee as an independent contractor can cost the business a bundle in fines and penalties. It has come up with twenty factors used by the IRS to determine whether an employer has enough control over a worker for that worker to be an employee. These are only intended as guidelines; the IRS has said that ultimately, the importance of each factor depends on the individual circumstances. So, the IRS will not simply accept the designation you or the person chooses to use, be that independent contractor, agent, partner, or the like. Even if you have a written agreement stating that the other party agrees there is no employer-employee relationship, the IRS will make a determination based on its own investigation. The line here is very questionable. Do we not interact and in many instances bow to the will of the producer or director, and are we not, therefore, subject to "control or direction"? Do we not agree that the director's vision of the play is the guiding principle we use to mold our designs? Read on.

The list below can be used as a guide for potential employers in determining who should be hired as an employee and who can be contracted as an independent contractor. It is believed that if the answer is yes to the first four questions, then the person is probably an independent contractor. But yes to *any* of questions 5 through 20 means they need to be a worker subject to employee status.

1. **Profit or loss.** Can the worker make a profit or suffer a loss as a result of the work, aside from the money earned from the project?

2. **Investment.** Does the worker have an investment in the equipment and facilities used to do the work? (The greater the investment, the more likely such workers are independent contractors.)

3. **Works for more than one firm.** Does the person work for more than one company at a time? (This is not conclusive, since workers can work for more than one employer at a time.)

4. **Services offered to the general public.** Does the worker offer services to the general public? (Does she or he take out ads in the newspaper?)

5. **Instructions.** Do you have the right to give the worker instructions about when, where, and how to work? (This shows control.)

6. **Training.** Do you train the worker to do the job in a particular way?

7. **Integration.** Are the worker's services so important to your business that they have become a necessary part of the business? (This shows the worker is subject to control.)

8. **Services rendered personally.** Must the worker provide the services personally, as opposed to delegating tasks to someone else?

9. **Hiring assistants.** Do you hire, supervise, and pay the worker's assistant? (Independent contractors hire their own staff.)

10. **Continuing relationship.** Is there an ongoing relationship between the worker and yourself?

11. **Work hours.** Do you set the worker's hours?

12. **Full-time work.** Must the worker spend all of his or her time on the job?

13. **Work done on premises.** Must the individual work on your premises?

14. **Sequence.** Do you have the right to determine the order in which services are performed?

15. **Reports.** Must the worker give you reports accounting for his or her actions?

16. **Pay schedules.** Do you pay the worker by the hour, week, or month? (Independent contractors are usually paid by the job or on commission.)

17. **Expenses.** Do you pay the worker's business and travel expenses?

18. **Tools and materials.** Do you provide the worker with equipment, tools, or materials?

19. **Right to fire.** Can you fire the worker? (An independent contractor can't be fired without subjecting you to the risk of a breach of contract.)

20. **Worker's right to quit.** Can the worker quit at any time, without incurring liability? (An independent contractor has a legal obligation to complete the contract.)

In the past, I have lost with the IRS over the issue of whether a crewmember who said he was a business, and even provided me with an invoice on business letterhead, was legally acting as a business, or whether he should have been considered an employee. Insist that anyone under your control be either employees of someone—the production company or a union contract—or your company must take the appropriate deductions. If the production company cannot or will not do that, then it may be better to walk away from the situation.

We had a case where the IRS came back to us three years after a gentleman had been "hired" to work on a specific project, a project that we said from the outset was not an offer of continuing employment. He took his wages in the gross amount saying he'd pay the taxes. Yet years later the IRS determined that he had not paid the taxes on his wages; therefore, we were liable to pay both the employer as well as his employee portion, even through we had paid him the gross amount. The IRS publishes over 350 free booklets explaining the tax code. Publications 15, 15A, 937, 334, and 505 are of particular interest to our types of business. They can be obtained by calling 800-TAX-FORMS (800-829-3676) or downloading from the IRS Web site, *www.irs.gov.*

To help ensure your reliance on the fact that the people working for you are independent contractors, you should obtain as many of the following as possible, says attorney Stephen Fishman in *Hiring Independent Contractors: The Employer's Legal Guide.* Actually, his list is even longer, so check the book for his comments in full:

* Certificate showing they have insurance, including general liability and workers' compensation if the contractor has employees that will be working for you also.
* Any licenses or professional certificates they possess.
* Business card and stationery.
* Copy of advertising or yellow page listing.
* A copy of their fictitious business name statement.
* A copy of their office lease or photo of the office or workplace.
* Their unemployment insurance number.
* Copies of 1099 forms issued to other employers.
* If they are sole proprietors, copies of the past two years' tax returns showing they have filed Schedule C, Profit and Loss from a Business.

I feel that these are more good reasons to bring in designers under a USA union agreement. The designer is viewed not as an independent contractor to the show or producing entity but as your employee. You, as employer, have "hired" an individual whose status is in question.

On the other side, it is best to insist that the production company hire the design assistant directly so that the designer does not incur that liability plus the added paperwork and responsibility for the payroll.

Safe Harbor Protection

An employer does have some protection from the IRS disputing the classification of a worker. IRS Section 530 provides hiring firms with refuge if they meet three relatively simple and straightforward requirements:

* Employer filed all required Form 1099s for the person in question.

* Employer has consistently treated all those involved in similar work the same.

* Employer relied on trade common practice in the industry of long standing.

While the last point may sound confusing, it means that if you can prove that other people do it that way in your same business as a normal, day-to-day practice, it will probably be accepted by the IRS. It is also possible for the IRS to accept a tax attorney's prior written advice to the employer, or to rely on past court decisions or IRS rulings regarding other firms in similar situations.

By the phrase "common practice... of long standing" the IRS means that 25 percent of similar businesses follow the practice of hiring independent contractors for the position in question. If the hiring firm can prove that this is the case, it will have met the safe harbor requirement. However, there is one area in which you could be caught if you hire someone to work under you to fulfill the agreement with the producer. Let's say you get real busy and hire a designer to fill in for you or outright handle a project under your company name. The law here says that that person cannot be protected on the basis of the safe harbor clause—and "designers" are specifically cited in the law. This is all covered in IRS Section 1706. Essentially, then, you are serving as a middle man, and the other designer must pass all the requirements listed to meet the IRS standards as being in his own position of independent contractor.

Thus you could hire another designer as an employee and send her to work on the show. And you, as the owner of the company contracting with the producer, can still be an independent contractor to the show's producer. But, you could also hire a designer who meets the criteria as an independent contractor, pay her fee to her, and send her out under your company name, since you hold the agreement with the show's producer. The catch is that if the show is cancelled, the employee will still need to be paid; you can probably cancel the independent contractor's agreement and not be liable for the full fee. We do not have the "play or pay" clauses that star actors often get in their contracts for a film or television series that pays them even if their character is cut out of a project. In either scenario, the producer is still hiring an independent contractor and gets the benefits already discussed.

Although I know of no ruling regarding safe harbor protection in our field, there have been rulings for architects who were de facto employees of a large architectural firm for which they were not employed full-time, but rather contracted for a specific project. This would appear to eclipse all the rules imposed by the IRS, but be very careful and discuss your particular situation with competent experts. Besides the IRS, your state's unemployment compensation insurance agency and the tax department, as well as the U.S. Labor Department and the U.S. National Labor Relations Board, could weigh in on this very complicated issue.

Employee Leasing and Payroll Companies

One of the ways to avoid all these problems is to use a payroll service. And let's get this straight right off the bat: there is a difference between a payroll service and a payroll or leasing company. A *payroll service* is nothing more than an accounting firm that handles all the paperwork, computes the state and federal tax deductions, FICA, union vacation funds, and so on. It then prints the checks from the client's own account. It does not pay the worker directly. A *payroll company or employee leasing company*, on the other hand, actually becomes the employer. It covers all the legal obligations, including the person's workers' compensation insurance, and it pays the designer/crew member with checks from its own account. Technically, you are employed by the employee leasing company, not the show.

Many movie studios use this method. Sony Pictures Inc., for example, has a company called Beachwood Services that technically contracts the crews. Beachwood Services is the employer of record, and it "loans out" its employees to the specific show (see chapter 14). Therefore the studio has no obligations and its exposure is minimized in case of a claim. You are not part of the show's staff. It may seem like a sham because you were interviewed and told you had a position with the show's staff, but you must fill out the paperwork from another company and you become its employee. This system, which has been in place for a number of years, has stood up to legal challenges. And though I'm sure the attorneys for the studios and the unions both think they win something, I personally believe it sends mixed signals to the crew, who have a hard time feeling loyal to the show.

In recent years, we have all seen this as a trend for small businesses nationwide, as a means of keeping costs down and dealing with seasonal workers. They pay a fee based on the gross payroll for this service, and in return the company avoids all the bookkeeping and tax record-keeping, as well as costly insurance policies on employees. This works particularly well if you hire staff on a project-by-project basis. There are no costs when a person is no longer needed, and there is little threat from the IRS for errors in payments. Most of the firms in Hollywood can hire either on a union or non-union contract. How they can do this is a volume unto itself, and I believe that even the unions have given up trying to block this practice.

In fact, in a related method of employment, U/RTA (University/Resident Theatre Association) can act as the employer of record for schools and universities that cannot or will not be the employer, which relieves the designer of working as an independent contractor, plus ensures that he gets the health and welfare benefits of his union. To avoid the designer's dilemma, this group has a contracting arm and will, for a fee, become the producer of record. (More about U/RTA in chapter 13.)

One final word. You probably don't have the time to go back and get a law degree, but you can read up on the topics discussed here. There are several good books, among them Leonard DuBoff's *The Performing Arts Business Encyclopedia* and Rhonda Abrams' *The Successful Business Plan*. Also find a business law book for a first-year law student. It will teach you some of the terms and general tenets of the law you will be dealing with. I still use an old book written in 1996, but I suggest getting a more up-to-date version. Lastly, the government publishes many useful guides on business, so take advantage of them. You can check with the nearest U.S. Government Printing Office, or go online at *www.access.gpo.gov/*. The biggest problem online is that there are so many headings that it may be too confusing. Going to one of their stores (found in most major cities) will allow you to see the books and pamphlets themselves, and you can talk to a clerk who will be able to assist you. I have also had great luck when I have telephoned the Los Angeles store and simply asked the clerk to tell me what they had on a particular subject—but be prepared to be specific with your questions.

CHAPTER 7
Sales Methods, Technology, and Follow-Up

The next five chapters are even more important than the last three, if that is possible. We can hire qualified people to assist us in the legal and accounting aspects of our careers, but we must also deal with an area for which theatre schools rarely provide classes. If there are schools that encourage interdepartmental studies in marketing and interpersonal psychology, I have not found them. Why do I place so much importance on sales and marketing? Because virtually no one can avoid it. We are all salespeople, at least some of the time. Remember, no matter how "creative" you are, the person you are facing across the table is a *businessperson*. And he is trained to obtain your services at the cheapest price he can.

Making contact with a potential client (see chapter 8), as well as how to present yourself at the interview (see chapters 9-10), won't mean you have completed the salesmanship portion of your learning experience. There is not a day during your career that you should fail to consider how you speak to people, appear to people, and interact with people (see chapter 11). The talent you have is only a small part of what it takes to "make it" in the theatrical-entertainment industry. Get real; your potential clients need to be sold on your ideas. The dynamics in the room are very important, so how you make your presentation can be the difference between selling the idea or not. Ever think about that? You should, because positioning is very important in selling, and its importance goes double when making your presentation before the design team.

"It's nothing personal, it's just business." Ever heard that line before? Well, if you haven't, you probably will sometime in your career. Even if you have gotten past the producer, project manager, and managing director, and have struck a deal, it isn't over. You now get to sit in on a production meeting and attempt to "sell" your concepts. You have to give the impression to the rest of the people in the room that you know what you are doing and have a great idea, and that they should run with it. Do you really think they buy the idea just because you draw nice sketches of the costumes, or build a model of the set?

How your clients perceive you also depends on how you are dressed (this will be discussed in chapter 9). I have found that, depending on the type of client I am meeting with, a change of dress may be the key to making the right connection and ultimately signing the client. Your clothing must convey the same impression that you want the client to take away from the presentation.

In meetings concerning a corporate show, the client must believe that I am a businessperson, too. Or if I am meeting concert clients, I may want to impress them with how hip I am and show that I can run with the band. Or the casual style of the filmmaker or the mixed bag so often found in the television world may be what's required. And then there is the classic architect in a suit or sports coat and bow tie.

But before you get in the door to make an impression, your potential clients have to know about you. I trust everyone realizes through his or her own life experiences that it is often more true that the "best" designer rarely gets the job than the other way around. You, of course, are the best designer, or at least you had better start thinking that way.

There are many ways to market your talent. They are not the same methods that an actor might use. Yes, a few designers, like actors, do have agents. But don't deceive yourself; they are not going to get out and parade your name up and down Broadway. Their prime job is to make "deals," not look for work for you. But they still get 15 percent of all your fees whether you found the work or they did.

We will discuss interpersonal relationships and group dynamics in chapter 11 and why mastering communication skills is so helpful in meetings, interviews, negotiations, and production. These skills are not just techniques to learn for interviews; they also play a big part when you sit across the table from someone, and in her eyes you see, Okay, convince me you're the right person for this position. Do you know how to read people in meetings to understand when to speak and when to listen? Are you aware of the body language that takes place when you are interacting with others that can signal when to get close and when to move away from someone? Person-to-person communication is very difficult to master, so start learning such skills now.

This chapter deals specifically with sales methods and how to deliver your information to potential clients. No matter how much we would like to, we cannot simply sit at home and expect producers to call and offer their next Broadway shows. Somehow you need to get the word out to the market(s) that you are available and eager to work. The main part of your message should be that you are a skilled, creative designer/manager who would be an asset to the production. How is that done? Do you just stand on a hilltop and shout it out? Some people actually say that we should not be aggressive, that what is proper is to build our reputations slowly, and then we will be rewarded for our good work. Well, this author will never endorse a passive approach like that. Have I ever met or worked with someone who hasn't taken a proactive approach to attract more work and is still successful? Of course, there are those people who succeed strictly on dumb luck. There are also those who fall into a hit project and are propelled along for a time on the fame of that show. That may get them in the door, but as for being hired for another show, they must still go through the interview process and negotiate a fee.

However, in my thirty-two years of professional and educational work, rarely have I met top people who say they have not struggled for every show. They now know that they should have done more marketing to advance and control the direction of their careers. But lack of knowledge of how to do it and the stigma attached to "selling" held them back. They also say that the biggest problem is not having the time to market themselves when they are working; then, when a big project is over, they often have nothing lined up for the future. There could not be a bigger red flag than this, and it happens to almost every designer I know.

Again, I have to say this: *The best person for the job rarely gets the job.* What a shock! Am I really telling you that all your training and years of work will not be the determining factor in your receiving that big assignment or advancement in rank at your theatre department? YOU BET. Try another old adage: *It's who you know, not what you know.*

How many times have we seen educators advanced or designers given assignments that we feel we, or someone else, was creatively or educationally better qualified to receive? Why did they get it? I doubt I can ever fully answer that question, but it need not be a total mystery.

Professionals who train salespeople have a lot to say on this topic, and there have been many good books written on this subject. Unfortunately, they do not deal specifically with our area of work. Sadly, many designers choose not to read them because they feel the topic does not pertain to them. Nothing could be further from the truth. Yes, it takes a little digging, a little vision to see how sales training can relate to our work, but these books offer great insight and wisdom accumulated over many years for selling anything from cars to dress shirts. I have listed a few of my favorites in the bibliography, but go to any bookstore and you will find shelves filled with books on sales techniques, methods, plans, and ten-step programs designed to help you sell everything, from tangible products, such as cars, to the intangibles, such as accounting services.

If possible, take a course in marketing. If it does not fit within your present course of study, something may be available at an evening adult class in your community. Beyond that, try loading up at your bookstore with books, as well as self-help tapes and videos.

What Are You Selling?

Before we discuss specific material to prepare and ways to deliver them to potential clients, we must agree on what we are going to sell. Sounds funny, I know. We are designers and production managers, therefore we are trying to sell our design and managerial abilities to producers, right? Well, not so.

> *In most professional services, you are not really selling expertise—because your expertise is assumed... Instead, you are selling a **relationship**. (42)*

This is a quote from a book by Harry Beckwith called *Selling the Invisible.* In the broadest sense, then, we are in a "relationship" business. This goes a long way toward justifying why the "best" designer doesn't always get the job, and we will speak about this more in chapter 10. For now, let's concentrate on how we can design both materials and delivery systems to get out our message.

What Makes You Unique?

Psychologists tell us that we are all unique, a combination of where we grew up, our home and play environments, moral and ethical upbringing, and, surprisingly, least of all by our formal education. So, let's start there.

Are you basically a passive person who, when offered a project, assumes you'll get paid and accepts whatever fee is offered? Were you brought up to believe that good comes to the righteous? Are you looking for a nice, quiet teaching job? Do you feel that as a designer or stage manager you are a small fish in the big pond of ShowBiz where actors and directors get all the praise and money? Do you think that no matter what effort you make, in the end, you will not gain anything by attempting to better your situation?

What makes marketing and selling hard for a lot of us is that our family and religious elders told us that employers respond best to a hard worker; someone who gives 110 percent, nose to the grindstone; someone who is honest, loyal, meets the goals set by management, and doesn't cause trouble. And all that effort will bring you your just rewards. But we didn't choose an assembly-line job. We didn't choose a profession that uses numerical quotas or advanced degrees for making promotion decisions. We didn't choose a job that will end with a gold watch and a pension after twenty-five or thirty years with the same company.

The answer to all these questions may be, "No." However, that does not mean that we can't change. At the very least, you must believe that you can modify your perspective, so that marketing can possibly add new horizons to your life and career. This doesn't mean that you have to get aggressive and pushy. It doesn't mean that you have to be "hip" and attend trendy parties. It doesn't necessarily mean that you have to drop your friends and move to the big city. Nor does it mean you have to change your moral and ethical beliefs.

Just the same, I have to add this line I remember from a Marx Brothers movie: "The secret of success in show business is honesty and sincerity. Once you learn how to fake that, you've got it made." Not everyone in Hollywood fakes it, but you do need to be seen for what you can bring to the dance. A light shines on a person who is perceived by potential clients as a winner. A team player, a person who can accomplish tasks on time, on budget, and with creative solutions to any problem, is an asset to the producer. All the things that make the producer look good, too.

We will talk in chapters 9 and 10 about your personal appearance and interview skills. For now, we will assume you want to advance your career beyond the level you are at and have come to realize that it is not likely to happen unless *you* do something about it.

Marketing Tools

If you were born with the "midwestern work ethic" rooted deep in your bones, as I was, how can you break out of the pack? The truth, I hope, is that you already have what it takes somewhere within you, but you just need someone to encourage you. Luckily, I had a great mentor to help me. In the end, however, you are the only one who can motivate yourself to raise the stakes. It isn't easy, and you will not get many people congratulating you on your effort. But in the end, you will know that you did all you could to bring your abilities out into the open for potential clients to see. And remember, the odds of getting work go up exponentially over others who have not made this added effort.

There are many avenues that are used to get material to potential clients. Throughout this chapter, you may not always see the connection to your specific field of expertise, but remember that the majority of research has been done on selling consumer items and services. The big corporations use mass marketing strategies to bring in large amounts of revenue—and profit—so more is known about how mass marketing is done.

Only recently has there been an emphasis on marketing the intangible or invisible skills and services people have to offer, as America moves toward a service society rather than a manufacturing one. Although there are a few books geared to consultants, such as architect and engineering firms, almost nothing has been written about theatrical services, so you must try to find ways to customize these techniques for your own personal services. I will try and help in this area not only by explaining the techniques, but also by giving personal examples from my own experiences.

Networking

Marketing while on the job is especially useful. You can do it on coffee breaks or at lunch. Be attentive to the needs of the other designers and crew. Listen and learn about what they're working on after the present project, and keep in touch. You want to be the first person that comes to mind when they are asked about a position to be filled. Lisa Passamonte-Green, one of my partners, is fond of saying, "Remember—it isn't really who you know, it's who knows you!"

You need to have a way of keeping these contacts' names, telephone numbers, etc.; this can start with a simple list. The way to build your lists is from your day-to-day contacts with other designers and production people whom you may be working with or simply meeting for coffee. Nowhere do I find this method more accepted than in the film and television industry. Since most of that work is for short periods, everyone is always looking for work. Asking the other designers, production personnel, director, associate producer, and producer what they are working on next is an accepted practice. Everyone feeds on other people's information.

I learned an interesting lesson about lists a number of years ago, sort of in reverse. I had a friend who was up for a new TV series. The star wanted him because they had worked together for years in Las Vegas, but the studio had said no when the star requested him as the designer for the lighting. He called me and asked if I would be willing to consult on the project. The studio had told him they would agree to me as the consulting designer, and then he could be the lighting director during the show's run. When I asked why, he said I was on the studio's "approved" list. Approved list? What was that? I called a senior executive (a boating friend) at the studio and found out that it has people who regularly view tapes of shows and movies to look for design talent that they feel have the qualities they would like on their own productions, and compile a list.

Learning from that experience, I started taking down names of producers and directors, as well as other designers whose work I liked and wanted to remember. Then when I saw their names in the trade papers or saw them mentioned in a review, I would call or drop a note and congratulate them. Human nature tells us one thing: People like to be flattered! When you can throw in the names of or comment on other work the people you are speaking with have done, they are even more impressed with you—well, themselves—but it doesn't matter, you have made it to the next level with them. Now, they will take your calls hoping for more praise. But this takes us into a discussion we will have in chapter 11.

Direct Mail

We most often think of direct mail as the junk mail we get from shop-at-home catalogs, sales flyers, unsolicited offers for credit cards, and insurance. But there is a growing use of this method in marketing theatrical services. Some are direct offers of services, but there are ways to be more indirect. For instance, you can put together a short cover letter and a one-page resume and mail it to all the producers and theatres in your area or extended potential markets. The cover letter should always be addressed to a specific person, and be direct and clear as to the work you are seeking. That means that a letter addressed "Dear Sir" and saying you are a costume designer looking for "challenging opportunities" will get thrown in the trash quickly.

Companies who regularly use direct mail say that a return of 1 out of 1,000 is considered a landslide of responses. But they are working with thousands of names from phone books or lists purchased from other companies. If you fill out a warranty card on a product you purchased there is a questionnaire attached asking for your buying habits. This information is sold to other companies. We don't have such a service available to us in theatre, but many unions make a list of production companies who have signed the collective bargaining agreement available for members to use. But most people starting out will need to build their own lists.

The best thing to do is make the cover letter personal. Always get the name of a person to address the letter to, even if that means calling the production company and inquiring whom is in charge of hiring for designers and stage managers. Next, if at all possible, state something that makes it clear you are familiar with the work the company has done in the past. You may have seen the last production and been impressed with some aspect of the show, or you might quote a good review you read. Then state specifically the expertise you possess. Finally, ask for a meeting by saying you will call next week to see when they will be available to meet. Simply restated:

* Address a specific person.
* Make a connection to the work of the company.
* State your expertise.
* Request a meeting.

Never send out a full resume, photos, and clippings of reviews unsolicited. First, the postage will be costly. Second, almost all of the executives I have ever interviewed say they don't read or keep unsolicited resumes unless they have prior knowledge of the person. A few, very few, will pass them down to a production manager to look at. It is a huge waste of printing, postage, and time.

Another method that is becoming very popular is the postcard. It can be printed relatively cheaply and the postage is less than for a letter. Put a photo of a recent project on the front and a short note on the back stating the project, your contribution to it, and how the company can contact you. It is still best to address it to a specific person. Most professionals agree, however, that this method should be used only as a follow-up to a letter or first meeting.

Cold Calls

Salesmen know that the *cold call* is the hardest initial contact to make with a potential customer. It is referred to as a "cold" call because the person doesn't know you, or know why you're calling them—so they may be put off from the start. You need to have your "pitch" well organized, to make it clear why they should be talking to you in the first place. I have tracked my own cold calls over many years and find that I get an average of one out of ten contacts to return my calls or agree to a meeting using this tactic. Now, that does take into account that I do "qualify" many of the leads. Qualifying simply means that I have confirmed the name and title of the person before I proceed to mail any material. Also, I have used lists published in reliable trade publications or lists of companies and producers provided by my union.

Speaking of computers, you should be building a mailing list that can be used to send out follow-up letters, event postcards, and holiday greetings. There are several computer programs available. The leading one is called ACT!, which is produced by a company more familiar to computer users as the maker of Norton Anti-Virus programs—Symantec Inc. ACT! is a database program designed to keep and sort contact lists. It can even prompt you when to make a follow-up call. As I said earlier, one of the hardest things for designers and production people to do is to keep making contacts in the middle of a rehearsal. Yet that is exactly when you need to keep up a stream of calls to set your next several projects. A program like ACT! can help you organize calls so you don't waste what little time you have available. And with the advent of nationwide cell phone plans, there is no reason not to have it a goal to make two or three calls every day, no matter what your location. Early in the morning or during a lunch break is the easiest time for most of us to work into our schedules.

With what frequency should you call a person? The answer is normally every two months or during the three-month period before a new season begins. However, you have to get a feeling from the person. Some do not like to be called constantly and so your call may be a turn-off. What you should do is simply ask. How hard is that? Try, do you mind me calling once in a while to see what you are up to? What can they say but "No," or "I'll call you if I have anything." For that person, you move on to the postcards or holiday messages or only making a call when you know they have a specific project. For all the others, get on that phone!

No Thanks!

The cold call reminds me that we need to discuss rejection. It is very possible that when you say you just don't have time to make these calls, in truth, you are afraid of almost certain rejection. This is natural, because we are creative types and a lot more sensitive to criticism and rejection than the "A" list business types. But we need to work through this and understand that it is no more personal to be rejected than it is for actors. They are rejected for silly reasons, too: they are too short, too tall, too young, too old, too light-skinned, too dark-skinned, have an accent, don't have an accent . . . So, start making those calls.

Brochures

The next level is something that will take a serious cash commitment: *brochures*. For a long time, I hesitated about doing one. First, there was only one firm I knew that had one for television and corporate show lighting out of New York, and none in the theatre market. So, why should I spend the money?

The answer came to me as follows:

* It gave my design work status as a "real" business.
* Corporate clients expected it.
* I wanted to "appear" to be a major player.

Did my brochure accomplish these things? Yes and no. It did allow me to mail it to all the corporate show companies, and I did get responses. But did it directly contribute to my getting the design jobs? Possibly. Was it worth the expense? Indirectly. Sounds cryptic, doesn't it.

I think the best thing it did was make me take a hard look at my own work. Up until then, I had not considered where I ultimately wanted my career to go. I had to spend a lot of time finding and sorting through pictures and reviews, and assembling other background material, all the while asking myself if it was worth the time and expense. But I couldn't answer that because I didn't have a watermark to gauge what I expected to accomplish. I went ahead and spent almost $5,000 in 1975 to produce an 8 x 10, full-color, four-sided brochure. I then spent a few hundred dollars more on postage to send the brochures to my mailing list, many of which came back because I did not have an accurate, up-to-date list. Then did I think it was worth it? Actually, yes, because I also took them to meetings and was able to pass out four to six around a production table. Those people, in large measure, kept them, and even years later, I got calls based on people still keeping them around. It legitimized my company and, therefore, me in the eyes of business clients. In the eyes of advertising agencies, corporate show producers, and their clients, the brochure made a statement that I was a stable, ongoing business that would be around to accomplish their projects. Also, I found that the corporate show producers loved to include the brochure in their presentation to their clients because it added weight to their "team."

You need to collect brochures from other designers, design firms, rental firms, and related businesses to get a feel for the different formats that can be produced. Sometimes looking outside the entertainment business at brochures produced by other industries can give you some ideas that you can relate to in making your presentation unique. And today, with desktop publishing programs you can buy for your computer, most formats can be produced in your bedroom and come out looking very good. If you choose, a brochure doesn't have to be a glossy print multipage piece. In its simplest form, a single sheet folded into a trifold and taped shut can be mailed without an envelope and can be very cost-effective.

Or you might be tempted to consider what is often referred to as the "press kit" style, a printed cover or sticker on a folio with slots to hold loose material and a business card. That way, you can continually add updated materials, reviews, photos, and articles at any time. Another advantage to this style is that you can custom assemble a brochure for a specific client. Clients have very little patience and don't like to dig through material beyond what they are interested in. My personal view is that the folio or "press kit" style often appears jumbled and messy. Pages are of different sizes, colors, and paperweights, and are sometimes not even assembled in a logical order. So be careful. And though this method can be somewhat more cost-effective, you might be better served thinking long-term.

About that $5,000 expenditure, was it worth it? If you look at the per item cost, it was $5.00 per brochure (1,000 brochures). I believe the brochure "assisted" in getting me about a dozen jobs. Those jobs paid over $100,000 in fees, not including return business from many of those clients over the years. So, yes, it was cost-effective. But initially, to lay out $5,000 meant that I didn't eat a lot for a few months, so consider what you will be giving up in the short run while balancing that against potential long-term gains.

I did regret that the brochure was literally out of date the day it came from the printers. I had completed a big corporate show and started a TV series that really would have given me better photographs and some "name" client status. So, I had to immediately stuff additional photos, reviews, and articles into the brochure. That destroyed the nice, clean, organized layout I had worked so hard to create. And I didn't have the resources, either cash or time, to keep updating the material, so I had to wait a year before I could do a truly updated brochure.

Compact Discs

As a delivery system for resumes and brochure-type material, the *compact disc* is currently the hot ticket. We receive resumes on this format all the time from designers, as well as students looking for internships. In fact, my company recently decided to produce a CD in conjunction with a new brochure. Several factors came into the decision process. Admittedly, the cost was the least discussed issue, because we have the resources to operate the business on a sound financial footing. We have done several brochures over the years. They have been well received, and although it is still a problem keeping them up-to-date, I feel they are an effective sales tool. And it helps that our architectural and corporate clients use our brochure as part of their presentation to *their* clients.

But the problem of keeping one up to date is compounded by the fact that the firm has four principal designers and six staff designers who are all producing work that should be showcased in a brochure. In the past the answer was a four-page brochure and a document-style addendum that is sent with every brochure. It provides the lists of all the work in progress, recently completed projects, and short bios on the entire team. Although this has accomplished the "targeted" needs of marketing the firm to a wide range of clients, it is time-consuming to put together and expensive.

I recently asked some of our clients what they thought about the idea of offering a promotional CD instead of a brochure. The result of this nonscientific survey was very positive. The most telling was a response from a New York corporate show producer who said essentially that his company effectively uses this format to make presentations to their own clients instead of the old multiple projector slide show. The presentation is created in Microsoft Power Point and then burned onto a CD, so that the client can show it to other executives not able to attend the presentation. Furthermore, he said that the firm's president concluded that most of his clients had the capability of viewing CDs on their office computers; if the clients didn't have the equipment for that, the president assumed they were not big enough to afford the firm's services.

Now, if we are speaking strictly of offering our design services to legitimate theatre producers, this may still be a contentious area. But there is no doubt that we are in the age of the computer, and most people have access to a computer with a CD player.

The cost of producing a CD can vary a great deal. If you hire a commercial design house to produce it for you, expect to pay for their expertise, which can add up to thousands of dollars. However, you can purchase a program that allows you to use preexisting templates with step-by-step instructions, and you can create your own. While I am not computer literate enough to tackle this job, many of the graduate design students I meet have done their own, some with simple presentations and others with all the currently available whistles and bells. I believe that these younger designers will be the wave of the future; therefore, I fully expect to see more and more electronic presentations.

But even if the cost were equal in producing a brochure or a CD, I would say that the CD format is unquestionably the future of information presentation for the following reasons:

* CDs do not need to be copied in quantity, only what you need then.
* There is minimal expense when material is changed or added.
* They are cheap to mail.

The Telephone

Just when you thought you could avoid making those calls! There will always be a need for personal voice contact. Even with the Internet and e-mail, as human beings, we need to have a one-on-one connection to the person we are hiring. There is something reassuring about a live voice on the other end of the phone. When it comes down to it, that is why one person gets the assignment over another in every business survey I have seen. The personal call makes the client feel like we care enough not to just send an e-mail. Even when the potential client doesn't take our call, as long as they know we made it, there is a positive effect. With nationwide mobile phone service available for under $100 a month, it is a very cheap business tool for the designer who travels. Just think of the cost savings for long-distance calls alone. Plus, I don't know how many times I have been out of town and received a call for work that I might have missed if it had sat even a few hours on my answering machine. I can't even count the times a client has called with a problem that I can solve right then. I'm the hero of the moment because of the quick response, and that gains me major points with the client—who didn't even know I was in Hawaii lying on the beach!

A final word on phones. I very much dislike calling a business and getting voice mail, especially the electronic routing systems that take several minutes just to get to the person who might be able to help me. Answer your calls!

Callbacks take additional time and effort; they put the client off because she expects instant action on her needs. And once clients know you will respond quickly to their calls, no matter where you are, you are a key resource for them. I almost always take calls even if I don't recognize the name, and surprisingly, sometimes they turn out to be work. And yes, I do answer a lot of calls from tele-marketers, but I feel that the clients are important enough to suffer a little.

Press Release

This is one tool that has been around for a long time and should not be considered out of style. But while actors take great advantage of it, we designers do not exploit it enough. Yes, the project is probably completed before your release makes it into the trade publication. So, what makes it useful? Simple: name recognition. The more we get our names out into the production community, the better the chance that someone will see them and remember until we make that cold call.

Just don't forget the all-important five W's: Who, What, Where, When, and Why. Keep it short; one or two paragraphs in length is best. The use of adjectives in place of facts and relevant specifics dilutes the meaning and impact of the press release. Everyone is turned off by glowing superlatives. And try to think of places to send releases that are not directly related to the entertainment business, such as art magazines, architectural publications, and business journals. You just need to find a "hook" that ties your release to what the magazine sees as their target audience.

Business Follow-Up

To design professionally, one has to have a very high degree of organization. The scheduling of drawings, plans, construction, and load-in is a group effort that every one of the designers must adhere to or everything is thrown off schedule. So if we are able to accomplish this task in our creative work, why not in our business? I think the problem arises out of the fact that we don't see these skills in a business context. Specifically, we need a marketing plan. If you purchase a book, such as *The Successful Marketing Plan*, published by NTC Business Books, you will be facing a big, 8-x-11-inch format, 500-plus-page book. That is what it takes to organize a marketing plan. Charts, forms, and schedules to assist in planning the marketing of your product take up a large part of this book. Even if this is a little bit of overkill for the type of marketing you will be doing, I believe it will be an eye-opener. There is much in this book that can help you plan your marketing strategy, and I highly recommend you get a copy and read it from cover to cover.

However, here are a few tips for tracking your potential clients—and, lest we forget them, your present clients. We often learn that our last client may not have another project for months, even a year, therefore keeping our names on his lips is a must, no matter how great he said our last design was. "Out of sight, out of mind" should be the watchword for all designers. We may be as good as our last show, but even the best of reviews turns brown at the corners and is forgotten unless we keep marketing.

If you keep a computer-based program such as ACT! or even a file-card system broken down into months, you should keep reviewing it every day. If someone indicates that there will be a project coming up in the spring, you should say, Fine, I'll call you in May—is that all right? Assuming you receive a positive response, the card for that client should have this information notation on it and be moved to the May header.

I also keep a composition notebook in my briefcase in which I write notes and lists to myself. But it is imperative that this information is transferred to one of the more organized systems, or it gets lost. I keep a mini tape recorder in the car. Since I live in Los Angeles, I am on the road a lot, and it helps me to record reminders to myself, such as to contact a client or order color media. Some people even carry one on-site to record production notes rather than a note pad and pencil.

When to Follow Up

How do you know when to follow up? What time interval is best? This is a very tricky area. Some people simply do not like to be bugged. But a surprising number of people will tell you it is all right, especially if an experience with you in the past has been good. Also, a lot depends on your telephone technique.

First, about the interval between contacts. Most people say no longer than three months. I try to tie my call to the preproduction and scheduling season. In theatre, for example, the management or artistic director is probably setting the coming season in February or March and will be looking to start hiring directors in early January. That means designers should have their names in front of all the artistic directors, production managers, and directors by January or early February at the latest. And take note: You can be too early, so a little investigation into the booking habits of the people you want to contact would be time well spent. For example, the television pilot season is in February and March for shows that may be placed on the schedule the following fall season, so we need to get our names in front of those producers by early December. Corporate shows have somewhat of a season, too, especially the automotive shows. Early introduction to the dealers happens a few months before the introduction at the public auto shows held in the winter. Both offer potential work for lighting designers, scenic designers, and stage managers.

The Callback

Most books advise salespeople to make repeat contacts only when they have some reason for calling. Sometimes, that reason is pretty flimsy, such as, I'll be in the area tomorrow and thought I'd stop by, what time would be good for you? Worse is when the party actually answers the phone and you don't have your speech together. If you fumble now, you have lost valuable ground. Rehearsal is important before making a call. Plan out what you want to say that will only take fifteen to thirty seconds. Most executives, even if nice enough to take your call, don't want to chitchat away their days. And if you ramble, they will not be as quick to take your next call. That is why I like the postcard for keeping in contact.

Postcards

I really like the postcard idea, both for keeping in touch and as an advance calling card. Make up a card that has a picture of a recent project, and put your contact information on the back with the appropriate details concerning your involvement with the photo. You can have these printed in quantity at Kinko's or other copying shops for a reasonable price. The date when you send the card should be noted in the contact's file. Placing a call a week after mailing a postcard works much better than cold calling because the person has recently seen your name and will hopefully have reacted positively to the card. If you can't get through on a call, at least you have placed your name in front of them.

Web Sites and the Internet

This is the newest tool in the contact game. Opening a Web site for yourself or under your business name is very easy and not terribly expensive. Today a domain name costs $70 for a two-year license. Your site can be a duplicate of your CD brochure and resume, and it can have links to other sites. It can contain very up-to-date information on your current schedule and recent design projects. You can add articles and reviews you were mentioned in or have authored, or any number of additional items related to work. But don't put personal stuff, like, I just took a week to bike through Yosemite Park, and boy was that fun!

Getting a client to look at your Web site is good, but you have no way of knowing if she really did, or if she did, how carefully she looked at it. Don't send "cyber-trash"; it won't be read. I get a lot of e-mails from camerapersons and gaffers looking for work, since my name is on the union's list as a director of photography. And we also get a lot of lighting design students inquiring about internships and employment. Sometimes they have attached a resume or a downloadable .jpg file of pictures. I am very excited about these future possibilities, but I also think that we are still exploring this area, and that we're not yet sure what the protocol should be used in sending such material. Only the next few years will tell.

When you piggyback a Web site with the CD, the cost of producing such a combined package is probably cost-effective. My only problem is the quality of the photographic material. I have seen mostly very bad photos downloaded to Web sites or placed on a CD. But the newest digital photo process is producing higher and higher resolution; I now have a 5,000,000-pixel digital camera that functions exactly like my SLR 35mm cameras and is quiet enough that I can take pictures during a production. And because of the huge advances in digital photography, we can instantly add one of these images to the Web site. There's no delay of months while a new brochure is designed and printed.

For today's young designers, especially those working in multiple markets, I believe that this is the place to focus your limited funds for marketing. In 1975, we needed a brochure; today, you're not considered a professional without a Web site. Tomorrow I believe you will walk into an interview and be expected to pull out a CD for the person to load into their wall projector.

Agents

One aspect we have not spoken of is having someone else make these contacts for you. I know of a couple of designers who very effectively enlist their domestic partner or spouse as their own personal "tele-marketer." But I personally believe that the actual call should come from you. A spouse or partner can be very helpful in keeping the contact list up to date by calling potential clients firms to get correct titles and addresses. No executive likes to be referred to by a title that is below him or her.

I know some people who will be asking why I have not spoken more about agents. First of all, if you have an agent, you probably are not reading this book. Second, anyone who has spoken to an agent has learned that agents do not see their job as your personal tele-marketer. As one told me, "My job is to take the many offers my clients get and cull out the best and advise my client on which one to take." That implies that the kind of talent he was speaking of has several offers on the table at the same time. Wouldn't that be nice—but so would winning the lottery! And remember, agents work for many people who are trying to get exactly the same jobs. So, how much effort are they putting toward your career? Or are they just as happy if any of their clients gets the job?

They still get their percentage, don't they? That is why I don't use one. However, it has and does work for some designers, especially in New York. If you are thinking about acquiring an agent, you should consider the financial implications—the loss of 15 percent of your hard-earned fees, to begin with. You should also consider how you will feel about not being in control of your own career, and having to wait for the agent to call in order to know where your next job is coming from.

What I believe does work, and has worked for me for many years, is a partnership in which everyone looks out for each other. The partnership allows us to hire in-house people to do the record-keeping, updating, and mailing. This still requires a one-on-one approach to marketing, but the time saved in paperwork and filing, and the synergy among partners, is priceless.

When I look at the efforts our partnership firm, Visual Terrain, has made, do I feel that we have attained the best possible marketing plan? Do I feel I have reached a satisfaction level concerning our marketing methods? Absolutely not. We are always discussing ideas. And we try out new things. Recently we did a variation on an old idea that has gotten a very, very positive response. It is not a direct request for work, but it does exploit the company name, so that clients and potential clients remember us. What is it, you ask? Now, that is our marketing secret—you need to invent your own!

CHAPTER 8
Making Contacts

We have already discussed the methods you can use to get your name in front of prospective clients. Now we will bring in another element: how to find prospective clients.

There is no book you can read or lecture you can attend that will force you to keep your ears open for potential clients. My grandfather used to tell me that there are thousands of opportunities flying past our heads every moment of every day, but we rarely reach out and grab one. Some we turn over in our hand, and then, without giving them any more thought, release back into the ether. But we can increase our odds of finding a good opportunity simply by being aware that this is happening and reaching out more often.

Every successful designer you meet has a story about a completely unexpected event that propelled his or her career forward. Maybe it brought the biggest paycheck or the most publicity or a new client he or she had been unsuccessful in attracting until some strange sequence of events was set in motion. Do not disregard the chance encounters that happen all the time. And if you can stop and take a moment to think like a salesperson, you must say to yourself, How can I use this event to further my career?

Gatherings and Parties

I will never be accused of being a "party" guy who hangs around looking to get invitations, but parties and other gatherings are useful tools for the marketer. Some of the best opportunities for such chance encounters may be found at industry gatherings, award presentations, conferences, and private parties. Industry gatherings where people other than your peers will be in attendance are the best. If you live in a major city, there are many special charity events sponsored and attended by industry people, such as museum and AIDS benefits. There are also the standard charity gatherings, such as the Heart Association and Boys and Girls Clubs fund-raisers, that will probably include people you would like to meet. Attending performances, however, especially opening nights, does not work as well because the attention is on the people directly involved in the show, and it may be awkward if you start talking about other business.

Award presentations are a good place to be seen and shake hands, but no business here either is a good rule. But there is nothing that says you can't meet someone new, shake hands, and ask if it is all right to call. Then drop your business card in his pocket discreetly. When you call, the person knows who you are—or at least there is a name-and-face connection—so you have a much better chance of getting through to him.

Conferences are more difficult to use as a marketing tool, since they are populated mostly with other designers who are also looking for work. But there are conferences that cross lines, such as those for regional theatre associations that have a broad membership of directors, artists, designers, producers, and artistic directors. Here it is doubtful you can engage a potential client in a long private conversation, but at least you can make contact with a compliment about what wonderful work she or her theatre is doing.

A private party is a great way to meet, and often find time alone with, influential people whom you might otherwise never get quiet time with. Agents call it "face time." But do not get into such a party mode that you think you can make your career by dropping names. You eventually have to do good work to get hired again. I also feel that a lot more time is wasted than advantage gained in too much partying, but I know that is not an opinion shared by all.

No system is perfect. There are thousands of stories of how some method has worked for one person but has failed for a hundred others. The answer, if there is one, is, try everything. See what fits your personality and lifestyle and go with it. It is more important to be consistent in your approach than anything else.

Trade Publications

Beyond the fact that they provide continuing, professional education, trade publications offer important information about the entertainment industry. In fact, they are important not so much as vehicles for finding new clients, but as devices for tracking industry news and happenings and what your competition is working on. I take the view that advertising in these trade publications is not the best use of your limited marketing funds, but it is not a total waste, because the ad can be reprinted and used as part of your marketing package. I have, on occasion, been talked into taking out an ad in a trade magazine that is producing a special issue or section honoring one of my clients. That makes good marketing sense because you want to "keep" the client. And believe me, clients check very carefully who did pony up money to say "Thanks" or what a pleasure they are to work with—egos on overdrive, I know, but this is Hollywood.

So, why should you have subscriptions to the magazines and search the Internet sites? First, you need to build up your awareness of who the players in your field are. Then when you see a name you can match to a project or a company, you will be in a position to act. That is critical when, over a drink at a party or over coffee, you are introduced to a person who potentially can advance your career. Most people do not wear their resumes on their jackets, so if you are unknowledgeable about names and positions, you could miss an opportunity to make a contact that could be very beneficial in furthering your career.

The other thing the magazines can do is help build your creditability within the industry. Look at trade publications not only for the information they provide, but for who their target audience might be. Seeing the types of articles and who the authors are is a big help in deciding if you could write something that they might be interested in publishing. Most publications will do anything to get industry professionals to write for their trade publications, because they can only afford a small core staff with expertise in the field. They need you, the in-service professional, to write for them. You say you were hardly an English major and that your grammar is poor? Don't worry, that's why they have editors who will clean up the punctuation; you just need to give them the story. Then when the article is published, you can add it to your brochure package in your mailing to potential clients. Articles as short as five hundred words are used, which is little more than a couple of typed pages. You should contact the editor and ask what kind of material she is looking for, and discuss what slant you might bring to an article. She will be very interested in helping you along.

Many publications produce some kind of yearly resource of people, the-atres, production companies, agents, services, and so on. These can also be very helpful as you build a reference list of potential clients. As I pointed out earlier, nothing flatters potential clients or interviewers more than you telling them what great work they have done and being able to tick off a list of some of their accomplishments. Let the Ego Games begin!

Lists of Other Designers

Another list to start is one made up of other designers, technicians, and man-agers you have personally worked with, even if just for a day or two. It is often said that there are 100 people in Hollywood, and they have all worked together. The implication is that it is a closed society, but nothing could be further from the truth. The same closeness that brought them together often is the catalyst for flinging them apart. Some cannot keep up the pace, which can lead to burnout and dropout. Or they move up the food chain to producer. And you know, of course, that every actor in Hollywood really wants to direct! Grips want to be camera operators, camerapeople what to move up to director of photography, art directors to production designer—and almost everyone is clawing his or her way toward the top. There isn't a time or an area that doesn't see movement, either out or up, so don't be discouraged.

And what about those long-term relationships we hear about between a particular director and his design team? Well, so what? Go after someone else; there are plenty of others who are not so firmly attached to their "team." You have to think positive. But keeping in contact can pay off, even after years of unanswered calls to one of these producers. One day, the "team" isn't available and you want to be the name that comes to mind first.

The point is to get names, phone numbers, and addresses on everyone. I have worked many times for associate producers who a few months before were the catering person or the "go-fer" for a producer. Just because you are shy about asking for the information to add to your contact list, be very aware that others are not so shy! Never underestimate another person's drive, especially someone who is not as talented. Why do we see, time and time again, a less skilled or creative person get the job? Because she was pushy, she stuck to making call after call and sending letter after letter, to get someone to break down and give her a chance.

Another little trick is that when you get hired, the first thing you should do after you ask when you get paid is to inquire if the client has hired the other designers, the master electrician, the seamstresses, the prop person, the sound positions, and the carpenters. Why? Because then you have information to share with your contacts—designers, master electricians, seamstresses, and others—and they will then be beholden to you for getting them the job or getting them an interview or at least letting them know there may be something open. I often receive calls from people saying they recommended me for a show, and by the way, do I know of any work? I had a case where I was hired for a television pilot. I tried to get the producer to let me recommend other technicians; he said he already had everyone. When we all showed up for the meeting, it turned out everyone knew each other and was on very friendly terms. This seemed to shock the producer, who thought he had independently hired people without the "Good Ol' Boy Network." But the truth is that these people work because they also know to keep their ears to the ground. Getting wind of a potential job and following up as quickly as possible is the name of the game.

When you are sitting around at lunch or on a break, take the opportunity to quiz others on what their next project is and if they know whether the producers have hired anyone for your position. No one will be offended; it is part of the working landscape. Get business cards from those same people and exchange yours, too. Then put them on your ACT! program or card-file system with a notation of where you worked together and when.

One concert designer I know tells the story of standing backstage at an award show once and seeing a very big star sitting all alone in a corner. My friend was a huge fan and hesitantly approached him. They struck up a conversation about his music, and a few weeks later, the artist's manager called him to offer a design gig for the next tour. This is an example of "right place, right time," I know, but it can happen.

Magazines and the Internet

There are other types of publications that can be of help. In concert touring there have been two magazines for a number of years that publish the touring schedules of the bands. In recent years they have added the schedules of touring Broadway road companies, ice shows, the WWF, and other shows. *Performance* magazine, at 1101 University, Suite 108, Ft. Worth, Texas 76107-4273, and *Pollstar* magazine, at 4697 W. Jacquelyn, Fresno, California 93722, are the leading monthly publications in this field. Besides tour dates for cities and venues, they also publish the name and address of the management. These can be used to contact the management company about future work. I say future, because if the tour itinerary appears in one of these magazines, it is probably already too late to get hired. But you are now prepared to strike before the next one.

In recent years many online services have come about that offer to shop for presents, sell books, check out new and used car prices, and perform various other specific tasks. Now we have specialized companies online that target the film business, commercials, and TV productions. One that does help to designers and production managers who want to follow the concert business is called *ENCORE* newsletter at *www.celebrityaccess.com/news*. *ENCORE* publishes weekly listings of artists' availability worldwide, concert listings, an industry events calendar, and industry profiles, but these may only be found on the Internet. To get the full service, you must subscribe, which is a little pricey but very helpful if you are interested in the music touring business in particular.

SHOWBIZ DIGEST, at *www.showbizdigest.com*, is another online service that works in reverse. People pay to get listed with the service. You can post information on your work availability on the site. If you are looking for equipment or facilities for film or TV, the publication also presents a section of listings for these needs, which, in many cases, include direct links to the Internet site of the provider or seller. The *DIGEST* also has a production calendar that lists films and TV pilots or series with contact information on the producer and studio.

Theatre is not completely left out; many of the traditional theatre magazines publish annual listings. *American Theatre* magazine (Theatre Communications Group, 355 Lexington Avenue, New York, New York 10017, *www.tcg.org*) publishes a monthly listing of regional theatre schedules. There are notations on the producer, director, and other contact information when available. Others, such as *Stage Directions* magazine (250 W. 57th Street, Suite 420, New York, New York 10107), do annual reports of summer stock companies.

For technician, stage management, designer, and educational job listings, the most widely read publication is *ArtSEARCH*, which is also published by the Theatre Communications Group. It is put out twice a month, but for an additional charge you can gain access to the online version, which is updated more frequently. Besides these, there is a wealth of information every day in the standard trade publications such as *Billboard, Backstage, The Hollywood Reporter, Backstage West*, and *Variety*. All of these, and the publications in the next paragraph, are listed in the appendix. Although these may not provide contact information, they are still invaluable for learning who is in what position and doing what project.

There are also publications for corporate and trade shows, such as *Event Solutions,* and specialty publications for individual markets such as the new *Church Production* magazine and *Behind the Themes* magazine for the theme park market. *Lighting Dimensions* and *Entertainment Design* magazines deal with several production areas, including theme parks, architectural, corporate, and theatre, regarding lighting, scenic, and costume design. Their publisher, Primedia Business Magazines & Media, is well known as the producer of the LDI (Lighting Dimensions International) convention held each year, alternating between the east and west coasts. The United States Institute for Theatre Technology publishes two magazines, *Theatre Design & Technology* magazine and *Sightlines,* that deal with educational issues, as well as design and technology advancements. They also hold a job placement fair at the annual convention. A newer publication for concert and corporate production is called *Pro Lights & Staging News*, which uses a glossy newspaper format. It reports the business of design but also pokes fun at itself and others, as well as presenting cutting-edge technology.

And we haven't even discussed the proliferation of Web sites for theatre companies, designers, arts programs, manufacturers, books and authors, and crewing services. Since the offerings of online sites are changing so quickly, it is probably best just to do a "key word" search using Google or one of the other search engines on your computer from the paragraphs above and do some Web surfing. You will get a plethora of information, with the speed of the Internet plus "links" between sites for more information. The challenge will be not to get hooked on *surfing* the Internet and forget why you are online in the first place.

I cannot continue to list all those specialty magazines because they keep appearing and merging. And then there are the yearly publications that bring together lists or condense the year's monthly publications into one volume. Keeping up with this list is difficult (see appendix), but I have always maintained that it is a necessary evil on two counts. First, doing so allows you to obtain information on potential clients and collaborative designers, as well as keeping (particularly if you're a lighting designer) up to date on the fast evolving technology. I always have a stack of these magazines in my shoulder bag that I bring with me onto the stage or set. I scan and mark items of interest for closer reading and cataloging when I get back to the office. It is a never-ending job, but one you must become very familiar with if you want to keep advancing your career.

Now that we have found people to contact, what do we do? You should probably re-read chapter 7 to review the media and methods available to get a potential client to see your work or become interested in you. But in the end it still comes down to a face-to-face meeting with that producer, director, or managing director. *What have you got to offer? How can you make our production special? Can you meet our production schedule and budget? How old are you— you look a little young. Can you keep up with our pace (maybe you are too old for our team)?*

This business is a people business; we do not stand in our backyards and sculpt a statue and, when we think it is finished, take it to a gallery to be sold. We must participate in the "design process" with a very diverse group of people. Some like us, our values and ideas, and others, well . . . that is a little beyond our comprehension sometimes. But what comes out of all this is a unique creation that we will have been a contributing part of, for better or worse, when it is all said and done. On to the next project! Once you get your foot in the door for an interview or get hired and show up at the production meeting, you must deal with another human being, unlike our sculptor who can be aloof and shrouded in mystery. Making a connection with another person, especially someone you must interact with on a creative level, may not be natural for you. Don't worry, there are techniques you can learn. Interpersonal relationships and the ins and outs of negotiating are the next things that come into play.

CHAPTER 9

Personal Appearance

Henry David Thoreau said, "Beware of all enterprises that require new clothes." If you plan to spend your life secluded from all other human contact, you can follow Thoreau's advice. If you want to make it in business, pay careful attention to your dress and grooming. You don't have to be a clotheshorse to have your appearance be appreciated. *Dress for Success*, ever hear that one? Well, we are in a "visual media," are we not?

We don't think about it much because most of us consider ourselves *artists* and therefore immune from the corporate dress code. But here's a little secret: The bohemian look is out! Unconsciously, people equate sloppy appearance with sloppy work habits. Many highly creative people affect a casual indifference toward their personal grooming, but in reality, they think they are making a very calculated and purposeful statement. There is no getting around it. Of course, when you are working in the shop in paint clothes or hanging lights you are not expected to be in good clothes. Then again, read what took place at Sea World later in this chapter; there are always exceptions to the rule. And no one is suggesting that you need to dress to the "nines," not even for a first-time meeting or interview. But take a moment and think about how the person you are meeting will be dressed—not only the managers and businesspeople you come in contact with, but also in your work environment and other designers and coworkers.

Dress for Inclusion

My guiding principle is to try and match the person I am meeting with in my level of dress or, if I am meeting a producer or financial manager, maybe just a little below. That is to say, if you are to have a meeting with a managing director or a school's provost with the goal of securing more funds for your department, it is wise to go into that meeting looking like someone who understands business. Such an understanding is very often equated with your appearance. Ask yourself, do I look like someone who knows numbers and budgets? Does that mean a business suit? I can't tell you that it does as an absolute; you have to judge how the person you are meeting with might interpret your appearance.

The safest position to take is to follow this rule: Avoid extremes in clothing, hairstyle, and grooming. Women have always been given greater latitude for individuality in fashion, but the general rules still apply. Nido R. Qubein is a nationally known author and lecturer on communication. In his book, *How to Be a Great Communicator,* published by John Wiley & Sons, he suggests that you dress for inclusion. Look at the people whom you will be working with and let them be the general guide for your appearance. That may seem a little too formulaic, but as a statement of accepted practice in American business, I would seriously consider taking his admonitions to heart.

In cases where you have never met the management person before, how should you present yourself? That is always best handled by going with a business look. At least a nice shirt or blouse, sweater, or jacket is always appropriate attire without fear of overdressing. What business now calls "casual" clothes has moved some businesspeople away from the three-piece suit. Now it is acceptable in many business situations to wear plaids and prints, which are perceived as being more whimsical and creative and would be good for the person trying to project that image. One item that all business people frown on is jeans. Never go to a business office wearing even expensive designer jeans. If you are a stage manager or production manager, then there is no question that your dress must reflect a *businesslike* posture.

If you're not meeting with a business manager, producer, or showbacker, things can get a little easier. But your dress is still an issue that must be thought out before you attend a meeting, even just a script reading. I learned a long time ago that matching my dress to the meeting extended beyond the style of dress. I once wore a tour jacket that I had been given by a famous rock star to a meeting with a manager of another artist. I thought I was showing how "cool" I was and that the jacket would project the image that I was a player in the concert lighting game. But in fact the manager was offended because the tour logo on the jacket I was wearing belonged to a former client who left the manager on less than the best of terms. Can you say, multimillion dollar lawsuit? So no matter how good my portfolio was or how well I spoke concerning his client's needs, I had lost points in his eyes. I did get the job, by the way, but it took some intervention from a mutual acquaintance.

Branding

We are a society of "logo wearers." What a marketing triumph that has been for the clothing industry—companies have actually convinced the public to give them free advertising! Many see it as being cool or hip to be able to afford a particular designer. It's a status thing. But when it comes to the entertainment industry, be very, very careful where and how you "brand" yourself.

There are other ways of creating an identity for yourself that can work. One example was Chip Mounk, one of the first concert lighting designers. Chip always wore a hockey jersey. There was no special team, it was just always a new, very colorful, hockey jersey. It became his recognizable trademark around the touring world. He could be easily found in an arena or in a crowd of people to be singled out for an interview (which he loved to do). So, he used branding in a positive way. There are many other ways to do this, as well. I knew a professor, Lee Watson at Purdue University, who always wore a bow tie. Now, that is not so unusual, you say? Oh, did I mention that they were always made out of colorful bird feathers? I'm sure that he would have been well known around his campus in Indiana with or without the bow ties, but as a nationally known educator and author, he was instantly recognized at conventions and other gatherings because of his distinctive form of branding.

These are "calling card" types of branding for people to assume as part of their persona. Some men wear a particularly distinctive style of hat or cap. Many costume designers are known for their very colorful dress, which often seems to be in a gypsy theme with lots of beads and bracelets. That works to convey that they have a flair for design. This is a little harder for the lighting people to do. Should lighting people wear battery packs with illuminated shirts?

So it is possible to take this a little too far, and it certainly can backfire. But if you do have something that fits your personality, I say take advantage of the recognition it can give you and use it. By the way, avoid the sound or lighting guy look: balding with a ponytail. This is advice from another old road horse, who happens to still have his ponytail . . . and is balding—so he knows of what he speaks.

Speaking of branding, let's discuss the other popular forms of branding: tattoos and piercings. This is a very difficult area to discuss, because if you have already done it, you have made a very personal choice. Let me also say that my comments do not come from a conservative point of view. I have worn a diamond stud in my ear for many, many years. Now, that isn't considered much of a rebellious statement today, but it was when I was younger and had "road dog" hair (long and unkempt), as well as a full beard. I cut my long hair short several years ago because I chose, as my community service, to work in Search and Rescue for the U.S. Coast Guard and had to agree to meet their grooming requirements. That does not mean that I can't keep my identity when pursuing my design work in entertainment. I simply take out the ear stud when on duty. Piercing can be removed, but never tattoos. They never completely go away, even with today's laser techniques.

You must think of what effect these adornments will have on your careers and personal lives down the road. And one thing no one can predict is what those years will bring. Will you stay in theatre, or move on to theme park work and want to move up to management or go into accounting? You can say that "nothing" will ever change your mind, but I hasten to add that I was a child of the sixties. I was a folk singer with a record contract. Would I have believed anyone who told me I'd be doing anything else with my life right then? Most of my then-hippie friends now sport three-piece suits and live in suburbia! But enough said. You must choose carefully in this area, as it could not only have lasting effects on your business appearance but in your personal life as well.

Specific Work Areas and Appearance

The following illustrates some specific areas of work and what I feel may be your best guide to appearance and dress when meeting with executives and managers. Most of what I will say is really a statement of your respect for the people you will be meeting. Once on the job, the attire of those around you should be your guide. However, we are not in the very structured factory system where workers don't wear a tie, floor managers do wear a tie but no jacket, middle managers wear a sport coat and tie, and vice presidents and above wear three-piece suits—even when working out! In any work environment, if others are required or expected to dress at a certain level, then you should follow their example. If that bothers you, then move on; this isn't the place for you.

Las Vegas/Casino Work

Let us start with other areas of potential work. First, Las Vegas and hotel/casino work. When attending meetings with hotel staff, you will most often find the men in at least a tie, if not a sport jacket or suit, and the women in a business suit. Since your meetings may take you through the casino and then into the performance space, they would prefer you conform to the hotel/casino's dress code, especially if you are going to be around the facility for a long period of time and expect to interact with their employees. They will look kinder on you returning if you dress to their standards. Remember, you are dealing with highly paid business people who just happen to be running an entertainment-based business, not people who are in love with the idea of being in ShowBiz.

If you are coming into the hotel/casino as part of a "package" show or as a staff designer to a headline performer, the wearing of the artist's or show's logo is very acceptable. It quickly identifies you as part of that production and makes recognition easier for the hotel staff and security. Along this line, most tours issue laminated passes to their crew and staff, so wear that around your neck. Again, it identifies you quickly for the people who are on the lookout for you.

Corporate Shows

Very close to the above situation would be corporate shows. The producer who is looking to hire you is essentially an advertising executive, so the lines are well drawn. Especially after the in-house creative meetings, when you are to attend a presentation for the client, business attire with a tie is virtually mandatory. You will be introduced to corporate types who themselves must dress to business standards. For them to perceive you as being on their team, you must dress the part. During the actual production of the show with the client present, I have almost always been told to dress well, in a coat and tie.

Television

For television meetings, I have always felt like I should take the initial meeting in a sport coat without a tie. These producers are not as formal. Some are downright sloppy. But the norm is most often casual business dress for meetings. Once you are hired, then it gets looser, but I would say never go to a meeting at the producer's office in jeans. Even when you arrive to find the vice president of production in a baseball cap, jeans, and a tee-shirt that says, "This is my lucky day—I get to fire someone!" (This actually took place at a meeting I attended at NBC.) You must realize that they get to set the rules, and they get to break them. So until you become vice president of production, keep cool and dress for inclusion.

Film

Closest to television is film. But here, I can't even begin to recommend anything. You have all seen Steven Spielberg or Ron Howard in a baseball cap and a windbreaker jacket on the set, or even as guests on late-night talk shows. But then there is director Martin Scorsese, who always wears a coat and tie even while on the set shooting. But quite a number will be found wearing a "safari jacket." Need I say more?

Theme Parks

Most people know how the dress and grooming code works at Disney parks. The story goes that when they took over the operation of the Queen Mary, they fired the man who played the ship's captain because he had a handlebar mustache and refused to shave it off! So be forewarned. But all the parks have dress and appearance concerns, so don't be shocked when you interview and are told how much importance they place on this issue, even if you are applying for a behind-the-scenes summer job. They will hand you a very thick employee booklet that will define the park's dress and appearance code in language that makes it a top priority for workers. But there are exceptions, and often how badly they think they need you is equal to how much you can get away with. But why tempt the issue.

Concerts

The artists' managers are most often in a business mode because they are normally schooled in accounting or law and, if men, dress at least in slacks and an open dress shirt. They tend to be the most fashion conscious people I meet with on a regular basis. The line here is difficult. Yes, you want to show them that you are a road warrior, ready to jump on the tour bus. But at the same time, if you appear too far out in grunge or heavy metal gear in emulation of the band, management may have a hard time seeing past the dress into your mind. Remember, if you are going out on the road with a band, the management must be able to rely on you to get a million-dollar show up and running each day.

Theatre

Theatre falls somewhere in between all the above categories. I have met with producers who are managing a production that will cost millions of dollars to mount. (Remember that many Broadway shows and tours are now corporate sponsored.) They cannot afford to take a chance on someone they don't feel understands their business concerns. As for regional theatre, that is a mixed bag. Anything could happen. So, it is best to err on the high side and dress nicely.

Dress for the Position

As a designer, dressing nicer than the crew quickly identifies you. Nothing too nice, though. If you're dressed well, the crew respects your position—even more when you still don't mind doing some dirty "grunt work" alongside them. Jeremy Windle tells the story of his boss, Jim Miller, at Sea World San Diego. Jeremy worked summers while in school and was greatly impressed when Jim jumped into a filthy, muddy, motor pit wearing good slacks and a crisp white shirt to help sort out some multicable. That action, he said, "impressed the hell out of me." He started dressing like a designer after that, not like the crew. He was then perceived as a designer by the other crew members, who appreciated it when he would still help with fixtures or carry cable and get his clothes dirty. The dry cleaning bill is a small price to pay for respect from the crew.

And remember my earlier story about wearing the tour jacket of another artist! At one point, we talked John Denver into a jacket for the band and crew that said "Johnny and the Sharks—World Tour" with no mention anywhere of Denver's name. That was the band's alter ego when playing Rock n' Roll in their hotel rooms. So, we designed a logo and had the jackets made, which we only wore to go to clubs and play, or for those times we didn't want to be recognized. Later, this became my go-to jacket to wear to meetings or events with other stars . . . nobody ever asked, and I didn't tell them who it was. It was great neutral gear.

The first day on a new job, dress a little better than you think is expected. After all, you can take off the sweater, tie, or jacket. No one will put you down for trying. At the worst, someone will say that they don't normally dress that well for daily work. But the reverse is very bad. If that first day, someone has to tell you to "dress better," you have damaged a first impression that can never be taken back, no matter what you do in the future.

If you can establish a persona, by all means, use it to your advantage. Once you are in production and you feel comfortable with the other members of the team, dress can get casual, but it should never be sloppy for the design or management personnel.

CHAPTER 10
The Interview

What goes hand in hand with personal appearance is the "game" of the inter-view. Walking in cold to a first-time meeting with a producer is the most stress-ful thing you will do. I like to use the key word "cold" to remind myself that the first meeting with someone establishes the basis of the relationship for years to come—and I don't want to have that person feel "cold" toward me. We want the interviewer or a group of new people to virtually fall in love with us. Whether we are going to our first production meeting or going on a blind date, we want people to respect and trust us, and see our creative abilities. People get their most lasting impression in the first few minutes of contact. We will never be able to take back that impression. But as I also said, it is a game. The truth is, we cannot be ourselves at an interview. We must be on guard to make sure we put forward an impression that will be favorable—which is not unlike a first date. The difference is, we get to do it over and over again, sometimes more than once a day. Luckily, we don't have to do this so often with potential lovers.

Luck

I can't say this enough: we are involved in a "team" creative process. We know that what we are discussing in this chapter will never end with one interview or meeting. Have you ever heard someone say, "Wow, I got the job, but I guess it was just dumb luck because I was late, and I dropped my resume and artwork all over the floor. I couldn't find an example of a project I had just spent five minutes telling them was my best work, and I talked nonstop." Or how about, "I just sort of fell into the job because a friend was having lunch with this friend who said he knew someone who heard this producer had just fired the costumer." Or the time I was contacted about doing some work for the TV game show *Wheel of Fortune*. They had decided to take the show on the road. I got through the initial telephone interview and was asked to come to the pro-ducer's office for a meeting. The doors opened to the conference room, and at the head of the table sat a director I had worked with several years before on a pilot. He looked up and said, "Oh, you've gotten Jim to do this. That's great, we worked together before." The producer, who really hadn't hired me yet, looked around the table and said, "Sure," and I was in. It was my marketing to that di-rector, which I had started years before, that did the trick. If we met again, I wanted to make sure I had planted a positive memory of myself so he would re-member me. That association lasted fourteen years, until he retired.

Okay, there is luck in all of what we do. It was lucky he was the direc-tor rather than someone I didn't know. It could have gone another way. But you should always assume you are not going to be so lucky and prepare for every meeting. Did you ever go to your parents as a child and ask for a particular toy only to be asked why you needed it, and you were not prepared to justify it? Well, guess what; that will be the case for the rest of your life. It is better to be overprepared and have worked through all the possible questions that could be thrown at you than to come up short with nothing to say. And as we all know, if we take the time to prepare, no one will ask!

Game Plan

You need a game plan before you arrive at the interview or meeting site, even if it is just a casual get-together for an overview of the production. Don't go in "cold." There are a number of great books and audiotape programs available to help you to prepare for an interview. One book is called *Killer Interviews,* by Frederick W. and Barbara B. Ball and published by McGraw-Hill Press. Al-though these books and tapes are targeted at people seeking what we think of as a business position, you can use a lot of what is offered to give yourself a boost.

Preparation

It is not possible to prepare for every question an interviewer may ask, but it is quite possible to be prepared on the major issues and subjects that are likely to come up in the meeting. You should do an Internet search for information on the company and even the specific person who will be conducting the interview. And practice your thirty-second closing into a tape recorder or do it in front of a live person. A good friend would be your best audience, because then you can ask for constructive criticism.

Let's assume that you know all about yourself, so that is not where you need to put the greatest amount of time in preparation. But if you are inter-viewing for a job in an area where you have had limited experience, making sure you have all the facts together on any projects that you could call similar is well worth your time. Even if you have sent a resume in advance or have been recommended by another person, the interviewer may not know your pro-duction history. You can launch into a short synopsis of your background, but only if asked.

The preparation is more about learning all you can about the inter-viewer and the production company. What other work has she done? Who has she worked with that you know? Have you read reviews of her shows that you can quote from? What type of production is the company known for?

I had an incident years ago that illustrates why you should do even minimal research. I got a call to come to a meeting for a tour that was being set up for the recording artist Andy Gibb. My brain heard "Gibb," and I knew the band was the Bee Gees, who were very hot at the moment. So I ran out and bought a tape of their latest music. I was preparing for the meeting by being able to quote song titles and comment on their musical style. I got to the office of the manager and, without waiting to hear what he had to say, I started spouting off about how great the Bee Gees were and how much I loved the new album. I was quickly and not so politely told that Andy Gibb was *not* one of the Bee Gees but a younger brother with whom, it turns out, they did not get along. All I could do was apologize and ask what they were looking for—any way I could think of to change the subject. By the way, I did get the job, mostly because the road manager they had already hired was a close friend and stood up for me and the fact that I was honest enough to admit I didn't know anything about Andy Gibb.

Some of the things you should have tried to learn concerning the artist's management or former production is how well is the production capitalized, and what are the fee levels the company has paid in the past for similar design work? Will this be a specific project assignment, or is the company looking for a full-time employee? How does that fit into your plans? If you are not prepared to travel, and you know the job is for a road or touring position, don't waste the interviewer's time.

Some people suggest that it is worth taking the meeting so you can get a chance to have the employer put a face with your name for future opportunities. But when I asked professional interviewers about this, they were overwhelmingly against it. They feel you are taking their valuable time just when they are focused on hiring for a particular position that needs filling right now. If you tell them in advance that you are not sure you are able to travel, but you'd like to meet with them to get more details, they can say yes or no at that point. Notice that I didn't say that you are not willing to travel. Never make an absolute pronouncement in an interview unless you are willing to walk away.

In *Killer Interviews,* the Balls speak a lot about mental preparation for interviews. The fears we have associated with wanting people to like and accept us really come out when we are about to go into an interview. Lack of self-confidence and any negative view you have of yourself are tied to the success or failure you will have in the interview. Perhaps your last show ended on a sour note, or you got fired, or the reviews were bad concerning your design; whatever the reason to be down about yourself or your abilities, the effect is the same. Don't bring it into the interview room or it will sink you.

There are other questions you should be asking yourself before you arrive or even before you call for the interview. Will the type of production be acceptable to or looked down on by friends and family? What if the people you want to impress perceive this as a step backward in your career? Do you already know that the job pays less than you can afford to work for and meet your financial obligations? All these issues can burden you and weigh you down in an interview. These worries about your personal problems and concerns about whether you can do the job show in your face, which affects how things will go in the interview—unless you are a great actor, and if that is the case, you may be applying for the wrong job. An experienced interviewer will pick up hesitation or uneasiness every time. If you are applying for a design or management position, you do not want them to get the impression that you can't take pressure.

Do you think this project is a derailment of your career path? Are you taking it just for the money? The interviewer will see this, know you don't really care about the project, and assume you will not be dedicated enough to do the best job possible. Do not, I repeat, do not spend the interviewer's time telling him how you'd rather be doing Shakespeare. Are you interviewing for a head electrician or seamstress position when you have designed professionally already? Is the project so simple or easy that you feel it is beneath your creative ability to give your all? Or, on the other hand, is this an interview for a position that would be a huge leap upward and forward? Are you simply afraid of the unknown? Do you have reservations as to your own ability to handle the job that is being offered? In your own mind, are you overqualified, underqualified, too young, or too old for the position?

These questions do not need to be gone over every day or before every meeting, but it does require some serious time on your part to answer these challenging questions. You may find it best to talk them out with a close friend or mentor. Many people are too shy or afraid to let people close to them know they are frightened or scared. So, find a mentor, someone who is older, more experienced, and willing to coach you at times when you are questioning yourself and your talent. Find someone who is a good listener and will ask questions to move your thought process along, not make judgments about you.

Positive Attitude

The things above are all negatives that you do not want to bring with you into the interview room. Instead, what you need to do is bring in an overwhelmingly *positive* attitude. Such attitudes don't even have to be directly related to the position under consideration. They can be very general, such as simply saying to yourself, I know I can do anything I put my mind to. Or, I know I am a capable, focused person and very good at what I do.

We would all do better to have a positive attitude all the time, but life has its ups and downs because there are events totally beyond our control. One way to combat this is to have a positive role model in mind, or a phrase or quotation that you can repeat just before the meeting. Some people call it their game-mantra. No matter how you do it, approach the interview by visualizing a positive outcome before you go in. It all comes down to your honesty and sincerity. Believing you are the best person for the position and that you are totally committed to the task ahead is the key.

It goes almost without saying that interviewers are looking for signs that indicate an interest and enthusiasm for the job. So, what should go into your game plan?

* Prepare specific photos and graphic materials that relate to the project.
* Learn about the person you will be meeting with and the company.
* Be attentive and listen.
* Have your minimum fee or pay scale fixed in your mind.
* Prepare well-thought-out reasons the interviewer should hire you.
* Be prepared to ask questions.
* Practice your closing.
* Have a firm walk-away position.

Portfolio

While you are still in school, with the help of your teachers and possibly at a conference, you have had time to prepare a portfolio of your work. Get as much help in this area as possible. You must have a presentation that is organized and shows off your best work without excuses. If the photo isn't as good as it should be and you find yourself making excuses for it, drop it! If you can't get a set of plans reduced to fit the format of the rest of the presentation, forget it!

The portfolio should be in such a form that it can be set up easily for viewing by the interviewer. Never bring a portfolio that has to be turned and twisted for the interviewer to see your work. There is a growing trend toward using Microsoft PowerPoint, or even making your presentation using a CD that can be left with the interviewer. If you decide to go this high-tech route, do not assume the interviewer will have the necessary equipment; bring your own laptop, just in case.

The whole presentation should take no more then ten minutes. Practice and practice again. Cut down if you must, but make all this work in ten minutes. That may seem impossible, but working on it in the mirror or saying it into a tape recorder helps you become at ease and more confident in yourself. And you can time your speech until you get in the zone of approximately ten minutes. Interviewers normally have scheduled no more than twenty minutes for your appointment, and you will see them looking at their watches because they are starting to worry that they will be late for their next appointment. If they are late, you will get the brunt of their displeasure with a negative on the interview no matter how well you presented yourself. It is not impolite to ask if they need to wrap it up. If they say yes, offer to come back tomorrow or later that day. Actually, this gives you a chance to breathe and evaluate what has been said, or not said, and you can use the time to organize your thoughts and come up with an even stronger case for the next meeting.

In any event, you need to be prepared to shorten your prepared presentation. That also means that you must be prepared to jump around in your portfolio if a question is asked that you believe would be better addressed by other material.

That said, if you find that you are losing the interviewer's attention, cut the presentation short. Don't try to rush through the rest. Find a way to ask if the interviewer has seen enough, or find any other way that gives him an out. If he doesn't take the offer, that is a positive sign. If he says yes, he is running behind, cut to the chase and do your run for the roses. Give him your thirty-second closing and cross your fingers. That is always better than trying to cram too much down the interviewer's throat. He may not like you any better either way, but it is the polite thing to do. It is not uncommon for the interviewer to break into your well-prepared presentation with a question that makes you digress or skip material you feel is important. You want to keep a mental bookmark and find a way to return the presentation to where it left the track. However, if the interviewer says, all this is nice but it is not what he wants to talk about, don't force the issue.

Listening

That brings us to the most important sales tool known to marketing: *Listen* to the customer. Often the interviewer will sell for you. For example, if she says, we are looking for a person who can handle a union crew, of course you'd agree that you do handle union crews very well. If she says, you seem like a very well-organized person and that is what we need, are you going to say that you are not? But in both cases, would you have thought to mention either of these qualities on your own? Probably not. Most books on marketing will state that listening is *the* key to successful selling, that the great salespeople listen, and listen closely, to the customer before ever trying to sell anything. It is a proven fact that people, especially those in management positions, are more interested in themselves than they are in you. I hate to say it, but it is almost an obsession in our business. At times I think that theatre invented the *Me Generation*. And if you think we are only talking about performers, you better think again. Almost everyone who is successful in the entertainment business has an "A" personality.

But that can be used to your advantage. Let them talk! You listen and learn how you can fit into their world. Then bring out the things that fit into their vision of that world and show them how you can be part of it.

Never Interrupt

The other side of listening is to never interrupt. The interviewer is running the show. It's his show and he knows what he wants to say, so there is no way for you to guide the interview. If the question is long and complicated and you are bursting to answer, take notes. Then you can answer the question later, point by point. It shows you are attentive and well organized. You can also ask for clarification if the speaker gets off track, but only when he is finished or asks for comments. Generally, when we interrupt we have not heard the complete question and our answer really doesn't go to the point. We lose out both for being impolite and additionally for not answering the real question.

Never put down someone else, even if the interviewer does. Sometimes it is a ploy to see if you will take the bait. If you will talk about others, why wouldn't you do it concerning the interviewer or his company? And never talk badly about a former employer or company. Do not use slang or curse—no matter how informal you think the atmosphere. The person sitting on the other side of the table may look like a biker, but he may also be the deacon of his church. So, that brings us to sarcastic humor and off-color jokes. Avoid them both. Although some speakers recommend a joke to break the ice, be very, very careful. There are just too many ways to offend someone.

Finances and Logistics

The most important things to have clear in your mind are how you will respond to questions concerning financial and logistical issues. These are without a doubt the hardest questions to be prepared to answer if asked. The tendency is to go over and over your qualifications and why you should be hired, and not even think about how much you should be paid. What is often referred to as the "deal-breaker" figure—something that just barely covers your expenses, maybe—is what you must be prepared to hold your ground over or walk away. My belief is that we must factor in several things:

1. What do you need to pay your bills?
2. What have you been paid for similar services in the past?
3. Do you see this project as a stepping-stone to bigger things?
4. Can you set a deal-breaker point, such as:
   * No regular weekend work, because you have young kids.
   * That you cannot relocate due to family consideration.
   * That you will only take the design job, not an assistant position.
   * That you must have a signed contract, not daily hire.
   * That you will only work under a union contract.
   * That you must have health insurance and workers' compensation provided.
   * That you must have a deposit before you present the design or begin work.

You can add or subtract from this list. I only want you to consider how to handle these issues in the interview. Many times, you will be asked to make a choice: to take the job right then, or not get it. That is a pressure tactic that negotiators like to use. They want to get you rattled and, in your haste, get you to agree to less than you would otherwise accept. I'll be more specific about negotiating in chapter 11.

Some interviewers will sit back and say nothing. They know that puts a tremendous amount of pressure on the interviewee and will make you uncomfortable. They are probably testing you to see how you sweat. But if you have a game plan thought out in advance, you can accept the challenge. You can also prepare a set of questions you want the interviewer to answer before you decide whether the position is right for you. It is good to have these written down and even to pull out a piece of paper with them listed. This shows the interviewer that you are very well prepared and are not dealing purely on an emotional level.

You can also turn the tables on the interviewer. For example, ask him what he paid the last designer, or whether he feels that your position is key to the production. (If he says yes, you can hold your ground for a higher fee, since you will be a "key" element in the production.) Or ask him to define your responsibilities, to determine whether they've thought out the process themselves. Find out whether they've budgeted an assistant. Some will not like this, so it should only be used *if* they clam up. You can also very successfully use it in the situation where they are forcing you to decide right then and there if you will take the position based on their overview of the project's scope and fees as they have stated them. So that you do not regret a spur-of-the-moment decision later, you owe it to yourself and your family, to make sure the offer meets your minimal needs, both financially and creatively.

You also need to keep your ears open so you can counter and resolve any concerns of the interviewer. Some interviewers will even ask you directly to tell them your weaknesses. You should have prepared answers in advance to such questions. For example, what is your response if they question your lack of experience? Why have you not worked for that specific director or at that theatre before? Is the implication that you were not good enough in the past? This would make most people angry. But do not be drawn in; it is a ploy to see how you react to negative comments. Reply that the situation just hasn't arisen or been right and don't get defensive. And are you ready to answer any question concerning your scheduling, or whether you can dedicate yourself to the project? If you are also working on other projects, can you convince them you will make their project number one? You absolutely must do this critical kind of self-evaluation.

Honesty

It is very, very difficult to face our shortcomings, but better that this be done in the privacy of our home than to be caught making it up as we go during the interview. Never just cross your fingers and hope they won't ask the tough questions. So, we are not perfect and we don't all have the same experiences. You can counter these concerns by redirecting the answer to something that is not fatal to your candidacy. Explain how you overcame a weakness or learned a lot and grew from a particular experience. And, as they say, if all else fails, be *honest*. Interviewers may ask if you have been reprimanded for being too hard on people working under you, or been sued for sexual harassment, or fired for drinking. The trap is that they already know the answer and are just checking to see if you will be honest with them. On the positive side, if they know something negative about you and still call you in for the interview, they are willing to set it aside. But only if you are honest. What cannot be asked is anything about your sexual preferences, political affiliations, or religious beliefs. Check with the Department of Health and Human Services for a detailed brochure on these issues.

Passion

In *Killer Interviews,* the Balls tell us that even after all the preparation and practice with interview skills, a great interview takes more—it takes *passion*. In our business, passion would seem to be virtually palpable in the air. But on the theory that we should never take anything for granted, make sure you impress upon the interviewer that you want the project more than anything else. Say that you believe the team and you would be a good fit, that you cannot imagine a better time to do the project, and that you have worked and prepared your entire career for this challenge. These may sound corny, I know, but you'd be surprised how well it goes over with a business and management-type interviewer.

Closing

Lastly, the closing. I always relate this to the old prison movies in which the condemned man is asked if he has any last words. When interviewers ask this question, you don't want them to see the lump in your throat or the fear in your eyes. You must be prepared to ask questions or to reply that you are comfortable that they have answered all your questions. But it is a good idea to reframe a question that is positive. For example, you agree that the person they hire must be key to their getting the production in on time and on budget, and that you approach things exactly as they have said. And then ask if there is anything else they would like to know about you. That gives you a moment to organize your thoughts. Then launch into your rehearsed closing.

Openness and confidence are the characteristics you should show in the closing. Design it to do just that. It can be as simple as, there is no one or company that I'd rather work for right now. Or, I have worked hard to reach this point in my career, and I am confident I am the best person you will find for this position. Some people will say this is going too far, but let me just say that if you were on the other side of the table, what would you want to hear? Someone who "thinks" they might be able to handle the job?

And lastly, *ask for the job*. Now is not the time or place to be timid. The interviewers need to see that you really want the job. Turn the tables on them and ask, when can I get started? If nothing else, this will force them to tell you what the next step will be, such as an interview with the director, or a check of your references, and so on. Then you should ask when you should call them back. That way, you go home knowing what to expect next. It doesn't do any good to pace the floor wondering when the phone will ring. You can't put your life on hold waiting, nor should you.

What if during the interview you found out that you have mutual friends or business associates? Call them and ask if they wouldn't mind making a call to reinforce what a great talent you are and how well you would fit into the project. Or get opinions on points the interviewer made. Is that historically accurate as to how the company works or what it pays?

And lastly, something that never should be skipped, send a *thank you card*. Never miss the opportunity to put your name in front of the interviewer again shortly after the interview, even if you have been told that this time it isn't going to work out. Keep the door open by sending a note saying that even though the interviewer felt you were not right for this project, you hope she will keep you in mind for the next one.

This very situation just happened to me. I got a call from a live show producer who said I had been highly recommended by the owner of the theatre where he was about to remount a show. He went on to say the lighting designer they had used didn't think she was going to be available for the dates, so if I didn't mind, we could meet.

I brought what I thought were appropriate materials, but put special emphasis on the last show I designed in that theatre. I didn't have any idea of the style or material content of this show. We had what I thought was a good first meeting. At the end we discussed fees. I countered the figure he offered, but he didn't seem overly concerned. (I had to do this because the figure was lower than the fee I had last received at the theatre, and I didn't want to get caught in the spiral of reduced fees that is so difficult to reverse if word gets out.) Then he gave me a copy of the script and a videotape of the previous production. I took this as a very positive sign, and we concluded on that note of optimism.

I left with the impression that the company wanted to go with me, even if the other designer was available, but nothing had been verbalized to suggest that, just an impression I got from his body language. He said he'd get a final answer from the other designer very soon and let me know.

I sent a card the next day with the normal comments about our meeting being a pleasure, and I hoped he'd have a successful production no matter what the outcome of our discussion. Three days later, I got a call from him that the other designer was in fact going to be able to do it and that the company felt it was best to stick with her. I politely said I thought that was probably the best idea and wished him success, then added that I hoped we could work together sometime in the future. I mailed back the script and videotape the next day along with another note saying good luck with the show.

A month went by and I got a call from him asking if I remembered him. He went on to say the lighting designer was splitting her time between his production and another, which she had not told him about before she accepted the project, and now it was behind schedule. But more important, he did not feel the show was getting her best work. Would I be available to take over? Now, that is an awkward situation, at best.

It would not have been the first time I had stepped in to "doctor" a design that had not worked for whatever reason. But to walk into this production a week before opening would be walking a tightrope that I felt could have less than a positive ending. Luckily, rather than having to make a decision, I was already committed and had to decline due to my own schedule, the very thing that had gotten the other designer in trouble. And if I had taken it on I would have been splitting my time and could have wound up in the same boat. Yes, I would have gained a show, but ultimately I could have damaged a new relationship. It was better to bow out gracefully, saying I was sorry, but my schedule was now set for those dates. Perhaps next time. The P.S. to the story is that I have already received a call from that producer about starting meetings on his next show!

Informational Interview

I tell students not to wait until they are ready to graduate to call and set up an appointment for an interview with a firm or designer. Many employers, if they do not have a specific opening, will not take the time to see you if there is no opening. To counter that, call and ask for an "informational interview." In such an interview, you are ostensibly not looking for work, just trying to learn more about the designer or firm for future reference. It is a great way to get people to look at your portfolio without the pressure of an actual job interview. Also, you learn what the designer or firm would be looking for *if* they were hiring. The atmosphere is a lot more relaxed and the pressure is relieved.

Does this mean that you can't ask for work even though you've been told that there is none? You can show that you are willing to wait for an opening—you feel that strongly about coming aboard whenever the opportunity becomes available. You should ask if you can drop by or tag along sometime to get a better idea of how things work. Then follow up later with a specific date or inquire about doing so on a project that was mentioned. If nothing else, you get to see the designer at work for a day or two. That can be valuable insight for an interview with that person later, or just general information to sock away for another time and place.

It is also an excellent time to ask about their internship program. And if nothing else, get names of other firms and designers whom you might see, as well.

Form Resumes and Letters

With the availability of computers and programs such as Microsoft Office, it may seem like the easy way to write a business letter is to fill in the blanks on some form and send it off, thinking that you have followed the correct business practice. But most executives can recognize these forms, in which case your creative stock just fell. If you can't create a letter or resume of your own, they won't be interested in you for their creative team. Now, that said, you can't go wild and forget the fact that this is a "business communication" that has an excepted form.

One student said that his college gave undergraduates examples of letters to send to prospective employers for internship programs. In fact, many of the students just stuck their names on the letters and sent them out without personalizing them. The problem was that most sent the letters to the same people, so all were busted!

One student showed up at my office at about 6:30 in the evening without an appointment. Although I shouldn't have, I was feeling generous and took time to see her. But then she handed me her resume, which had been copied on preprinted stock that looked like crumpled paper. Why would I hire someone that gave me the impression that she was not neat? She may have been attempting to add whimsy to the resume, but it was a bad choice. Think your ideas through very carefully.

If your letter is going overseas, depending on the culture, there can be quite different formats used in crafting a business letter. Get a book that shows you what is expected. Also, check out what it might take to get even a portion of your letter translated into the recipient's language. A note of caution: the computer programs that do automatic translations leave a lot to be desired and need to be checked by a person fluent in that language. You could get your words mixed up and find that, instead of saying you would like to work with them, you have said that you would like to eat their cat!

I had one person send a small gift with her resume and cover letter. It was not a bribe, but a cute little bear. Was that appropriate? Not really, especially since we had never met. Don't get too personal, even if you know the person with whom you will be interviewing. Keep it all business; you can relax a little with some prior knowledge of the person, but don't drop your guard too far. The potential employer is in business mode, and any friendship should be put aside when it comes to hiring.

To recap:

* Be prepared.
* Listen.
* Have a positive attitude.
* Don't interrupt.
* Rehearse your closing.

If you remember these points, you'll make a good impression at any interview. You may still not get the job—remember, the odds are against you at about 10 to 1—but you will have done all you can to influence the outcome in your favor.

And who knows, weeks, months, years later you will be surprised by a call from someone you interviewed with, saying that although she was impressed and it just didn't work out that time, she thinks she has something that would be a perfect fit. So, it goes to show you: never, never write off an interview as a total loss. If nothing comes of it, so be it. But you should have learned something from the experience so that the next time, you are even better prepared.

CHAPTER 11
Group Dynamics and Negotiating Skills

Assuming we are all equal in our training, work experiences, and technical expertise, we have to believe that there are other factors in play when we search for the reason why some people get hired and others are rejected. Since it is only natural to feel that we are the best for the assignment, could it be that we asked for too high a fee? If not, what other reason could there be?

For a long time, I have seen that the difference often lies in the fact that some of us are simply better communicators. Although we were taught in school that communication skills are written or verbal, there is another component, the group dynamic. Some books and clinicians call these interpersonal relationship skills.

Writing Skills

Improving your writing skills is a must. If you are already out of school, this is best accomplished by taking an adult learning class. Our skill in using the printed word has been damaged by the proliferation of mass visual communication: television, radio, and graphics that replace the descriptive sentence. Today's advertising moguls make every effort to keep the printed word to a minimum, finding that clever symbols or visuals are more effective in getting the attention of the mass consumer. Couple this with a public school system that has difficulty producing college freshmen who can spell, punctuate, or write in complete sentences, and you have the picture of writing skills today. Twenty-three percent of entering college students must take remedial English classes.

Good writing skills do not cease being graded on the last day of college. The ability for you to communicate via the written word will always be a watermark by which people judge you. Being able to produce well-written specifications, grant requests, and business letters, as well as letters of introduction composed with clarity and style, are a key skill in any business situation. In Asia and Europe, in particular, the art of writing is held in high regard and considered to be a very desirable business skill.

A cover letter that goes along with a resume, for example, should be personalized for the prospective client. It should be a short letter, no more than one page, but it must be clear and to the point if it is to be read at all. Cold contacts are difficult, and the recipient must at least receive a letter that can hold her interest, and is neatly typed, appropriately formal, and grammatically correct. Don't think that a grammar or spell check program on your computer is going to solve problems. When it comes to sentence and paragraph structure, you must know that word processing programs only provide generally accepted guides and will not do the work for you.

Verbal Skills

Most verbal communication is between two people. Nido Qubein, in *How to Be a Great Communicator*, writes:

> *One-on-one verbal communication affords the greatest opportunity for precision, because immediate feedback can tell you whether you were understood accurately.... The purpose of most communication is to influence the attitudes and behaviors of those whom we address... So it's important that you learn to express yourself accurately and in a way that will accomplish your purpose concerning the individual you're addressing. (79)*

Most of us would do well to take a class in public speaking to learn how to clearly verbalize our ideas and organize them in a way that effectively communicates to the person(s) we are trying to influence, whether they are the managing director or other design team members. Sure, some of you draw very well, and if you do, you may be tempted to let your pictures do the talking. When you hide behind the drawings, you are not letting the pictures speak for you as much as you are sending signals that say you are not comfortable with people. This can be perceived as a sign that you can neither defend your ideas or yourself—and that could lead to outright bullying by the more aggressive members of the design team.

Given that the United Scenic Artists union asserts that you cannot provide drawings until after you have signed a contract for the project, what do you do? We must communicate well. The story goes that famed film costume designer Edith Head didn't have time to draw because she was doing up to fifty-seven films a year, resulting in over five hundred movies during her career. How could she keep up that pace? She had other people do the sketches, and she "sold" her concepts to producers through her effective communication skills! To get the job in the first place, you must have the verbal skills to express your ideas effectively.

One way to enhance verbal skills is to sit down with someone who does not know your job and try to explain a design concept to him. A big problem is that we often skip or leave out details because we assume the other party understands what we are talking about, when, in fact, he may be very ignorant of the specific workings of your particular design process. He may not grasp the concepts or the implications of costs, time, and labor to accomplish it. Being embarrassed to admit it, he remains silent. This is especially true of directors and producers who want the world to think they know everything about everything and are unwilling to admit their inability to comprehend design and technical terminology.

Listening Skills

We are all guilty of selective listening—and of inadvertently eliciting it in others. If your explanation of a design concept is too drawn out, for example, you will probably lose any likelihood of convincing your listeners about it. People will just nod their heads without really caring to understand what you are saying anymore.

According to Robert Bolton in his book *People Skills* (published by Prentice Hall), there are four basic communication skills that are critical to satisfying interpersonal relationships:

* Listening.
* Assertion.
* Conflict resolution.
* Collaborative problem-solving.

Business consultants and employment executives rate a good listener very highly when it comes to defining a successful businessperson. Bolton says studies have shown that 70 percent of our waking hours are spent in communication. Of that, 9 percent is writing, 16 percent is reading, 30 percent is talking, and the largest portion—45 percent—is spent listening. This means that 75 percent of our communication time is spent directly communicating with another human being. If you then take researchers' view that 75 percent of oral communication is ignored, misunderstood, or quickly forgotten, then you have the basis for people not understanding instructions or abstract concepts, such as a design solution. In the book *Are You Listening?* (now out of print), author Ralph G. Nichols writes: "It can be stated with practically no qualification that people in general do not know how to listen" (149). Hearing and listening are two distinct things. According to Nichols, hearing is a word used to describe the physiological sensory process by which auditory sensations are received by the ear and transmitted to the brain. Listening, on the other hand, refers to a more complex psychological procedure involving interpretation and understanding. Besides this internal process, there are other elements to good listening:

* Posture.
* Eye Contact.
* Body Language.
* Attentive Silence.
* Reflective Attention.

Posture

Posture, as any actor will tell you, communicates as much as dialogue. Perhaps this is a reflection of our ability to really listen to the words. Many authorities say listening is affected by how we sit and other physical influences. Good listeners follow these rules:

* Face the speaker squarely.
* Incline the body toward the speaker.
* Maintain an open posture (don't cross your arms).
* Don't violate the personal space of the speaker.

In the book *How to Read a Person Like a Book,* the authors Gerold Nierenberg and Henry Calero analyze a full range of emotion as exhibited through the posture and mannerisms of both the listener and the speaker. In regard to confidence specifically, they say:

> *Confidence can bring about self-control, and the reverse is also true. . . . A confident person is likely to talk without hand-to-face gestures like covering the mouth and nose- and head-scratching, so in reading gestures for confidence, one should watch for a doubt or other negative gesture that would contradict the feeling that is being projected. A proud, erect stance, often seen in the man who has accomplished much and knows where he is going, is also a clear indication of confidence. (93-4)*

Eye Contact

Effective eye contact is believed to express interest and a desire to learn. But remember, do not stare at the interviewer constantly or blankly. Good eye contact enables the interviewer to appraise your receptiveness to what she is saying. Finding the appropriate distance to position yourself from someone cannot always be controlled by the listener. Your interviewer may be behind a desk or table. If the location is the interviewer's office, a chair is generally already positioned at what the interviewer feels is a comfortable separation between her and you. Do not pull the chair up unless requested to do so. If you are standing face-to-face with an interviewer, watch for reactions from him, which might indicate his comfort or discomfort with your proximity. Cultural differences affect the optimal distance for conversing. In America, for example, three feet is a comfortable distance, but in Japan and Korea, that is too close. Be culturally sensitive and check with someone who has conducted business in whatever country you may be interested in, and discuss proper business manners before you take a meeting with someone you do not know.

Body Language

Body language was a popular subject for books dealing with the singles scene a few years ago. In business, it is very possibly of equal importance to listening. One researcher claims that a mere 35 percent of the meaning of a communication is derived from words, and the remainder from body language.

The important facets of body language described by Bolton in *People Skills* are facial expressions, clothing, and grooming. We have already discussed grooming and clothing issues in chapter 9. In *How to Read a Person Like a Book*, Nierenberg and Calero address the issue of facial expressions as follows:

> *During a business negotiation one can observe a wide range of facial expressions: At one extreme is the aggressively hostile negotiator who sees a negotiation as an area where a "do or die" situation exists; he typically looks at you with his eyes wide open, lips tightly closed, and corners of his eyebrows down, and sometimes he even talks through his teeth with very little movement of lips. At the other end of the spectrum is the individual who approaches the negotiation table with impeccable manners and a choirboy look of half-closed or somewhat droopy eyelids, a veiled, slight smile, and peacefully arched eyebrows without any furrow on the forehead. However, he is probably a very capable and competitive individual who believes in cooperation as a dynamic process. (29)*

Many of us believe that if another person does not look at us while either listening or speaking it is because he or she is trying to hide something. Michael Argyle, in his book *The Psychology of Interpersonal Behavior,* observes that people look at each other between 30 and 60 percent of the time. He also notes that when two individuals look at each other more than 60 percent of the time, they are probably more interested in the other person physically than in what is being said. As Nierenberg and Calero point out:

We have also found that people tend to have eye contact more when they listen than when talking. They also employ a gaze aversion when asked questions that make them feel uncomfortable or guilty. On the other hand, when asked a question or when reacting to a statement that makes them feel defensive, aggressive, or hostile, their eye contact increases dramatically. You can sometimes clearly see the pupils dilate when a person is thus aroused. (34)

Other important indicators will signal resolve or questioning. Vocal cues, such as tone and inflection, as well as gestures, which promote self-image and energy level, can also be observed. Be aware of your own attitude and body language, and watch the interviewer for clues as to how he or she is receiving your ideas.

Assertiveness and Other Behaviors

About 5 percent of the population communicates assertively. Just as there are specific ways to increase listening abilities, there are practical methods for developing assertiveness. Much research and experimentation has been undertaken to see how we can increase our assertiveness.

It is widely believed that assertive people are more comfortable with themselves and therefore others feel at ease and more comfortable with their ideas. The most striking thing that Bolton found about assertive people is that they like themselves. They appear to be in a much better position to feel good about themselves than are submissive or aggressive people, he says. Notice that assertiveness is not the same as aggressiveness.

Assertion is generally credited with reducing a person's fear and anxiety. Assertiveness training has been in vogue for many years. A class might be the answer for increasing your skills in this area. Bolton contends that most people are predictably submissive or aggressive, at least in the majority of business situations. The goal of assertiveness training is to help individuals choose their behavior effectively, not to have them behave assertively in every situation. Sometimes, it is wise to give in to orders. Other situations may call for you to defend your ideas aggressively. The point is to be in command and to be able to consciously choose your approach.

On the other hand, aggressive people express feelings, needs, and ideas at the expense of others. They tend to overpower other people. They feel they must always win in arguments. People who behave submissively, on the other hand, demonstrate a lack of respect for their own needs and rights. Other submissive people do express their needs but do so in such an apologetic way that they are not taken seriously.

When you are trying to make a sale in business or promote your concept for a design, you should consider these behavior patterns and choose yours appropriately for the situation. Your ability to consider and choose your behavior can be of great assistance in controlling the direction and ultimate outcome of the conversation.

Conflict Resolution

Unfortunately, it is impossible to avoid conflict in the highly energized world of entertainment production. Conflict disrupts, and ultimately destroys, relationships. Once it erupts, it is difficult to control.

When we are acting as part of a design team, presumably trying to achieve a collective art, we are often in a love-hate relationship with the other members of the team. It is true, particularly in the artistic community, that while we may love our colleagues for their creative flair, we may simultaneously hate their behavior because they don't have *people skills*. Everyone is trying to assert his own personal views at once. How we deal with that situation is the resolution part of the formula.

Conflict can have its positive aspects. It can prevent stagnation, stimulate interest and curiosity, and foster greater creativity. What we must learn is how to harness it and prevent unproductive conflict. To resolve conflict, Bolton suggests three steps to follow:

1. Treat the other person with respect.
2. Listen attentively to his or her ideas.
3. State your views, needs, and feelings clearly.

The respect you show to the others is contained in the attitude you convey by your specific behaviors. The way you listen, the tone of your voice, your look, your selection of nonaggressive words, and your body position all convey respect.

For many people, it takes a lot of conscious willpower not to show disrespect. It is hard to treat other people as equals when we know our own ideas are better. But so much more can be accomplished through the conscious use of conflict resolution methods, because others will most likely give you respect in return. We listen, but all the while we are prepared to say no to the other person's idea—often not even taking the time to consider their idea, totally fixated on our own. But can we really say, I hear what you're saying, I'm just not listening?

After we have demonstrated respect for the speaker, we can use the following to bring about resolution:

* Restate the problem presented by the speaker.
* Brainstorm possible solutions.
* Select the solution that will best meet both parties' needs.
* Plan who will do what, where, and by when.
* Implement the plan.
* Evaluate how well the situation turned out.

Unless a clearly defined understanding of the other person's view of the problem is reached, the exercise will be completely undermined. It is important to arrive at a clear, concrete, succinct statement of the problem to be resolved. Define the problem not as a win-lose situation, but in terms of each person's needs. If you can find a resolution that covers both parties' needs, then you have a win-win situation.

Brainstorming

This is simply the free and open exchange of all possible solutions without evaluating the merits of any right away. Try for a shotgun method with many possible or even crazy solutions. Disregard how silly ideas are, or which side they will most benefit. Quantity is better than quality at this phase of the game. Do not try to clarify or say no to any idea; listen to them all. Research findings have found that it is important not to come into a problem-solving session with the attitude that there is only one solution to the problem—yours!

Only after every idea, no matter how far out, has been listed can you eliminate those that do not meet any of the group's criteria. Some compromise will ultimately be necessary to resolve the problem, and a perfect solution that pleases everyone will be impossible to achieve. But tomorrow is another day and maybe the tide will go your way.

After a solution is reached, take time to make sure everyone understands exactly what each party will do, and when and where. It is important to keep up your part of the bargain no matter what the other person does. Your good faith will often prod the other party into living up to his end of the agreement.

The final step proposed by Bolton is very important. Once you have actually used the plan to resolve a problem, review it to see how it worked. The goal is to be able to use the method with confidence the next time you encounter conflict.

Studies on group dynamics point to the fact that taking the time to consider others as part of our own creative process is necessary for success in collective creativity. Whether attempting to sell ourselves to a potential employer, or a design concept or idea for a show, or a product, good communication skills are at the center of daily interaction on the job with others. They are part of the total creative/businessperson.

Negotiating Skills

Negotiating involves a series of techniques. To arrive at a successful resolution to a conflict researchers have learned that both sides need to win.

This discovery spawned the term *win-win negotiating*. When we try to resolve a design issue within the creative team environment, we must always view the situation as one in which we are searching for a win-win solution. How can we win, yet have the other party feel they have also won? Embracing this idea will go a long way toward achieving your goal in a conflict situation. Negotiating should not be seen as the only technique used in such a situation, however; it is such a broad topic and, admittedly, the most often used way to resolve conflict that we will spend the rest of this chapter discussing it. You can find many books on conflict resolution and interpersonal relationships to gather lesser known and used techniques that will bolster your arsenal for future business battles.

Techniques

One of the leading authors on this topic is Stephen Kozicki. In his book *Creative Negotiating*, he makes a statement that I feel fits our theatrical business to a tee: "Negotiating is the art of reaching an agreement by resolving differences through creativity"(3).

Every day we are negotiators in our personal lives, dealing with wives, husbands, kids, concerning who cleans up, who takes out the garbage, who waters the flowers. It is all done with some kind of negotiating technique. "Johnny, I'll give you an allowance for taking out the garbage," or "Honey, please do me a favor and clean up the yard," are all forms of negotiating. Some are more successful than others, and if they don't work we probably resort to yelling and demanding. Although such tactics are not good negotiating techniques, they are sadly not uncommon in the business environment, either. Negotiating takes place only when everyone involved thinks that he or she will get some benefit from the transaction. The trick is to figure out what each party wants. All too often, there is a hidden agenda that may not even seem relevant to the issue at hand. What is necessary is seeing through all the huffing and puffing and posturing to get to the substance of the issue.

For instance, I wanted my fee increased on a show I had been doing for a number of years. The studio had just sent a memo around saying there would be no raises that year due to the ratings decline of the show. I was a "loan-out" (see chapter 17) to the show, not a full-time employee of the studio. The fact that I was not a "staff" employee may have put me in a weaker position. It is harder—and often expensive—to let a staff member go, whereas the studio or show has no obligation to the loan-out person beyond the stated, short-term, very specific time frame. How could I go to the production manager and negotiate a raise? I went to him and said that I understood the studio's position with a tighter economy, but I felt that my work warranted an increase. I waited, hoping he would agree, which he did. He even went on to praise my dedication to the show. I'm sure he thought his sympathetic response was safe, because I knew he couldn't give me a raise. Then I said, perhaps there was another way he could show his appreciation for my contribution to the show. There was silence, so I asked him out of what budget he got funds for vacation replacement crew. He said the studio had a contingency fund specifically to pay for vacation replacements separate from the projected running crew costs, and that the studio actually paid these costs without deducting them from the show's budget. (I wasn't aware of this: I had been paying my replacement out of my own fees. He never even showed up on the show's payroll before. My agreement stated I would be there from 7:00 A.M. until approximately noon, five days a week, fifty-two weeks a year. If I wanted time off, I was told I had to pay for the replacement out of my own fee.) I suggested that he could put my replacement directly onto the studio payroll.

He thought about it a moment and agreed. Why hadn't this been mentioned before? It didn't affect the show budget, and it wasn't cheating the studio. The reality was, no one thought to mention it before. Thus, I could take vacation and keep the salary for those days, which in the past I had to use to pay my own replacement. Although he did not give me a raise, thus maintaining his boss's edict, he was able to keep me happy. I didn't get a percentage raise, but the actual fee for the fifteen days off amounted to almost a 12 percent raise!

Now, I had not gone to my production manager on a whim. I had done my preparation by talking to other production managers on the lot. I investigated the difference in how the full-time employees and the "loan-out" employees were treated financially. I spoke to other designers from my union about their deals at the studios, all with the goal of finding a way to make my request for a raise a win-win situation, otherwise I was not going to ask for one at all. To put myself into a conflict situation that I knew I couldn't win would not have proved anything—and probably would have damaged my ability to negotiate with this manager in the future.

Joint Problem-Solving

Another way of saying win-win is joint problem-solving. Joint problem-solving revolves around interests instead of positions. The production manager's position was that he could not give out any raises, so I changed the situation into one of interests. We were both interested in rewarding me for my good work. Joint problem-solving can generate better results for both sides. It saves time and energy by cutting out the posturing. And it usually leads to better working relationships, which can be very beneficial in the future.

My preparation had been done long before I found the right opportunity to speak to my production manager concerning a raise. I knew that most negotiations were won or lost on timing. You must look at the problem not only from your side, the demand, but also from the other side, the response. We know from childhood that when we demanded something from our parents we seldom got it. We knew what the response would be, yet we went ahead and put ourselves in a situation that was not winnable. Why?

Most people, from friends to business associates, do not consider the consequences of their actions prior to making demands. They also do not consider the other person's position. If they did, in many cases, they would not make the demand, because they would realize it would only create hard feelings or ill will. Both are difficult to overcome later on, especially in a business situation. Our friends forgive us, or they are not our friends. Our business associates hold grudges—so beware!

Mutual Agreement

William Ury, coauthor with Roger Fisher of the book *Getting to YES* and author of *Getting Past NO*, both published by Penguin Books. In his latest book he discusses the five important issues to take into account along the way to a mutually satisfactory agreement:

* Interests.
* Options.
* Standards.
* Alternatives.
* Proposals.

In order to come to an agreement, both sides must be satisfied. It is thus best for you to figure out not only what you want from the negotiation, but also what the other party will likely want. Ury says that the single most important skill in negotiating is the ability to put yourself in the other person's shoes. Try imagining how the negotiation would look like from the other side.

How has that person behaved in past negotiations? Is there anything that has happened to the other person in recent weeks that could change her attitude toward you? You can even talk to others who know the person to assess how she handles negotiations. The more you find out about the other side, the better your chances of successfully influencing her. I can't go into great detail on all five points listed above. I hope you will read the authors mentioned to get a more detailed explanation of these principles. I merely wish to open the door to your mind.

Options

The purpose of identifying each side's interests is to see if you can devise creative options to satisfy both of them. Ury also says that inventing options for mutual gain is a negotiator's single greatest skill. Although it may not be possible to get everything you want in the exact form you request, there are ways of stretching things into other shapes that equal the same conclusion. Perhaps an additional fee of 10 percent is not possible, but an agreement for another show with an increase then would be agreeable to both parties.

A common mistake in negotiating is to dwell on only one possible solution. Your original position was to get 10 percent more for the job already undertaken. By communicating to the other party your desire to be included in additional work, you may get him to lock you in much sooner than you thought. Avoid planting your feet, folding your arms, and pouting. No resolution will happen that way. There must be something "won" on both sides. After laying out your demand or idea, it is wise to say, okay, now how can we make this mutually profitable or workable for both of us? This shows that you are not making demands; it avoids putting the other party on the defensive, but shows you are willing to negotiate the issue.

Standards and Alternatives

Is there a standard you can use, a watermark of sorts? If you are negotiating a design fee, for example, what is the United Scenic Artists fee schedule for this work?

Do you feel you deserve more, and, if so, how will you justify a higher fee? What did this client pay you in the past? Is this a bigger production, is there less time to build it, or are there more days involved in rehearsal? All these factors can be used as a guide. It is easier for the producer to accept a standard she is familiar with than just pay whatever fee you ask for. So, think before a meeting about what standards you can quote in your negotiation.

You must also know what your alternatives are before you go into negotiations. The purpose of negotiating is not always to reach an agreement, for agreement is only a means to an end. The purpose of negotiating is to explore whether and how you can better satisfy your interests through compromise.

Walk-Away Position

Before you enter a room to negotiate, you must have already decided on your *walk-away* position. Your walk-away position is the key to negotiating power. You *must* prepare a walk-away position before beginning negotiations. In the matter of a fee negotiation, what is the absolute minimum fee you can do this project for and pay your bills? If you do not have this figure firmly in mind, you are lost. A good negotiator sitting across from you at the table (and producers are good, experienced negotiators) will be able to exploit you if he couches his offer in a lot of fill, but the bottom line is actually below your minimum. The "fill" is what they use to clutter up the offer; they hope you'll lose sight of what you will actually receive that is of real value to you. You may not even realize what happened until after you have signed the agreement and walked out the door.

This is sometimes referred to as the used car salesman's ploy: Suck the customer in with a flashy new car and hope he forgets he came in for a used one.

You must have prepared a proposal to counter the other side's offer, which we will assume is too low. You want to select an option that satisfies your interests better than your walk-away position. You should actually have several proposals ready to lay out. Besides your ideal offer, what would satisfy your basic interests sufficiently enough that you would feel that you had still "won"? And finally, what is your bottom line, your lowest possible position, your walk-away or final position?

Now, here comes the hard part. Once you have moved on to your walk-away position, you MUST walk away if it isn't met. No hesitation. That is why your position must be clearly and completely thought out. Does this mean that you lose the project? Not necessarily. Many times, the other party will agree to the position, knowing that she will lose you if she does not. What you have missed in the beginning of the negotiation is that the other side really wanted you. Instead of this becoming a conflict, it should have been a joint problem-resolution meeting.

A word of caution: NEVER, reveal your walk-away position to the other side until you absolutely feel you must walk away, otherwise the negotiation then turns into a "demand." Since there is nothing left to negotiate, the talks usually come to a halt.

Group Negotiating

Although the discussion thus far has been framed in terms of a conflict be-tween two people, everything said would be useful in a group situation, as well. There is a lot more to learn about techniques that can be used success-fully in negotiating—many more than we have room for in this chapter. But in the end, they all come down to a need for people to communicate. Ideas, desires, values, and dreams are all intertwined in a good negotiation, so ne-gotiating is an ongoing part of our creative lives. Make the most of the re-sources used in negotiating.

Negotiating should be viewed as just another tool we can use to achieve our personal goals, as well as the team goals. Will you win them all? No. But compromise and conflict resolution go hand in hand with our art form. The ul-timate conclusion to any negotiating is that both parties walk away without any personal animosity. You cannot attack a person's character or his intelligence. We often marvel at lawyers who can argue and yell at each other in a negotiat-ing session and then turn around to say, how about the families get together for bridge, which is just beyond our comprehension. But they have been trained to leave the negotiations at the door and not take them into their personal lives. We need to do the same thing. If you meet with a producer and cannot calmly reach a mutually satisfactory agreement, never take it personally. He may even have used the tactic of saying your last project wasn't well received, whether it was or not, in an attempt to get you to lower your fee. But often, that is only a ne-gotiating ploy or you wouldn't be sitting there. He wants you, just at the cheap-est price he can get you to agree to.

When it comes to a creative team discussion in which you are negotiat-ing for anything—from time on the stage, to paint for the floor, to focusing the lights, to getting more crew—always end the meeting with handshakes or warm remarks. Don't let anyone leave the room with bad feelings or a negative im-pression of you.

CHAPTER 12
Theatrical Unions

I was raised in a union household. My grandfather was the union representative for the International Brotherhood of Firemen and Oilers, a railroad workers' union. Our town, Joliet, Illinois, was the hub of the EJ&E Railroad. Adolph was a working man himself—no fancy office. He went to the train yards everyday in his bib overalls, and when necessary, he would talk to a man with a problem or who had been causing trouble and get his side of the story. Then he'd walk to the railroad office and discuss the issue with the bosses, one on one.

Sometimes he fought for a worker, sometimes he agreed with the bosses and would suggest punishment that, I know from being at his side on more than one occasion, was usually agreed to because everyone knew that Adolph was a fair man.

Being raised in that environment obviously makes me supportive toward unions. I saw what good the strength and unity of a large workforce could have on workers' ability to receive evenhanded and fair treatment. So naturally I wanted to join a theatrical union when I graduated from school. But I found it more difficult to do so than it was in my grandfather's days. While still in graduate school, I worked summers at NBC Studios in Burbank, California in the special effects department, and as a carpenter out of IA local #33 as a "permit worker," who is someone who does not hold membership but is allowed to work when the local can't find a member to fill the position. (IA is short for IATSE, the acronym for International Associations of Theatrical Stage Employees.) In those days, 1968 to 1969, I was told it took an average of five years working on call as a permit worker to finally be voted into the local.

I really wanted to get into the United Scenic Artists (USA), which was part of the Brotherhood of Painters, Decorators, and Paperhangers of America at the time, but they didn't have much of a presence in Los Angeles in the 1970s. USA represented designers on Broadway. When I assisted Jules Fisher on *Jesus Christ Superstar* at Universal Amphitheatre, and later helped him open the Schubert Theatre in Century City, California, with a show called *Mary C. Brown and the Hollywood Sign,* I was not approached or offered membership. But I wanted to join, so I went back to Chicago, since I was from the area and knew a few USA members there, to take the entrance exams that are required as part of your admittance to the union. I passed and was admitted to USA local

#350 membership as a lighting associate in August 1973. USA, under the Painters Brotherhood, had not made many inroads into the small Los Angeles theatre community. And frankly, the theatre designers were a small part of that organization. Most of the designers hired for the big shows at Los Angeles' Music Center came out from New York. After going through all that, though, I didn't use my card for many years, mainly due to that fact that I was sidetracked by Rock n' Roll touring for the next ten years.

As I attempt to explain today's union business, please understand that I am a West Coast designer, and that carries some bias against East Coast designers who feel that the world of design only revolves around Broadway. I have always viewed the design business as a global enterprise, not limited to a few square blocks of Manhattan. Those of you wishing to go east need to contact the appropriate local or go to an informational meeting to learn more about how membership is handled there. What follows is a short outline only. The contact information for many of the unions' national offices and some of the locals are contained in the appendix.

What is most important to understand is that there is always a supply of talent (designers, technicians, and craftspeople) in the entertainment field that is greater than the demand. You can benefit because the unions help improve your odds in such a market. By receiving their list of potential employers who have previously hired union designers, you can go armed with contracts the union has negotiated as your collective bargaining agent.

By definition, a guild is not a union. In the distant past a guild was an association of like-minded workers who banded together to discuss common interests. Although a union is partially defined as a collective bargaining group formed to protect workers in an industry, the dividing line between the two was blurred years ago. You will also find "unions" using the word *Association* in their title. The accepted line for years was that a union insisted that its members' only work under a collective bargaining agreement with companies that had negotiated with the union for worker protection. A guild was understood to be looser; it only offered members advice and sometimes form contracts, but it did not exert control over whom they worked for. But even this distinction is no longer a clear-cut or useful guide.

Costume designers belong to the Costume Designers Guild, for example, which, depending on the job description and the jurisdiction, is either local #892 of the IATSE or Motion Picture Costumers local #705. If you are a scenic designer and wish to work as a production designer or art director, your IA local is #876. You will need to look into IA local #847 to become a set designer or model maker, and local #816 to be a scenic artist. However, these lines have also blurred as United Scenic Artists now can contract a number of these positions in television and film. The spread of USA's influence is growing now that they are part of the IA.

If you are trained in theatrical lighting and cannot meet the qualifications set forth by the unions as a television lighting director (both IBEW—the International Brotherhood of Electrical Workers—and IATSE have this classification), you might want to join IA local #33 for stage and television stagehand work in Los Angeles and local #1 in New York to learn and gain experience. For film work as an electrician, see local #728. To really push the envelope, try for local #600 as a director of photography, as I did. This does not even begin to cover the other locals that involve the people working in editing, sound effects, laboratory technicians, story analysis, publicity, and so many more. The IATSE has fifty-five separate classifications of workers in film, television, theatre, and trade show businesses that they represent through some 500 affiliated locals, so you must do some research on your own design field or craft.

The following is not a definitive explanation of each union's area of influence or their contracts. For that, you will need to contact the group you believe can best support your efforts and discuss membership and the union's goals one on one. I have also included a few stories about my own experiences, for a small, personal window onto how the unions have affected one designer's career. But everyone is different, and your needs are not my needs. So, though I support unionism, I believe the decision ultimately has to be yours as to how the unions fit into your career plans.

If you cannot gain membership yet, or simply do not wish to join, consult an attorney and get a basic design agreement drawn up that covers the key points I have outlined in chapter 14.

International Alliance of Theatrical Stage Employees

The IA or IATSE (the full designation of which is International Associations of Theatrical Stage Employees, Moving Picture Technicians, Artists and Allied Crafts of the United States, Its Territories and Canada, AFL-CIO, CLC) is the largest collective bargaining group of theatrical workers other than actors, musicians, directors, and producers, with some 103,100 members in North America. As the actual name implies, it represents not only the traditional stagehand but designers, technicians, and artists in the United States and Canada. As just mentioned, the IA has fifty-five classifications of workers in film, television, theatre, and trade show businesses, which is why you will need to go onto its Web site at *www.iatse.lm.com* or contact the international office in New York to find out which local would represent the work you wish to pursue.

Although the IA's long tradition in theatre is foremost in most people's minds, it also holds the majority of collective bargaining agreements in Hollywood with the major film studios, television networks, and production companies. The international leadership negotiates the collective bargaining agreement on behalf of the film and television locals with the Alliance of Motion Picture and Television Producers. The IA is also an integral part of production, distribution, and exhibition of film and video. Among its membership classifications are art directors, set designers, set decorators, scenic artists, set painters, grips, electricians, property persons, set builders, costumers, makeup artists, hairstylists, camerapersons, sound technicians, and editors.

For designers, it brings the strength of a much larger labor union back to us, since the United Scenic Artists became part of this organization. The USA-829 is chartered as a "national local" (all the locals were combined into a single organizational structure with one president, thus eliminating redundancy and jurisdictional disputes, enabling the presentation of a united front in negotiations, and hopefully effecting better representation). USA controls thirteen of the categories in the IA. This "national local" idea is a trend in the IA. The Cinematographer's Guild locals banded together to form a national local several years ago, now called local #600, in an attempt to resolve such disputes.

Early Concert Touring

When I got involved with the fledgling touring music business in the mid-seventies, there were no unions directly involved on the tours, only the stagehands at the arenas and other venues where the tours stopped. The IA was hardly alone in thinking touring music artists were a fad and would fade quickly. I appealed to the IA's international office to convince them that these were workers who needed the union's support and protection. But I could only persuade one man, Al Di Tolla, who later became the international president. He was a national union representative, and we began to formulate a way to bring the lighting crews who worked for my company, Sundance Lighting Corp., into the IA family. But it wasn't easy. First, we tried to get the locals to take in these young workers. But as I have already mentioned, there is a long history of a rigorous process for gaining membership, and they were not about to just give cards away.

But Brother Di Tolla came up with another idea. There was an Associated Crafts Technician (ACT) card, and its membership was structured unlike the other locals. Although I don't believe the classification is still available, when it was, I once went to an IA convention as an official delegate representing this group. ACT members could work in a "union" hall as part of the road crew. But local autonomy is a jealously guarded right of IA locals, so we were still subjected to some uneven treatment. On the whole, however, I believe most knew we were trying to do the right thing.

Even though I was designing those tours, I never was able to get the Painters Brotherhood to see the uniqueness of the business and its potential. And since I owned my company and was not a salaried worker, frankly they didn't push for me to work under a USA contract. The IA locals took a live and let live attitude, not wanting to upset the local promoter who was hiring a lot of its members. So, the project simply faded away after a while.

A former high-ranking union official recently told me that he realizes that the IA dropped the ball and doubts it will ever become a major force in concert touring, other than providing local stagehands. All this because the leadership just thought it was a fad—a fad that today is a $13.5 billion industry. I certainly don't blame anyone; there were priorities and limited resources, and the IA needed to pick its fights carefully, as it still does today. However, things have changed, and designers can utilize the USA contracts and agreements in touring, as well as with the other media we have discussed, such as corporate meetings and parties, auto shows, some television and video, mural painting, and theme park work.

The Yellow Card Show

All major theatrical shows touring under an agreement negotiate with the international office of the IA for what is called a *Yellow Card Show*. Why is it called that? Because tradition has it that the "card" that the head carpenter carried, which listed the road crew and how many stagehands had been agreed upon for each location, was printed on yellow cardstock.

Essentially, the Yellow Card stands for the pre-tour agreement on how many stagehands will be hired to tour with each of the traditional four departments: carpentry, electric (sound is under this department on a Yellow Card show, but not when discussing department heads for an in-house IA crew at a theatre), and props. Generally, department heads and possibly a rigger will travel with the show, so it also lists how many union people will be hired locally to complete the manpower requirements agreed upon prior to the tour starting. Riggers, follow spot operators, and run and strike crew are needed. The card also lists by name and IA membership number the heads of departments and the traveling crew, so that the local can be sure all the people have been authorized to be on the tour. There is an IA requirement for a member to have a "Road Card" before he or she is eligible to work outside his or her local's jurisdiction.

That permission must be given by the local for the member. Then a "Pink Contract" (so called because of the traditional color of the paper) is drawn up that details his or her position, salary, per diem, and other special conditions issued to the worker for a specific production. While the Yellow Card details the whole show's needs for stagehands, the Pink Contract is the individual members' authorization to work on the specific show.

All the important information is printed out on the Yellow Card and sent to the business representative of the local that has jurisdiction for the theatre or arena at which the show will play. Letting the international office of the IA negotiate with a show's producer prior to the start of the tour has been found to be a very effective system—especially in light of the fact that up until recent years, most producers were almost always based in New York near the international IATSE office. Since the individual venues really don't care about how many stagehands are hired beyond their in-house staff (usually the department heads only) after the negotiations, everything else is really handled between the international office and the local IA that has jurisdiction for the venues the show will be playing. Sending the Yellow Card in advance of the tour makes sure the local had time to arrange for the additional manpower required.

Why have I taken the time to explain issues and procedures with stagehands, when this text is for designers? Because as designers of touring shows, most of you will not be traveling with the show, yet you may want "your person" placed on the crew to look out for your design interest. Knowing how the unions contract the crews is essential to successfully negotiating on behalf of your people. And you need to be able to discuss this issue with potential employers from a position of knowledge.

All the crews who went on the road for me in the early years of concert touring carried the ACT card. We were touring with a lot of the major artists of the day: Linda Ronstadt, The Eagles, John Denver, The Osmonds with Donny and Marie, The Captain and Tennille, Frank Zappa, Rod Stewart and the Faces, and many more. However, we were never able to get a Yellow Card because the rules said that all departments had to be card-carrying union members, and I was never able to get any of the touring sound companies to join the union. Today, there are non-Broadway-type road shows with a Yellow Card, such as dance and trade shows, but I still don't know of any Rock n' Roll tours under the union label.

United Scenic Artists

When the need for a union for designers was recognized as far back as 1891, a group called the American Society of Scenic Painters was organized. Although it has gone through many affiliation changes over the years, that group is currently the national local USA-829 of the IATSE. It is headquartered in New York and managed via five regional support centers rather than locals. The offices are listed in the appendix.

If you are a costume, scenic, lighting, or sound designer in theatre who aspires to work for the major legitimate theatrical producers, and especially in LORT (League of Regional Theatres) and on Broadway, membership in national local USA-829 should be your goal. Its constitution specifically does *not* limit its categories to just theatre work; industrial, as well as many other media specialty areas, are included.

Membership normally requires passing an exam, which showcases your technical knowledge of the craft as well as your creative abilities. Although there are ways of circumventing the test—such as an open enrollment period, often with reduced initiation fees (given the person had substantial work experience in professional theatre) to attract designers back to USA after many years without a LORT contract)—it will be necessary for most of you to take and pass the test. As of 2002, local USA-829 has been on a major campaign to enlarge its membership, so there are incentives being offered that could make joining even easier for established designers. You should check with the regional support center listed in the appendix or call the national office in New York for further details. The Web site *www.usa829.org* is complete and can be a good source of information.

USA has been a part of IATSE since around 1998. And though the IA designates it as USA-829, it is not a "hiring hall" like a stagehand local. There are several ways you can work under the protection of the union's contracts. First, secure a design assignment from an LORT or a League of American Theatres and Producers show or any one of hundreds of other signature companies that have pre-negotiated agreements with the union. If the production is not already a signatory, and not all the designers are members, you can use what is called the "Individual Artists Agreement, Project Only Agreement." This form contract can probably be used in any crossover media (USA-829's official working term for any project outside traditional, legitimate theatre), and it gives a wonderfully flexible avenue for a designer. The "Designer's Resource Booklet" issued by the local helps clarify minimum wages, terms, and working conditions as a guide in your negotiations.

Fully explaining why membership in USA-829 is so desirable for a designer would take up this entire book. Short of that, what is most important for you to understand is that utilizing the union as your collective bargaining agent assures you of certain minimum fees as well as health and pension benefits.

And this doesn't mean that you receive only the minimum fees. Many designers do negotiate higher fees. The USA agreement was meant to avoid the problem of a designer being considered an independent contractor. Whether the show's producer or the theatre is the employer of record or some outside firm doesn't matter. Simply making sure the designer is covered for health, welfare, and workers' compensation insurance was the real victory of the union. Even if you have established a legal entity as a business, putting together a pension plan and obtaining health insurance is costly and a hassle. The union's plans are already in place via these agreements, and the employer makes a percentage contribution to the plan for you. If there is a dispute, the union goes to bat for you, which means you don't have to hire and pay an outside attorney.

What the union is not is your *personal* agent. It does not go out and look for employment for you. You must still market yourself. And the freedom to do so is, to me, a big plus. I get to choose when and for whom I design, not wait for a phone call to "report" to a job site.

The recent resolution of a new LORT contract after six years will, I believe, be the shot in the arm the union needs. Under that agreement, you will need to become a member to work for a signature LORT theatre. The specifics should be discussed directly with the regional office of USA.

International Brotherhood of Electrical Workers

Theatre is not a place you often find this union, but they do have a presence in the trade show world, long a contended area of the IATSE, as well as in some television studios. On the West Coast, local #45 represents the thirteen western states for people primarily in the fields of broadcast, television, and recording engineering. This is a branch of the same union that provides electricians who wire your house, so undoubtedly you will deal with some branch of the union if you are designing lighting for architecture or involved in the installation of lighting in a retail store, home, or museum.

National Association of Broadcast Employees and Technicians

While I have not spoken of this union, I believe you should be aware that while its focus is not directly on designers or most of the theatrical descriptive jobs, it is a union that has some effect on our lives in entertainment. Technically, its title is NABET-CWA (the last three initials standing for "Communication Workers of America"). A 1993 affiliation vote now places NABET as a "sector" of the CWA. While NABET comprises about 10,000 members and CWA represents more than 600,000 telecommunications workers, you would think that a strange pairing. Not necessarily so. With cable and satellite communications and the megamerger of television, cable, and "Webcasters" with streaming video into one conglomerate, the workers sought to unite. NABET was founded in 1934 specifically to represent employees in broadcasting (television, radio, film, and production) at NBC and ABC. In the following years, radio was added, and by 1965 the first film local was incorporated. In recent history, the union has concentrated on the engineering departments but also, at select stations, camera operators, lighting technicians, and sound engineers.

Actors' Equity Association

As a designer, AEA, or Equity, will probably never concern you, but if you work as a stage manager, it will. There has existed a lingering hard feeling on the part of many USA and IA members, because Actors' Equity, as well as the other artists' unions AFTRA (American Federation of Television and Radio Artists) and SAG (Screen Actors Guild), have never supported the IA/USA unions on work actions and strikes.

However, since Equity has, for over eighty-eight years, controlled the hiring of most stage manager positions on the national theatre scene, those of you attempting to proceed in that career path will need to consider membership. To join, you must sign up for Equity's candidate program and document fifty weeks worked at accredited theatres. Here, too, the biggest reason for membership is the strength of the union's contracts and collective bargaining position with theatres.

Equity (British)

This is the English version of Actors Equity Association. Formed in 1930 by a group of West End performers, it, unlike its American counterpart, is also the trade union for the entire spectrum of arts and entertainment professions, not only actors but singers, theatre directors, dancers, choreographers, stage managers, variety and circus artists, television and radio presenters, stunt performers, and fight directors, as well as theatre designers. It does not have counterparts in various entertainment fields outside of theatre as we do in America, for example, AFTRA and SAG. Nor do they have a line between artists and designers. Even directors, as well as the actors, are in one union. You must be a United Kingdom or EU citizen to belong.

Other Entertainment Media

Even if you choose to design in a field not widely accepting of the unions, in my opinion, the contracts and support materials alone, as well as the continuing education offered to members on health and safety issues are worth the price. Then, when and if you suddenly find yourself offered a design project in theatre or an area where they have agreements, you are ready.

Once we step outside the bounds of traditional theatre production, we enter the much-varied landscape of union versus non-union work opportunities. As I have already stated, touring concert work will probably not force you to belong to a union. Most of the theme parks are not affiliated with unions for their technical employees or designers. Corporate shows have a wide-open position on unions. Some do contract with the unions, but others do not and are very vocal about their position. However, you can still try the Individual Artist contract, which we discussed earlier in this chapter, when negotiating with them.

If you wish to work in film there are over fifty local unions, guilds, and associations, which hold jurisdiction over some part of the work in film. Most are under the IATSE banner, but there are exceptions. There are several unions that have a portion of their members employed in theatrical venues. While everyone will think first of the Teamsters, the other unions that have members doing the same jobs as the IATSE members are the International Brotherhood of Electrical Workers (IBEW) and the National Association of Broadcast Employees (NABET), both discussed earlier. They represent the electricians, camerapersons, and several other technical positions in many broadcast television studios, as well as a few film studio positions.

Some people mistake the initials ASC or BSC after a cinematographer's name as indicating union membership. Actually, what these acronyms mean is that a person was elected to a society, the American Society of Cinematographers or its British counterpart, both of which are discussed in chapter 13. For their union participation, these select few cinematographers most often belong to a section of the IATSE called the International Photographers Guild, or IATSE local #600. It is another of the new breed of locals that is national in scope. It provides one charter that covers the whole country instead of a region or city. This allows the members to work as directors of photography, camerapersons, video controllers, and still photographers without running into local jurisdiction problems when they travel on location to cities outside their area of residence.

Unions Outside the United States

Canada is the country that puts the "International" into the name of IATSE. The British and Australians have unions that do not have reciprocal agreements with the American unions. In many cases, you are required to join them even if you are only in Britain or Australia temporarily—in effect paying a union tax, as you receive no benefits for your limited time in their country. Asia, especially Japan, has only in-house unions, no national organization of theatre employees.

If you intend to move to one of these countries, you must do a lot of research into the rules that govern foreign workers and find out if it is possible to obtain a work permit. It can be extremely difficult. Understand that the United States is virtually the only country that will grant a foreigner a work visa to enter the country and supplant a U.S. citizen. This is a very big fight that the unions are waging against the administration. The I.N.S. rules state that for a producer to bring in a foreign worker he must prove that the person holds exceptional status within her occupation, and that no legal worker can be found to meet the needs of the employer. The rules appear to be circumvented all the time while our government apparently welcomes foreign workers even with the union's specific objections. The IA has taken the lead in the fight to close this loophole without success. When American designers and workers travel overseas to work, on the other hand, most other countries have a tight control against foreign workers, so check with the country you wish to enter before thinking you will be able to work.

Union Contracts

We will fully discuss what constitutes a contract in chapter 14, but here we need to learn a little about union contracts, specifically the USA contracts. If you work under most other IATSE locals in an entertainment media, you will probably not sign an individual contract. Rather, you will be considered an hourly- or daily-rate employee. Those wage scales and working conditions have already been set through collective bargaining with the employer. In most places, a single sheet "Deal Memo" is filled out (see chapter 14).

However, if you are hired to design a theatrical set, costume, or light plot, then you would use the USA contract. In the first place, these contracts make life simpler and save your money. Since lawyers from both sides have previously evaluated the contracts, you do not need to suffer the time and expense of having your own lawyer draft one for you. Second, they contain provisions for housing, travel, and expenses that you would have to cover if you didn't know better. Form contracts such as these provide big financial savings to designers, not only in the hourly fees an attorney would have charged, but also in specifying your working conditions.

They are written in a convenient form that only requires filling in a series of blanks, and then the agreement is sent to the local to be checked and countersigned. If the local finds anything that is lower than its standards, you will get a call, thus saving you from a potentially costly mistake.

Additionally, you will be eligible for a health plan and pension benefits that, as an independent contractor, you will not get from the employer. For more details on contracts and other agreements see chapter 14.

Fee Schedules

The beauty of the USA agreements with LORT, and Broadway producers in particular, is that although minimum fees have been negotiated for various theatre sizes, number of sets or costumes, and design positions, you can still negotiate a higher fee. Even if you are not experienced enough to qualify for membership in USA, the fee schedules it has developed are a handy watermark that you can use in your own negotiating.

I have never worked for the union minimum, either in film or television. Outside union jurisdiction in other media, I have avoided working under scale by applying the union fee schedule, as found in the *Designer's Resource Booklet*. This is not a boast; it is simply a statement to let you see that you can do even better. But the truth is that if there were no unions to fight for the negotiated minimum figures, we all would be making far less. Everyone benefits from the unions, whether you want to belong or not.

My grandfather used to tell me that the railroad workers that didn't have unions still benefited because he was creating a watermark for them to use to better their own lives. I have done the same thing many times. When a producer puts you on the spot about how much you are going to ask to design, you can mentally compute the union fee, and then you can ask for what you wish. This way you will avoid asking for something that is far lower than what others in your field get for the same work.

Unions have been much maligned, and many people today feel their time has passed. After all, most people feel that their employers are paying decent wages and that they are looking out for their workers. Yet every once in a while we have a big reminder to the contrary.

For most designers starting out, or those already deciding to take their career track into the newer entertainment waters, the union's presence is going to be spotty, but only if you let it. If you tell your potential employers that you wish to use the union's contract as a basis for your deal, you may find they are willing to go along. A lot depends on how strong your position is and how the producer feels about unions in general. You have to remember that some producers do not see it as being in their interest to have you be protected. But if they will discuss it, a case-by-case review can be authorized, and the union's business representative will often go with you to work out the details. If not, he will review the agreement to make sure your rights are protected. If you are dedicated to making it on Broadway exclusively, then there is no doubt you will need to gain membership in USA.

So, consider the benefits of union membership:

* The unions have already written a series of contracts that you can employ.
* They have already negotiated agreements with many theatre companies and producers.
* They have sets minimum fees and working conditions.
* You will receive pension and welfare fund coverage.

All unions have such pension and health funds; however, each local may have varying eligibility requirements for its plan, so review these very carefully when you join.

That is why you need unions. It wouldn't be at all hard for any group of theatre designers and technicians to sit down and tell horror stories of non-union jobs gone bad. So, why do people continue to fight membership?

I think it is because of the very independent natures of the kind of people who become designers or want to work in the creative field. But this is a habit that you need to overcome if you are now going to approach what you do as a business. Thinking logically about the issue, there are pros and legitimate cons that you must personally think about and discuss with others.

But I believe we need to support the theatrical unions more than ever. Yes, there is a sacrifice sometimes. Because of our membership it is possible that we may not be offered work from a particular producer. But when it comes to my working in a safe environment at a fair wage, I don't mind not working for someone who probably will not live up to the agreement, anyway. Without an organization to look at the bigger picture, we can easily fall prey to the sleazy producer who talks a good game. Who do you turn to—your lawyer, a collection agency, your older brother? Support the theatrical unions; they are working in your interest.

I firmly stand behind what I have just said. Nevertheless, there are potential markets for our talents that fall outside the unions' sphere of influence. Whenever I have gone to my unions with a potential project that is from a producer who is not a signature to any collective bargaining agreement to which I belong (both USA-829 and IATSE local #600), they are open to working things out. The worst case is a producer who refuses to sign, no matter what pressure is brought to bear. Then, as a union member, I could face possible censure or expulsion. If you run into such a situation, see it as a big red flag warning that this producer may not be supportive of the designers and crew, either, and ask yourself if you even want to work for him. He could be a new producer, or it could be a production company that the unions may not even know about or have not had a chance to negotiate with yet.

Notice that I did not say the reason was because a particular media was an area of entertainment where the unions do not claim jurisdiction. Some group or local, within the IATSE, USA, or the IBEW, will undoubtedly claim jurisdiction. *When it comes to stage managers (SMs), the Actors' Equity Association has rules that govern actor members working on a production without an Equity stage manager. So, SMs have it a little easier when it comes to knowing whether their union, on a theatre production, will protect them.* However, if an actor chooses to work on a non-Equity production, he will almost assuredly not have an Equity SM to protect him. And the actor is opening himself to fines and sanctions if he has not received permission from Equity to do the show. The rules are very involved, and this is not the text to fully discuss Actors' Equity rules, but the point needs to be made that a SM virtually must be a union member if the lead actors are members of Equity. If union (usually AFTRA or SAG) actors are used in a television production, the stage managers(s) may or may not be in the union. However, if the director is in DGA (the Directors Guild of America, the SM will be in the DGA, also. In this case, note that they are part of the DGA and not AEA.

But there is a difference between *claiming* jurisdiction and actually having formally come to an agreement with the producer—especially if the production company is outside of network TV, major film studios, LORT, or Broadway theatre. Frankly, the unions often don't have enough available manpower to go through the long process of first arranging a meeting with the workers, getting the required signatures from these workers to necessitate a vote, setting up balloting with the proper governmental supervision, and so on. Even if they win the right to represent the workers, they now must negotiate with the employer for a specific contract. All this takes time. And if the management is against the workers organizing, there is always the picket line, which just lengthens the process. Besides, it takes time to rally members to walk the line, and this tactic doesn't always work. I don't think the unions really like to resort to it. A production company formed specifically for one show or movie just isn't worth the time, resources, and people involved.

If there is a vote and it is for union representation, the good news is that the workers on the payroll that day will be offered union membership as a grandfather clause. This is, especially in Hollywood, about the only way to get a card in some of the locals.

Now that USA has a new LORT contract in place, theatrical designers will have consistent working conditions with benefits at the many member theatres. However, the actual fee, anything above the contract schedule, is still up to you to negotiate. I would also suggest that you ask any producers who are not signatories why they are not. Surprisingly, a few will say they have never been approached. In that case, call the union rep, who will set up a meeting to discuss the benefits for both sides.

In the end, the decision to join a union, if you qualify, or to work outside of the established union structure, is yours. You must go back and think long and hard about what your goals for yourself, your family, and your career ultimately must satisfy.

CHAPTER 13
Professional Organizations

There is wide disagreement among designers on how effective or useful participation in what are called "professional organizations" can be for your career. I use the term in quotation marks because there is much confusion on what that term really means. Some of the groups listed below do require some level of expertise to join; others see their mission as one of basic education, continuing education, or support for experienced professionals, as well as introducing the profession to novices who are interested in their field. This is why there are so many opinions as to what they are or are not. Are they worth your time and money to join or not?

I personally feel that as creative people we cannot afford to stop learning. Although I am an avid reader, I cannot be aware of all the new ideas, equipment, and techniques that are available. The myriad options offered by these organizations creates a problem in and of itself. It is impossible to attend all the lectures, conferences, and meetings of all the groups that interest me. Also, the cost of membership is nothing compared to the financial burden of flying to their conferences and meetings with the associated hotel and meal expense— and not only the direct expense but also the lost billable time and productive research and design days. These must be weighed against what you personally feel is the payoff. If you are just starting out, even the cost of membership can be a strain on your budget.

Then there is the literature you receive. I get so many magazines and periodicals that I keep them in a backpack that I carry with me to the stage or studio. When there is a coffee or lunch break, I pull out a stack and go through them, marking interesting items for further study. The commercial publications I receive add volumes to the pile of professional magazines and journals I subscribe to.

On top of all this, if you become active in these groups, which are mostly run by unpaid volunteers, you will start being asked to be on committees and boards. You can find a good deal of your fee time taken up with phone calls, e-mails, and meetings. So, what is the plus side?

I believe in giving something back, and in doing so, growing and learning more, myself. The process is never ending. If I agree to participate in a forum or write an article or lecture at a college, I then search for the answers by reading more, studying more about my craft, and trying new techniques in my production designs. All that, to me, is the real payback. To be challenged by questions that cannot be answered easily forces us to continue to search for solutions and higher wisdom.

When you were still in design school, you probably came into contact with the largest of these organizations, the USITT (United States Institute for Theatre Technology), or if you were interested in acting or stage management you became aware of Equity (Actors' Equity Association). The first is a very diverse group of students, educators, and professional technicians and designers that is bonded by a common interest in sharing and learning about advances in theatrical design and technology. The other is a working union. But they both have their place in our professional lives.

What I am going to present here are short statements about the nature and makeup of a number of organizations (for which you can find contact information in Appendix A). You will have to pick out the ones you wish to investigate further to see how they fit in with your goals. Some will meet your immediate needs, but do not be too quick to discount others that could bear fruit as you grow in the industry. You can go on the Internet and get a tremendous amount of information from Web sites to begin your research. Then I suggest you attend a lecture, conference, or meeting of the group to see how well they fit your needs. As for groups such as Actors' Equity, see chapter 12 in which we discussed unions. Although I have provided addresses for contacting these organizations (see appendix), please understand that they may be out of date by the time this is printed, so check their Web sites for the latest information. Also, I have not indicated any dues structures, as these too fluctuate and are best determined at the time you are thinking of joining. If this list seems heavily weighted toward lighting organizations, it is due to the fact that they have more professional organizations than the other crafts. If I have omitted any of your groups, I would like to know so that I can include them next time.

United States Institute for Theatre Technology

The USITT is a nonprofit, educational organization headquartered in the United States, and is one of the Centres of OISTAT (the International Organization of Scenographers, Theatre Architects, and Technicians), which is headquartered in the Netherlands.

With 3,800 members, USITT is by far the largest association of theatrical designers in the United States. It was founded in 1960 to educate, set standards, and build bridges between all of the world's theatrical designers. All the basic design and technical disciplines—scenic, lighting, costume, props, makeup, theatre technology, theatre architecture, rigging, stage management, and sound—are well represented by individual commissions. With a solid footing in the educational community that has remained strong, the institute has in recent years tried to attract a larger component of working professionals. Its annual conference is attended by designers from all over the world and is a central gathering place for meeting and interacting with other designers. It also encourages regional chapters to facilitate meetings for discussions of local interest. There are also a number of student chapters at colleges and universities around the country and Canada. With three publications, *Theatrical Design & Technology, Sightlines,* and *Costume Research Journal*, it reaches a diverse group of designers with many interests. Membership is open without qualification.

Canadian Institute for Theatre Technology

The north-of-the-border component of USITT is CITT. Although CITT does a lot jointly with USITT, with the south-of-the-border neighbor even collecting dues covering both groups, the Canadians maintain a separate Institute. CITT members are very involved with the USITT Annual Conference, even serving on its board, but they also hold their own workshops, conference, and trade show, as well as other developmental sessions in their own country. In addition, they operate the Web site for both the USITT and their own group. They serve as the Canadian Centre for OISTAT and publish a magazine called *Stageworks* for members.

International Organization of Scenographers, Theatre Architects, and Technicians

This is the umbrella organization, called OISTAT, for its thirty-eight Centres around the world. Its mission is to stimulate the exchange of ideas and innovation, and to promote international collaboration in professions that support live performance. Further, it encourages lifelong learning and respect for the integrity of all cultures and celebrates the diversity as well as the similarities of those who work in support of live performance. OISTAT was supported partly by the government of the Netherlands for many years. Now, however, it must rely on dues and contributions from the Centres. The executive committee is composed of members from Centres all over the world. OISTAT does not publish its own magazine, but member Centers contribute some fifteen journals that members can pick and choose to receive for an additional change.

The main event for OISTAT is the International Quadrennial, held in Prague every four years. Centres from around the world provide exhibitions, and the meetings and panels have an international theatre flavor.

The Association of British Theatre Technicians

The British organization of designers is called ABTT. Members come from manufacturing, architectural, theatre design, and technology fields. Becoming a member as a student is encouraged because full member status only comes when you have been an associate member for two years, are over twenty-five years of age, and have two members sponsor you, or have worked professionally for five years and had a position of responsibility for two years. Information about vocational training, degree programs, and NVQ (National Vocational Qualifications) certificates is available through the Association. ABTT holds an annual theatre show in London that is highly regarded throughout Europe. More recently it has added a theatre engineering and architecture conference.

The Society of British Theatre Designers

The Society was founded in 1971 with the objective of deciding on the most appropriate union to negotiate for designers. Since then it has developed and diversified. Its aim now is to enhance the standing of British theatre designers at home and abroad. The Society produces a quarterly newsletter called *The Blue Pages*. It also produces a yearly *Register of Designers*, which is circulated to directors and theatre producers as well as the national and regional theatre, dance, and opera companies in Great Britain. In a rather unique arrangement the SBTD is incorporated within the Association of British Theatre Technicians (ABTT). Membership is open to any theatre designer—set, costume, or lighting—who is working professionally.

Association of Lighting Designers

This group represents lighting designers in all fields in the United Kingdom and the rest of the world. It is run by volunteers. It exists to provide a resource and forum for discussion and development of artistic and creative aims among designers from the fields of theatre, television, architecture, education, industrial and corporate presentation, and manufacturing. Among its aims are: to further the art of lighting design and raise the professional status of the lighting designer as a member of the creative production team; to actively promote the education of lighting designers and to be available to act as an advisory body in the field; and to represent the art of lighting and to ensure that members of the Association operate within its professional code and terms of contract as far as possible.

This group grew out of the Society of British Theatre Lighting Designers because the Association of Lighting Engineers wanted to embrace all of the entertainment fields using lighting. The group boasts over six hundred members, roughly half of whom are professional designers, and the others are associates, students, and corporate and related organizations. Membership is granted to those who have worked at least one year as a professional lighting designer in which the principle income was from design work, who are proposed by another professional member of the Association, and who submit details of their production experience, programs, photos, brochures, and contracts.

International Association of Lighting Designers

This is a group more geared to architectural lighting design. However, there has been a tremendous crossover in recent years of theatrically trained lighting designers who have found work beyond the stage door, in television and concert lighting in particular, and this association is worth looking into for a lighting designer who wishes to widen the scope of her design efforts. There is a membership structure that recognizes people outside of the mainstream of architecture and an educational category. The group publishes a bimonthly magazine and holds seminars, lectures, and interactive workshops on topics of interest to the professional lighting designer. There are annual awards for excellence in installation lighting, and recently the Association established the Lighting Industry Resource Council (LIRC) to provide a forum for members and manufacturers to discuss current topics, trends, and issues in the lighting area. It is very involved in establishing lighting illumination standards, especially in what it terms the "quality" area.

Illuminating Engineering Society of North America

This is one of the oldest design organizations. It was founded in 1907 to establish scientific lighting recommendations and to disseminate this information to all interested parties, and it is the recognized authority on lighting in North America. The Society has over seventy technical, research, and design and application committees to study and report on all aspects of lighting. *Lighting Design + Application* is its journal, published monthly, and it also publishes a biannual technical journal that includes the latest information on lighting research and technical developments. The *IESNA Lighting Handbook* is recognized worldwide as the most authoritative and useful reference in the field. It contains lighting research, theory, facts, and applications. Although it is not strictly a theatre group, it does have a committee called the TTFL (Theatre, Television, and Film Lighting) that holds separate meetings to discuss specific issues relating to these specialty areas. IESNA holds regional conferences and an annual conference each year in the summer. There are over 120 IESNA sections and chapters in the United States, Canada, and Mexico with a total membership of about 9,000, plus 400 sustaining members. Full membership only comes after a minimum of five years of professional work, but there are programs for associates and students.

The Professional Lighting and Sound Association

PLASA is probably the best known group in Europe for lighting and sound design in live entertainment. PLASA's publication, *Lighting & Sound International,* is highly regarded, and its annual conference, the PLASA Show, draws designers and technicians from Europe, Asia, and the United States. It was also among the first to use an online newsletter, *PLASA Online News,* to speed the delivery of news to its members. The newsletter is also accessible via its Internet site. PLASA does have a very large contingency of manufacturers in its membership, but it is still an excellent publication to read and conference to attend.

The International Costumers' Guild

This is an umbrella organization of sixteen chapters:

* Australian Costumers' Guild
* Greater Philadelphia Costumers' Guild
* New York/New Jersey Costumers' Guild
* Beyond Reality Costumers' Guild
* Northern Lights Costumers' Guild
* Chicagoland Costumers' Guild
* Costume Guild UK
* Costumer's Guild West
* Greater Bay Area Costumers' Guild
* Greater Columbia Fantasy Costumers' Guild
* Rocky Mountain Costumers' Guild
* South Bay Costumers' Guild
* Southwest Costumers' Guild
* St. Louis Costumers' Guild
* Utah Costumers' Guild
* Western Canadian Costumers' Guild

This is a worldwide organization of costume professionals and hobbyists. It is also a nonprofit, educational organization designed to "promote the educational, cultural, literary, artistic, and theatrical advancement of costume design and construction, and the influence of costume (clothing), fabrics, and design upon societies and cultures."

It publishes a magazine, *Costumer's Quarterly,* which is full of articles on techniques, events, and items of interest to costumers. Costume-Con is its annual four-day conference with workshops, lectures, and competitions. Most chapters also publish their own magazine or newsletter.

The Costume Society of America

This is an organization dealing with the costuming industry, its history, future, and education. They are an advocacy group for professional costume designers nationwide. Their annual magazine, *DRESS,* contains articles from leading authorities in the industry. They hold an annual meeting and symposium each year.

The Costume Society of Great Britain

For over thirty years this group has encouraged and supported the study of all aspects of clothing. With over a thousand members across the world, the Society studies all aspects of clothing. Their publication is called *Costume* and is published every year, and its *Newsletter* is biannual. It presents the latest research on all aspects of dress from all over the world, from prehistory to the present day. It also reviews recent books and exhibitions. It holds a weekend conference with speakers and an opportunity for members to present research in their subject area.

Audio Engineering Society

This group has been around for over forty years and is the only professional society devoted exclusively to audio technology. AES sections serve members in forty-seven geographic areas throughout the world, including Australia, Canada, Europe, Japan, Mexico, South America, as well as the United States.

The Society holds two annual conferences, one in the United States and one in Europe, with sites chosen in or close to high-density membership areas. The technical council and its committees respond to the interests of the membership by providing technical information at an appropriate level via conferences, conventions, workshops, and publications. In that regard, the Society publishes a variety of anthologies, standards, drafts, convention reprints, and other information documents. *The Journal of the Audio Engineering Society* is the official publication available to members.

The Stage Managers' Association

This professional organization was created by and for stage managers. They have created a network through which they can share problems, ideas, and stories. They do provide educational projects for themselves, as well as try to educate those whom they work with. The Association's members work in theatre, dance, opera, industrials, events, and other venues. It is not a labor union; its members belong to the DGA, AEA, AFTRA, and other unions.

The Themed Entertainment Association

This group targets professionals in the location-based entertainment industry who play a key role in the development and production of theme parks, entertainment centers, casinos, resorts, museums, themed restaurants, location-based entertainment, and themed retail stores. The TEA goes beyond the designers to encompass writers, architects, operations, filmmakers, set builders, audio and video systems designers, special effects designers, and management. The TEA is involved in industry standards, conduct of members, and networking between members. It also produces annual awards in the field of themed entertainment. It operates an online job placement posting service for members as well as providing an educational seminar and speakers and writers bureau. Its publications are *The Network* and a recent publication geared to European members called *Behind the Themes*. It also publishes a wonderfully rich volume called the *TEA Project Development Guidelines Book* that is the resource for learning the complete story of how a themed project is put together.

Academy of Television Arts and Science

ATAS was founded one month after network television was born in 1946. It is a nonprofit corporation devoted to the advancement of telecommunications arts and sciences and to fostering creative leadership in the telecommunications industry. In addition to recognizing outstanding programming and individuals and engineering achievements for prime time and Los Angeles area programming for the Emmy Awards, the ATAS sponsors meetings, conferences, and activities for collaboration on a variety of topics involving traditional broadcast interests, new media, and emerging digital technology. The academy publishes *EMMY* magazine, produces the ATAS Hall of Fame show, and through its foundation is responsible for the ATAS Archives of American Television, the ATAS Foundation Library at the University of Southern California, the College Television Awards, the Internship Program, the Visiting Artists Program, and the Faculty Seminar programs.

Membership is limited to those directly involved in one of twenty-six categories of production of television programming. There are peer groups for each area of the membership that set further standards for membership, such as a minimum of twenty-five hours of nationally aired program credits. These peer groups meet to discuss and vote on technical and creative matters brought before them. The peer groups also serve as a focal point for seminars and meetings of mutual interest to members. The voting for the annual Emmy Awards is restricted to qualified members in specific areas of the Academy. ATAS offers a screening program for members to see new works with the added bonus of providing post-screening discussions with the principals involved.

American Women in Radio and Television

This group may be a stretch for this book, but it shows that there are groups that try to appeal to niche groups beyond a specific field. The group, although it attempts to advance the technical and creative knowledge of its members, is more concerned with networking for its members.

Established in 1951, AWRT has been the leader in creating awareness of the role women can and do play in the entertainment media. It is the leader in advancing women in the media through idea exchange, networking, and providing entry-level opportunities for women. Its annual awards show is televised nationally.

The American Society of Cinematography

The ASC is world-famous in the film business. It started out as a "Club" in 1913 for New York cameramen, who were the first generation working in the new motion picture industry, and it has grown in status ever since—as indicated by the fact that the listing of ASC after the name of a director of photography on film or television credits is a symbol of excellence. Election to the Society is closely guarded and does not come easily. It is strictly by invitation only.

Although about 800 people have received the coveted title, only about 250 are currently actively involved in production. ASC produces a wonderfully rich monthly magazine called *American Cinematographer* that is also sold on newsstands in Los Angeles; subscriptions are available to nonmembers as well. It also produces a yearly Award show honoring work by both film and television cinematographers. It runs a screening program that includes after-screening discussion with the cinematographer and director.

The American Society of Theatre Consultants

The primary objective of the ASTC is to inform owners, users, and planners about the services that theatre consultants offer and about the value of those services to the achievement of effective and economically viable performance and assembly facilities, whether large or small, new construction or a remodeling/renovation project. To qualify for membership, you must demonstrate a broad range of capability and experience. The ASTC members have individual and collective interests in providing unbiased, functionally sound, and practical consulting and design services to owners, users, architects, and engineers or performance and assembly facilities.

Entertainment Services and Technology Association

ESTA is a nonprofit trade association representing the North American entertainment technology industry. Its members include dealers, manufacturers, reps, service and production companies, scenic houses, designers, and consultants. The Association addresses areas of common concerns such as technical standards, customer service, equipment quality, business practices, insurance, and credit reporting. ESTA publishes *Protocol* as its journal, as well as a newsletter called *Standards Watch*. It also presents annual awards and is a sponsor directly involved with special sessions at LDI and the USITT conferences.

For full membership in ESTA you must be a commercial organization in one of three categories: dealer, manufacturer, or affiliate. There is also a place for international and individual members who are not U.S. commercial concerns, but they are nonvoting.

University/Resident Theatre Association

It may be questionable whether this group belongs in a chapter devoted to organizations that you can join, but I do not think it fits into the union chapter either, so here it stays. The U/RTA has been working for over thirty years to build a consortium of professional theatre training graduate programs and associated professional theatre companies. It sees itself as a liaison between the professional and educational theatres. While much of its work involves the schools and professional theatres with training programs, it does offer a couple of unique services. Its National Unified Auditions and Interviews, which are conducted in New York, Chicago, and Los Angeles each year. Some 1,200 students attend these auditions each year, and they are not limited to actors. Interviews for design specialties and management positions in seasonal employment and stock companies, as well as for professional producing organizations, take place at these audition and interview sessions. The other unique program is CMP, or the Contract Management Program. Through the Association U/RTA offers complete contracting and employment service to organizations that, for many different reasons, are unable to directly engage professional, union artists. Institutional policy or state government regulations may prevent a university from contributing to the union pension and health funds that are mandatory with most union contracts. A small theatre company or presenting organization may not yet have developed the management staff or expertise capable of dealing with union contracts, weekly reports, and the federal and state paperwork requirements. In essence, U/RTA becomes the employer, "The Producer of Record," on behalf of the organization. Since it maintains agreements with Actors' Equity Association, the Society of Stage Directors and Choreographers, and United Scenic Artists, it is able to integrate professional actors, stage managers, directors, choreographers, and designers with students, both on stage and in the classroom.

The member theatre training programs and professional theatres believe in the integration of educational and professional theatre. They are committed to the development and expansion of high-quality professional theatres and training laboratories, where advanced students and professional theatre artists work together to encourage achievement in production and performance.

There are also many more groups that service niche or regional interests, such as:

* Women in Film
* American Film Institute
* Theatre LA
* Theatrical Management Association
* Directors Guild of America
* Producers Guild of America
* The Stage Directors and Choreographers Foundation
* International Touring Personnel Association
* The American Society of Lighting Directors

In the accompanying appendix, I have tried to list all the organizations I have any information on or found in a trade magazine or annual. I know there are bound to be others out there. I apologize for any omissions and ask that people write to me so I can add them to future editions. But remember that you can go online with a good search engine, and maybe you'll find the ones I missed or new ones that have formed in the interim. I encourage you to do so. Maybe you will find one that suits your interests better than those above. In any case, your association with one or more of these organizations is just one step in a lifelong pursuit of knowledge. This knowledge will propel your career into the future. Choose wisely, but when you do, please become involved and contribute. You will gain much more than you give.

CHAPTER 14

Contracts and Letters of Agreement

In my grandfather's day, a man's word was all that was needed to seal an agreement between gentlemen. In my father's day, a handshake was good enough to make a binding agreement between men. In today's world, there had better be a written agreement with a video record and a neutral third party present—and I'm not sure that would even hold up in some courts. I am not a lawyer, but I have studied the law, particularly where it affects me as a designer, because I feel the necessity of understanding my agreements and contracts with clients. I have also pored over many a rental contract. But nothing—*nothing*—prepares you for the games that can be played if the other party wants to change or disregard the issue outlined in a contract.

Now before I scare you off, understand that although we may think all lawyers are snakes, just remember that you will appreciate having the baddest, meanest snake in town on your side if push comes to shove.

It isn't that people lie about what they'll do if you design their show. Let's just say they sometimes have memory lapses or forget to tell anyone else about the conditions of the agreement they made with you. It's not uncommon to hear, oh, didn't someone tell you that the start date was pushed back and you need to stay until Thursday? (When you needed to be in Memphis on Wednesday!) Or, how about, we never said we'd pay for your assistant. These cases sound almost comical, but unfortunately they are not farfetched.

For instance, a hotel was not prepaid as per your agreement. So you pay—after all, you need to sleep. Then it takes months to collect reimbursement from the client. Or, a check is drawn on a bank account in Muskogee, Oklahoma, and you later find out that it has insufficient funds. It's now a week or two later and the client swears the funds are good; just redeposit the check. It could take a couple of weeks to get this straightened out, and how are you to pay your bills in the meantime?

Before you decide that this only happens in non-union theatres, think again. I could quote stories from virtually every entertainment area and design field to further illustrate my premise, but they all have the same last line: I should have checked the contract more closely before I signed it.

Having a contract or a letter of agreement is no guarantee that you will avoid these problems, but it helps ensure that the basically honest client will adhere to the conditions of the agreement. Really sleazy clients, contract or not, will take advantage of you, so don't even try to go head to head with them. They are pros at getting around agreements. It is no contest, you're a featherweight to their Don King.

Defining a contract is pretty simple. *Black's Law Dictionary*, the recognized work in the field, has three pages of definitions for the word; I offer the last three definitions to put it into some perspective:

> *CONTRACT*
> * *A promissory agreement between two or more persons that creates, modifies, or destroys a legal relation.*
> * *An agreement, upon sufficient consideration, to do, or not do, a particular thing.*
> * *It is an agreement creating obligation, in which there must be competent parties, and mutuality of obligation, and agreement must not be so vague or uncertain that terms are not ascertainable. (394)*

Contracts can be either written or oral. Although oral contracts are sometimes enforced in courts, they are very difficult to enforce without unimpeachable corroboration. So have your priest or minister by your side at all times, and if Johnnie Cochran is the attorney for the other side, that may not be enough.

Do you need a contract for every job? No. But whatever you decide, stick to it! Consistency in business dealings is very important, both for yourself and to establish professionalism in your business. If you try to individualize each project's financial terms, you will quickly trap yourself. For example, you might fail to ask for a deposit on a project, then find you need cash and ask the client for a deposit. The client asks why you need it now, as you didn't ask for one the last time. Don't you trust him? Of course you don't trust him. But what do you say to his face? The same is true if you don't ask for signed contracts from most clients. It is always harder to justify an action in one case and not all the rest. It is also easier for you to stand your ground if you are consistent, because you know it is the right thing to do, and the clients will come around. At least they do most times.

Uniform Commercial Code

The UCC, as it is generally referred to, was first published in1952 as a code of statutory law derived from common law, commercial custom, and case law covering business practices and then adapted by forty-nine states to make it easier for interstate business transactions. It currently consists of ten articles and a recent revision (not yet accepted by all states). This is a substantial publication, but you can buy what law students call a hornbook, a text with instruction in rudimentary understanding of a subject, to more easily interpret it. I use James White and Robert Summers' version, published by West Publishing. And a rudimentary understanding is all you need. The rest is up to your lawyer. According to many legal experts, one of the wisest moves a businessperson can make is to get a copy of the UCC and have a general understanding of the code. You should also purchase your state's adopted version of the UCC for reference concerning business practices, including contracts and leasing laws.

Non-Contracting Situations

Now, before we go any further, I must point out that I am talking in general business terms here. Once you are a member of a design or technical union, the rules of the game change slightly, which we have already discussed in chapter 12. One of the prime reasons for unions is that we cannot trust the clients to pay us what we are due. And in contract negotiations, the unions are our best lines of defense.

But there are times when a contract isn't necessary or simply can't be accomplished. When can a non-contract situation be reasonably safe? In two cases:

* A one-time show
* An ongoing client relationship

In the case of a one-time show, it is best to get the fees paid up front before the curtain goes up—a deposit of half the fee before you begin work with the remainder due the day of the show is the industry standard. One reason for the deposit is to have time to make sure the check clears the bank—that way, you can only get stiffed for half the fee. Make sure that the deposit covers all your out-of-pocket expenses, such as the cost of hiring other people or rental equipment. The thing you do not need is to get behind in your payments to other businesses, subcontractors, or employees whose loyalty you will need for the next project. Cash is second best, for reasons we will discuss later. A certified check or cashier's check drawn on a local bank is actually the best. The company's business check is least desirable if there isn't time to clear the check before you do the work, in which case you have nothing to hold back to force payment.

I have mixed feelings about insisting on payment the day of the show. Usually everyone, including myself, is way too busy that day to deal with this issue. It is difficult, and demeaning, for you to be forced to chase the client around to get the check (or worse, cash). Getting cash is a problem, because you don't have a place to secure it, and carrying it around can invite disaster. One road manager I know had his briefcase fly open as he was exiting a cab, and $20,000 went flying.

In actual practice, final settlements after the show are more common in the concert field. However, you're giving up your best leverage. Some theatres will agree to pay you from the box office prior to settlement with the artist's representative (usually the road manager). But get such an understanding in writing with the producer beforehand, so there is no allegation that you tried to steal money from the box office. The theatre cannot give you funds in an inappropriate manner. It comes down to how confident you feel about the client and that you will get paid. I learned the hard way that if I have any doubts, I shouldn't take the job, or if I do, I should get it all up front, period. The only times I have gotten burned were when I wanted, or needed, the income so badly that I didn't listen to my gut. Reams of contracts will never make this situation come out in your favor, but a little common sense should prevent you from getting stuck in the first place.

In the early 1970s, I was asked to fly into Chicago to do a one-night concert for a client I trusted. We agreed on the fee and I received a ticket in the mail with a hotel confirmation letter. After the show, the road manager came up to me with an envelope. Inside I found my fee, $2,500 in cash (a big fee in those days). Well, okay, I hung around for the load-out and then went outside to get a cab to the hotel. I didn't know that the gate would lock behind me, and I found myself alone at 2:00 A.M. in a rather seedy part of town with no cabs in sight. So, I decided to walk to the hotel, which was about ten blocks away. I sweated the whole time as I made my way past bar after corner bar in an unfamiliar neighborhood. So if you don't want to elevate your heart rate, don't take cash!

The second category for possible "no contract" work is an ongoing client relationship. I understand that the best advice would be to always have a contract, without exceptions! I know I will hear a loud cry from the unions supporting that position, but, sadly, reality sometimes dictates different circumstances. The day-to-day situation is that there isn't always the time to arrange a contract, and a trusted client will be offended if we constantly badger her for a signed contract—not because they do not intend to pay, but because it is a nuisance that takes up time. But if for some reason the trusted client doesn't pay promptly, you shouldn't get mad—you could end up killing the golden goose. Even a good client can screw up because there are so many people, business managers, road managers, and personal managers, accounting firms ... anyone could drop the ball. You have to make every effort to avoid an embarrassing situation.

A safety valve is to put everything into a simple letter, fax, or e-mail. A simple note could say:

> *Thanks for asking me to design the lighting for Nancy Drew's appearance at the Fairmont Hotel in San Francisco on January 23, 2003. I will need to fly from Los Angeles prior to that date, and I understand that you will arrange prepaid airfare. The room has a standard light plot to which I will make adjustments. You said I could spend $1,000 on additional fixtures if I need them, with an additional expendable budget of about $350. The crew is all from in-house, and I was told the load-in is at 8:00 A.M. on the day of the show. The fee and per diem we discussed, $1,000 and $50 per day, are great. And since the gig is this week, you can have the check for the fee ready when I get there, but I'd appreciate the per diem in cash. I look forward to seeing everyone and working with Nancy again.*
>
> *Best Regards,*

With such a note, you thus send them an outline of what your understanding is in regards to what you are expected to do. They do not even have to reply, although it is best if they do. With e-mail, you can get a delivery receipt with many services. This is legally spoken of as a "quasi-contract." *Black's Law Dictionary* defines it as:

> *An obligation similar in character to that of a contract, which arises not from an agreement of parties, but from some relation between them, or from a voluntary act of one of them. An obligation springing from voluntary and lawful acts of parties in the absence of any agreement. (89)*

Another way to make this a little more secure is to ask for a small amount, even $200, as good faith money that can be messengered or FedExed overnight to you. Of course, that begs the question, then why not get half the fee sent? Well, that depends on your relationship with the artist and management. Most courts may view the client's deposit check as an agreement in principle. It is a form of a simple contract, without the formalities. The key here is that they have given payment in accordance with what you asked for in the letter. When it comes down to facing the choice of whether to do a contract or not, you will have to apply your best judgment. Lawyers will naturally tell you to always get it in writing. They are absolutely correct, but on a day-to-day basis it is not always practical, physically or financially.

Contract Situations

The advisability of a contract can never be understated. View it as an insurance policy. Is it worth the expense and time to go to court if the contract is not adhered to? If it comes to a court fight to collect, it will be a very long, expensive undertaking. The sleazy client is probably counting on just such a long, drawn-out process to dissuade you from proceeding with litigation.

In one case, I decided that it was not worth it because the amount owed was only $500. A year later, the producer needed me and agreed to pay up as a condition of having me do the new project—all the while contending it had just been an oversight, and he never meant not to pay the bill. Right.

As I said, there are disreputable clients who know how hard it is to go to court and are counting on that fact. So, why have a contract in the first place? First, you are giving yourself the peace of mind of knowing you have clearly laid out exactly what you are to do and what the client is to do for you. In a nutshell, that is exactly what a contract is: a meeting of the minds recorded on paper so that each party can see and understand exactly what they have agreed to do.

A contract is required when you are a member of a union such as the United Scenic Artists (USA) or International Alliance of Theatrical Stage Employees (IATSE). And although USA merged with IATSE several years ago, the designers in theatre still work most often under specific USA agreements and contracts. For stage managers, the standard Actors' Equity contracts cover your position most of the time. (Some of the specific agreements used by USA were discussed in chapter 12.) There are exceptions due to regional or a few states' right-to-work laws, but the fact that a collective bargaining agreement has been reached saves the designer or stage manager a lot of trouble and worry.

Such union contracts apply mostly to those involved with legitimate theatre, film, some corporate shows, and a few theme parks. The concert industry has yet to accept formal union coverage for touring concert shows. Some designers are able to get the promoter or artists' management to allow USA to represent their interests. But without a collective bargaining agent such as the union, there is no way to have a standardized contract that is accepted by the majority of producers and managers in a field. In the early eighties, there was an attempt to develop a standard agreement for touring, but it never gained wide acceptance. That group was formed by many of the lighting and sound rental companies who were working in touring as the Professional Entertainment Production Society, and I was its first president. We developed a form contract, but we were never able to get a major promoter or artist's management company to sign it. So, interest fell, and sadly the group disbanded three years later.

Some designers are insisting on the USA contract for work outside of the mainstream theatrical productions, in a few cases, winning the right. Technically, if you are a member in good standing and the producer of the show (not covered by other collective bargaining agreements) is willing to sign the USA "Individual Artists Agreement, Project Only Agreement" with you, she can do so without obligating herself to other union employees or agreements. This way she can contract you through the union and you will get your welfare and health contributions.

Will a contract fully protect you? Don't bet your life on it. I had an interesting $20,000 lesson years ago. The group's road manager, the person I had been dealing with throughout the planning of a tour, signed the contract. Several weeks into the tour, I pulled the crew and equipment because the group was not keeping up with the payments. I was forced to cut my losses and withdraw from the tour. When I finally got the group in court, its lawyer contended that the tour road manager did not have the authority to sign on the group's behalf—even though I had called the same lawyer to ask him if the road manager could sign the agreement! It took a year to get a judgment (I eventually won), but it took two more years to collect. For the record, the reason I finally prevailed was that the judge agreed that since the band had made some payments as called for in the agreement, then I had an implied understanding and therefore had the right to assume I was dealing with a valid contract. By the time I collected, paid the lawyers and process servers, and figured in the lost interest on the money, I was the loser. But I insisted on proceeding because I felt it was important to make a point. I can't say if that struck fear in any of my other clients, but I never had to go to court again—probably because after that experience I have been much, much more cautious and insisted on a fully executed agreement with a deposit check.

Letter of Agreement

A letter of agreement can be thought of as a less formal contract. It should contain all the parts that constitute a contract. The general difference is that a letter of agreement lacks the legalese, such as *whereas* and *wherefore. Black's Law* defines it this way:

> *The coming together in accord of two minds on a given proposition; in law a concord of understanding and intention between two or more parties with respect to the effect upon their relative rights and duties, of certain past or future facts or performances. (89)*

Black goes on to say, "Although often used as synonymous with 'contract' it is a wider term." So, although a letter of agreement does not have to conform to all the essential parts that are required in a formal contract, the modern understanding is that most knowledgeable people write such a letter while keeping in mind a contract's necessary parts. Simply withholding the formal language makes it appear less forfeitable, but it should have equal weight in court.

As a rule, a letter of agreement takes much less time to get signed than a contract because most businesspeople see the word "contract" at the top of a page and immediately go running to the $225-an-hour attorney. With the letter of agreement they seem to be less likely to spend the money. I have not gotten formal contracts back from the group's attorney before a six-week tour was completed. Should you continue to work on the tour? A judgment call. You probably already have your bags packed or are out on the road with the artist. And there will probably not be anyone on the road that has any authority to sign it, so you either cut and run, or stick it out, hoping everything gets settled satisfactorily. Bottom line, if the checks are coming per the agreement and everything is being taken care of on the road as far as accommodations, travel, and per diem are concerned, I personally would stay.

There is no guarantee in getting letters of agreement back, either, but clients seem less threatened by their appearance because they are generally written in simple business letter format.

One situation that does require some form of a contract is when you are providing work for a major film studio, television network, or theme park owner. They all have large legal departments with a gaggle of fresh-faced, young lawyers with nothing to do but try to find something wrong or questionable. That's how they earn their keep, and they have no incentive to provide a timely turnaround of the document.

Besides, if you do not have a contract, they do. And I can virtually guarantee the studio's will be a lot longer than yours. Now, you will definitely need to pay your attorney to go over it, thus not only costing you time but money. The studios have also developed some interesting shorthand agreements that are approved by the unions, in some cases.

The Deal Memo

There is a rather unique form of contract, used by the Hollywood studios in particular, called a "Deal Memo." This is a form contract that they have developed with all the boilerplate that protects them from any harm you do to anyone, and in some I have seen, even giving up your right to binding arbitration. They provide for a series of blank lines that are filled in with the person's name, social security number, address, start date (sometimes, end date), and daily/weekly pay rate. Whether there is a box fee (tools provided by the employee or makeup by an artist), the rate is also provided for in this format.

The issue of the end date has always been interesting to me. Generally, the memo is for a daily or possibly a weekly rate; therefore, the studio has no obligation to give notice that you will not be needed any longer after the end of the last day of the memo—that is, that day or at the end of the week. They don't feel they need to give you time to secure other work. Now I realize that in some cases unions have a hiring hall and you simply would go back on the list for the next job. But with designers, this is not normally the case. There are availability lists with some design locals but they are not hiring halls and will not "send" you out.

These forms have been gone over by the unions, exercising the collective bargaining rights of their members, and have been agreed to so that bringing on a worker for a day, a week, or a full season is easier. Are they fully enforceable contracts? The only leverage the union has is that the pay rates and working conditions cannot be less than the collective agreement base scale. Beyond that, you are at the mercy of the studios to agree and sign it or not. The studios and producers really do not care, but you must sign to work.

Loan-Out Agreements

Another term seen mostly in Hollywood is "Loan-Out" agreement. These were started by movie stars as a method for them to place their finances in a corporation in their control, which allows them to write off business expenses, such as an assistant, office, cars, and other quasi-business items plus have the protection of a corporation for liability. They either take a salary or draw funds from these companies as needed to cover their personal needs. Effectively, then, the employer is hiring the company and the company is loaning out the actor for a specifically contracted period or project. Thus, the actor is not an employee of the studio, and the studio's exposure for wrongful acts by the contracted loan-out person is reduced. This may seem like an odd distinction, but the actor/designer must still belong to any union with which an in-force collective bargaining agreement has been signed by the producer or studio. But the fees can be paid to the company, not the individual. Understand that the union will have the production company or studio deduct the union's collective bargaining agreement percentage of the wages, based on the gross check paid to your loan-out company. What you take in salary from your own company does not concern them. Annual or quarterly union dues are billed directly to me as the member of record, even if my company pays it. Designers, cinematographers, and higher level technicians now use this form of contracting quite regularly.

What Makes a Contract?

In order for a contract to be prepared by your attorney, he needs to know what you have agreed to do and what your clients are going to do for you. Many years ago, then, a lawyer and I devised a list of seven points that I need to have answers to before I ask him to draw up an agreement. I think this list makes understanding a contract much easier, because it shows exactly what elements are normally part of a contract. It is not in legalese and is only used as an example.

Who Are the Parties Involved?

This is not as easy as it might appear. Often the person you have negotiated with has no legal standing or power of attorney to execute the agreement on behalf of the party actually paying the bill. Ask who has the legal right to sign the document. An even better way is to type, in the space below the line where the client is to sign, a line that says "on behalf of XYS Productions." Then if a person who did not have such authority signs, he would be perjuring himself. So, the signature of an unauthorized person may still not obligate the other party, but you probably would have legal redress against that person and he probably would not chance that.

By the way, do not sign the agreement with anything other than your legal name, even if you have a business. You are acting as an agent for the business, but you, or your legally designated representative, must only use your names with "on behalf" of the company.

What Are You Going to Do for Them?

Basically, this is a job description. Be specific and include things you assume everyone knows a person in your position would do. If you feel the list is too long, you may attach it at the end of the document in what is called the "rider." But do list everything you are going to do or provide.

What Are They to Do for You?

Pay you. But how much, how often, in cash or check, daily or weekly? Are they paying travel expenses? Are they paying per diem, and if so how much? Is there going to be overtime pay, or is it a flat fee? Payment schedules that are simple and straightforward are the best. Accountants like round numbers that get paid on a regular basis, such as on the first of the month or the last Friday of the month. Are they to pay you for out-of-pocket expenses?

Make sure that all these issues are specified in writing. Specify what type of expenses, such as blueprinting, telephone calls, and expendables used in the production, such as notebooks, tapes to record rehearsal, and Xeroxing costs. If the job is outside the United States, is the per diem to be paid in U.S. currency? Be specific. By the way, have a very serious conversation with your CPA before you agree to fee payment schedules, per diem, or anything that may involve taxes paid in other countries. Some can be avoided, others cannot, but you do not want to be penalized for the additional costs if it's not necessary. The employer should compensate you for any loss due to local tax laws.

What Are You Providing?

Yourself, an assistant, a full crew, equipment . . . exactly what are they getting for their money? Details are important. Will it be a five- or six-member crew? Do crewmembers get single rooms, or are they doubling up? After you start the job is not the time to bring up these points.

When Does the Project Start?

You need to know dates for the start of rehearsal, when plans and sketches are due, due dates for shop drawings, as well as when you are to be on site. And finally, you need a closing or clear date so you can book other work. If we are discussing a theatrical or concert tour where you are expected to stay with the show, when will it end? If the producer says it is an open-ended run, don't sign the contract. A tour you expected to run at least six weeks could get cancelled after the third week, and you would have no recourse for lost wages.

Or the producer can say the run is continuing. Without a specified closing date, you might find yourself working for far longer than you had anticipated, without any additional compensation. Again, you will have no recourse for wages lost.

Do You Need Added Schedules or Riders?

After the body of the agreement or contract, you have the option to add a "rider" that details more specifically items outlined in the contract. This is a legal part of the contract and is accepted even when not directly attached to the contract at the time of its signing. This is a generally accepted practice in the industry. I bring this up because often an artist signs a contract to play a date in a city months before the event and probably long before the designers are hired and the show design is put together. There would be no way to have all the details filled in that far in advance. So, the "industry standard" can be used to justify the promoter getting additional demands for crew and time long after they have signed an agreement with the artist.

In the legal sense, any "schedule" must be part of the body of the contract, and a "rider" is attached to the contract. The rider is also very helpful in creating documents when removing equipment from the United States.

A *carnet* is a legal document that is internationally recognized by customs agents. Basically, it lists all the equipment you are taking out of the country by serial number and descriptive word picture. For more information, see the section in chapter 15 on what a carnet represents and how it operates.

Who Are the Responsible Parties?

How will the payment be made? Who will issue the checks and from where? Often they come from a business manager or accounting firm, not the client. You want to know who to contact in case of a late payment.

Can You Trust the Client?

There is an old saying: a contract is only as good as the people who agree to it. If one party has no scruples, printed words will not keep them honest. You must develop a sense that tells you, in your gut, if you can trust the client.

If this is true, why even bother with a contract, a letter of agreement, or a loan-out form? Like a lock, a contract acts as security between two basically honest parties. Do not pin all your hopes on a contract or agreement. What if a dispute erupts after the show? Can you afford the time and expense it will take to adjudicate the dispute in court? This is one of the really good things that unions like USA can do for designers: they will fight for you if you filed a proper union contract with the local.

In the final analysis, you must believe the client is willing to live up to the conditions as set forth in the agreement, or no litigation will make it right. If you're at all unsure whether you can trust the client, get your money up front, preferably in a certified check. But, as hard as it may be, the best option in such a situation is to take to the highway and say, thanks for the opportunity, but I think I'm going to pass on your project. You'll probably mourn the loss of income for a time, but in the end, you will have made the best business decision.

Small-Claims Court

In most states you can, without the cost of an attorney, sue a client in small-claims court for unpaid fees. Check with your local court system for specifics. As private citizens we have the right to appear before this court and confront the other party without all the formalities of a regular court proceeding.

Although the maximum amount you are allowed to sue varies from state to state, California appears to be among the highest at $5,000, with New York at $3,000 and Massachusetts at $2,000. Check with your state's consumer affairs office for detailed instructions and directions in filing a claim.

In California, the filing fee is only $20, until you have filed more than twelve cases in a twelve-month period, and then it is raised to $35. Also, in California, as in most other states, an attorney cannot represent you in court, but you can consult with one prior to appearing. A judge or commissioner hears these cases and will guide you through the process by asking questions of both sides, usually rendering a decision immediately. There is an ability to appeal the decision, and it is not necessarily a winner-take-all situation.

In general, if you are suing someone or being sued, you must physically appear and represent yourself. Even a large corporation cannot send its attorney. It must be a person directly involved with the issue. If no one appears for the other side, which often happens, you will most likely be awarded what you have requested. The other person cannot appeal in that case.

Then you need to collect. With the decision of the court in hand, you can then levy the person's bank account and place a lien on his property. This is most often done with the assistance of the sheriff or local police agency. Don't try to drive off in the guy's car, or you'll be seeing another judge.

I have gone to small-claims court as well as to superior court in pursuit of money due me. On the basis of experience, I can say that if at all possible, use the small-claims court. Even if the amount due is larger than the maximum allowed, the savings from lawyer fees and wasted time can offset giving up some money.

Mediation

This is another possible way to come to a resolution regarding a contract dispute or debt collection issue. It is a nonadversarial, out-of-court alternative used to settle disputes. You and the other party must agree to binding arbitration in most cases, but in others there is no requirement that the mediation must resolve your problem. Court action can still be perused if this doesn't work out. It usually takes just one session of two to three hours with a volunteer mediator in a neutral location to discuss and attempt to resolve the dispute. Eighty percent of California disputes brought to mediation are settled. Mediation is especially helpful in situations were you wish to keep a businesslike relationship with the client. As a businessperson, he or she understands the separation of you as an artist from your business and may not hold the matter against you personally. It's just business, after all.

I do not presume to have more than a layman's knowledge of business law and, more specifically, contracts. I too must rely on a good attorney who is willing to help me with my negotiations. But with a little research and reading of the basics of business law and contracts, you can talk intelligently with the client and attorneys to get your needs understood and, it is hoped, keep you out of the courtroom.

CHAPTER 15

The Contract Rider and Follow-Up

We just learned what a contract contains in chapter 14. A rider is, by what the law calls "trade usage" or "custom," an attachment to a contract. Or, put another way, you are allowed to attach a document, after the fact, which provides detailed schedules and descriptions. All this should be supported by a line in the original contract that says that such a rider is to follow and is currently not attached to the document. Otherwise, it could be looked upon as a new contract. Since we learned in chapter 14 that an agreement creates, modifies, or destroys a legal relationship between two or more parties—all of which are implicit in what is referred to as "offer and acceptance—what is it that the artist offers the promoter to accept this rider? Riders are not exclusive to musical artists' contracts, and we should understand that a rider can be attached to virtually any contract. All the designer's needs for the show will be attached to the artist's contract, because the artist is the one with clout! What is the consideration for the other party? That is where the "trade usage" words come into the equation. Some lawyers have told me they also like to give a list of the departments that will be in the rider so there is no misunderstanding: for example, lighting, sound, staging, and band gear.

In the entertainment business, we usually think of the rider as being something that is added to a musical artist's contract. In it, they would detail the items they will need for their performance, such as a grand piano, a piano tuner, a drum kit, and so on. Additionally, special requirements concerning sound reinforcement equipment and lighting equipment could be spelled out. And don't forget those dressing room needs. What brand of wine, the number of towels, maybe a vegetarian buffet, or M&Ms (without the brown ones), need to be listed so the local promoter can arrange for them. (By the way, the brown M&M thing was started just to see if the promoters were really reading the rider, not out of ego.)

The fact is, however, you can use the rider with your personal contracts, as well. Although it is better if it is done in an attached "schedule," which actually comes attached to the contract, a rider could be an accepted form if anticipated in the original agreement. If you are designing a show and will need an assistant, but are not sure of the actual details, the rider could be the perfect place to detail how many weeks and whether the producer will hire the person or you will bill him for the person's time. Will the producer be required to re-imburse you for long-distance telephone calls, blueprints, or construction draw-ing? What about a visit to the site to check out the theatre? And who gets the plane tickets and hotel room reservations? These are just some of the questions that can be detailed in the rider.

Outline Form

There is no legal format prescribed, but use common sense. Probably the form of an outline is best.

A. Design Assistant
1. Fee per day, $250.00
2. Total days required, 12
3. On-site days required, 4
4. Per diem, $38.00 per day away from home (see chapter 17)
5. Hotel, paid by producer (single room, nonsmoking), 4 nights
B. Expenses
1. Long-distance charges, $100.00 maximum
2. Blueprints, 3 sets of drawings, estimate 6 drawings per set
3. Purchase of research materials, $150.00 maximum
C. Expendables (Lighting)
1. Color Media, estimate $300.00
2. Patterns, estimate $260.00
3. Tape, line, and black-wrap, estimate $114.00

The above may be in fact the whole rider, or a much more detailed one can be written for a Rock n' Roll tour, which contains parts that you submit in your capacity as production manager or lighting designer. But usually, someone else, like the road manager, will gather all the parts from lighting, sound, road-ies, and band members and collate them all into one rider.

Details Are Essential

Why is such detail needed, you may ask. Well, in the case of concert promoters we assume they know that a band will have special needs, but just because they have the financial resources to promote a concert doesn't mean they know any-thing about production. It is always best to approach a project as if no one has ever done one before, so you need to present every detail, no matter how small.

I have been in the position where I knew the building and the power hookups from previous trips to the building, but didn't bother to detail the power requirements to the road manager. We walked into the building and I shook hands with the promoter's representative and asked when the house electrician would be ready to make our connections. He looked at me and said, "No one ordered power." Of course my reaction was, how could anyone be so stupid as to think we were going to do a concert without power, but I held my tongue. It was not his place to second-guess what the show needed. He was just dealing with the information he had been given. We could have been running the show on our own generators, for all he knew. Now, you can say that is ridiculous—and it was—but I had no legal recourse; he had done what he had been contracted for, no more, no less. Of course, one of the stagehands made the connections and all was right with the world.

Even in the case of a theatre producer, do not assume *anything*. Always detail specific items that involve financial consideration, either in cash or in kind (items such as hotel rooms, airfare, stagehands, house equipment, etc.), and even program credits; assume nothing.

One of the reasons I place so much importance on the rider is that it shows the producer that competent production personnel are involved with the show, and that alone should give a sense of security to management that the coming production is being handled professionally and is well organized. By taking the time to write a clear, full, and accurate rider, you do your homework, and that helps to anticipate problems before they rear their ugly heads. There is no substitute for good planning in any area of production. We are all aware that Murphy's Law does exist: *If it can go wrong, it will go wrong.*

And let's face it, when we are involved in designing and mounting a production, it is a unique creation. It has never, ever existed before. Inherent in that statement is that we must consider all the possible ways things need to be structured and how to prevent problems.

Pre-Planning

Recently, I was on site with a production manager at a project I had done the previous year. There were no changes scheduled for this year's show, and yet we both looked at each other and at the same time said, Now what are we forgetting? "Simple" can be the toughest type of production, because it is very easy to become complacent and think that the work is going to be a snap. Put your mind on autopilot, skate through it, collect your check, and go home. Is that what you think? Well, I hate to be the one to break your bubble . . . that is *exactly* when trouble comes. Never underestimate the importance of pre-planning. And the rider is the key to pre-planning. I often do a rider outline even if the production is not going on the road. Even if I will be in every meeting with the producer, designers, director, and facility management, I have my list in front of me. If not, something will get missed. Once we are on site, I hate to hear the line, oh, by the way, did anyone mention that we need six follow spots?

If you are designing at a LORT theatre, you probably will not have any say over the staffing or crew. They are usually hired for the season, and we are usually hired to design one production. If we are working in television or film, there is also the likelihood that the stagehands are union workers hired by the facility, so we do not normally become involved in the crew's contractual arrangement with the facility. If we are doing a Rock n' Roll concert tour, as I have said earlier, there is not much of a chance that the road crew will be all union. Many will be, but it is very doubtful that it will be a Yellow Card show, so we need to get involved in supporting the crew. If we are speaking of lighting and the manager has hired one of the many full-service rental companies, they will provide the crew. In so doing, they will be the one to say, based on their extensive experience in assembling shows for the road, that X number of road crew with X number of local stagehands at each stop will be needed to accomplish the work.

If the manager comes to you and says that seems high to him, what is your opinion? You need, in a managerial capacity, to be able to respond. Just to agree with either side leaves you in a tight spot. On the one hand, the rental company is going to be the one making sure your design is done correctly every night. Yet the manager is paying your fee, and you need to look out for his bottom line. If you have not taken the time to really look at the needs of the system and how long it will take to assemble, you have done yourself and the client a disservice—which, in my eyes, makes you less than professional.

This is not a problem limited to lighting. Scenic designers who wish to design touring sets cannot simply place the burden on the set construction house. In the design process the management will need to have a reasonable understanding of the space the set will take in the trucks and how long it will take to assemble it. Do you know?

Theatre traditionally leaves such matters to the M.E. (master electrician) or head carpenter, but I don't see how a designer can sit down to a blank piece of paper knowing there are only three house electricians or two staff carpenters and not have this be a major consideration in the design.

This is equally true of costumers who do wonderful drawings but have not considered the construction problems, the personnel available, and the time it will take to execute the designs. This is also not an issue that should be put off for the production managers to work out after the fact. They are dealing with budgets and crew allocations that are greatly impacted by what you can intelligently discuss with them early on in the production design phase. We, as professional designers, owe it to the producer we are hired by to know the physical needs of our designs. And the best way of understanding this is to build a rider as we are designing. I sit with a quad pad next to my table and make notes as I design, such as reminders of assembly time for an effect, or expendables I will need, and so on. Does that truss need to be made special, and who and how will that be done? So many details arealso unanswered in a scenic design. Who will paint the set and how long will it take? Do you, as the set designer, know the painters at the theatre or shop that is going to build the show? How slow or fast are they? Are you asking for an unusual brush technique that they may need to practice first, and has time been built in to teach them? These are the kinds of issues you need to be aware of during the design process.

Carnet

If the show is to be transported out of the country in which it was constructed, we must deal with the *carnet*. This document is a customs manifesto that is checked before the items leave the country of origin and are then rechecked when they are returned. It sounds funny, but every piece of scenery and every prop must be labeled with the show name and a number, no exceptions. Believe me, the producer will not be happy if her set is delayed in customs because of inaccurate paperwork. Now it may not seem like a set is something that would be built out of the country, but there are many cases of sets being built in Canada, or lighting being hired for a Broadway show from a Canadian rental house, or vice versa. They need this paperwork to make the entry and exit of their equipment smooth.

Information in the rider can help to prepare that carnet. The only thing that a rider does not contain that a carnet requires is a serial number on each item of value. There are a lot of things on a rider that have nothing to do with the carnet, but since the key information is extracted from the rider, it is always wise to assemble a very complete document.

The production manager really handles the hardest part of this process. He must coordinate the materials that come from each department, plus the artists, and assemble them in a logical order.

This book is not specifically about touring, but you can refer to my other book, *Concert Lighting: Technique, Art, and Business* to see examples of carnets and contract riders. After all parties check everything twice, it is taken to the booking agent or manager to be sent out to the facilities that have already signed the artist's contract to present the show. That brings us to the next step: *follow-up.*

Technical Follow-Up

When it comes to this type of follow-up, our problem is often logistics. Did the information go to the right person? And if it did, was it accurate, clear, and useful information?

Logistics actually encompass both areas, if we think about it. First, often the information needs to be gathered from several sources. Seldom does information on a production get to the correct party on the first try. It is up to the designer to deal directly with the shops. However, when it comes to analyzing the bids received, then the designer should have given a sound, clear evaluation of each bid. And you know that has little to do with artistic merit. Producers are interested in the bottom line and how it will fit into their schedule, first and foremost. Referring back to chapter 10, The Interview, it is always best to have already thought of what shops you might want to work with and why. Then if asked, you have a ready response and are not caught off-guard without any intelligent reply. Conversely, if the producer mentions a shop with which you've had bad interactions or from which you've received poor workmanship, you'll have an alternate suggestion ready. Just make sure you can back up any accusations by citing overcharges or late deliveries; don't make generic criticisms like, "They suck!"

Let me go back to the contract rider for a moment. This is usually the document we are trying to make sure has arrived at the proper location, be it the theatre or concert promoter's office. The gap comes between the office and the person who is to act on the information contained in the rider. Usually the production manager or road manager is given the task of coordinating all the individual departments' requests.

Limited Design Staff

Sometimes the rider is only about a couple of areas: sound and band equipment support, and lighting. For the majority of concerts there is an audio mixer and a lighting designer/director on board when the tour hits the road. It is rare to hire a professionally trained production manager, whose sole duty is to deal with the backstage needs. Instead, that duty most often falls on the lighting director. I say it this way because many times, the actual lighting designer does not tour, but trains and sends out another person to "direct" the lighting. In either case, that person is usually the only designer on the tour, and therefore everything to do with staging falls on his shoulders. So it is incumbent on that person to have some knowledge of the sound needs, staging (including risers, stage width, and depth), and dressing room needs (although the road manager normally handles this last area).

The actual items listed in the rider must be checked in advance. Dan Wohleen, who was the production manager at the Greek Theatre in Los Angeles for years, said that follow-up was a big problem. Too many tours rely on the rider getting to the correct person at the facility. And if it does and there are questions, it is often difficult to get in touch with anyone connected with the tour to get clarification. All too often, it ends up as a screaming match at the loading doors the morning of the show. Dan says he worked very hard to avoid such confrontations, but they do happen.

Words with Different Meanings

How can they be avoided? First, by using clearly understandable writing techniques. Often syntax is to blame for confusion. A British artist's staff may use a term without thinking of how that word is understood in America, or vice versa for Americans going overseas to Asia or Europe. Americans are famous the world over for our use of slang expressions, but I have found more confusion when it comes to the other side. Not that Americans don't use slang prolifically, but most American slang is understood the world over. Americans do not, however, always know European slang nearly as well, which leads to misunderstanding. So, check your slang at the door. An excellent reference is a book called *Theatre Words* published by OISTAT and distributed in the United States and Canada by the USITT. This book gives 1,258 theatre words in French, English, German, Spanish, Swedish, Italian, Dutch, and Japanese with additional words in Russian and several other eastern European countries. This is a must-have book for anyone touring or designing outside of North America.

Who Receives the Rider?

Unfortunately, the fact that you sent the document registered or requested a return receipt has little bearing on whether the correct party actually received it. An accurate address is not enough, and sending it care of an unnamed production manager is asking for disaster. You must take the time and go to the trouble to find out the responsible individual's name, address, and telephone number. Sending it care of the facility manager or producer is also not a very good idea. I have seen countless riders sit in producers in-boxes without ever getting to the people who need to act on the information.

Promoter/House Contacting You

Once we are sure that the person who is to act upon the information received it and can reasonably understand the document, the battle is only half won. This is not a one-way communication. Often there is a need not only for a response to a question but for changes to be made in the rider. First, the promoter may not agree to something that is going to cost him money, or it may be a physical impossibility, such as the stage isn't as deep as requested. Now the facility needs to contact you to get the changes agreed upon. Did you include accurate information on how to be contacted? Or is the production manager filtering all the changes back through herself—if so, how can she be contacted? Cell phones have made this whole process so much easier, but not foolproof.

A very good idea is to include a sheet with check boxes for major items that the receiving person can check and send back so you have a physical piece of paper that says she will do what you requested. And a follow-up phone call is an absolute must in any case. But here, sadly, I have been burned. I have had very cordial telephone conversations with people at distant facilities only to arrive and find that nothing was done.

The Internet

This is a new and very useful tool in the follow-up game. Almost instant communications can be handled continents away even with language differences. Some services allow for "receipt notification" so you know that the Internet addressee received your communication. But you cannot be sure without a direct reply that it got to the right person, so a return e-mail should be requested, to ensure receipt. That is, even today's wonderful electronic communications must be viewed as a tool and not the total answer.

One last word about touring shows. The other thing the Internet has provided us with is a resource for information on facilities around the world. Most facilities now have a Web site where you can download technical equipment and personnel rosters from the facility. Some even allow you to use a CAD program to download the plans of the facility. This has been a great help in determining what you will find when you arrive. But, again, use Web sites as tools in your investigations and don't stake the farm on their accuracy; many are not updated as often as they should be.

Technical follow-up is just as much a part of the game as business follow-up. Not only are you protecting your design by insuring that all the correct information has reached the person who can act to insure everything will be in place, but also you show the client that you are organized, reliable, and thorough in your work. That will stick in the client's mind and you *will* be paid back many times more for the good impression, as well as insure yourself that the design was done as you wished.

CHAPTER 16

Employment:
Freelance, Academic, or Staff

There are three basic roads that lead to work. The independent contractor or *freelance* way is considered the most difficult. You must search every day for the next project. Being associated with an educational institution has many rewards. But clearly the main focus must be on being the best teacher you can, and furthering your design career must be secondary. The reward for good teaching just could be a secure job for life via "tenure." Since the business world has nothing like academic tenure, the next best thing could be a staff position. Here you could have a very long relationship with a theatre or production company that conceivably could last your whole career . . . but don't count on it.

Freelance Positions

So what if freelancing is the most difficult. The search for work can bring a rainbow of challenging projects that will keep you at the top of your game. What you must do is take everything you learned about marketing and do it over and over and over again. In other words, you had better be looking for your next job while you are doing the current project, or sooner. The worst thing you can do as a freelancer is become complacent while working on a big project and forget that no one is picking up the tab once you are finished. And if you wait until the project is completed, it will be too late to fill the void that will likely follow.

Hollywood show business executives are sometimes accused of spending more time looking for their next job than doing the job they were hired to do. And that presupposes that they can do the job they were hired to do, doesn't it? But that is another book. We, as designers, never have that problem. We know our business, and we are good at our jobs, right? Right, because to get a job you must have the confidence in yourself to believe you are the best person for the assignment. Confidence is your biggest gun on the battlefield of business.

Whether you have years of experience or are just starting out, never let them see the fear in your eyes, so goes a line from an old movie I saw late one night. And as someone else said, *What is the worst they can do, fire you?* Darn good advice. Because getting fired is not the end of the world. We are in a business of personalities, and sometimes they don't mesh. Actors get fired, directors get fired, and designers get fired, so we must always be on the lookout for that next assignment. You can't let it tear you up inside. It happens, and it will always happen.

For you to be a successful freelancer, you must have your network of contacts working at all times. This is where skill in business organization comes in handy. Can you recognize a name overheard at a party as someone you should make contact with? Can you keep a call and follow-up contact list going? Can you keep yourself open enough to see opportunity coming for a direction that you didn't expect?

Most entertainment designers fall into this work category. There are fewer and fewer staff positions for designers in theatre. Even the fast growing field of themed entertainment seldom has designers on retainer or staff beyond a specific project. So as designers, we need to hone the business skills already discussed.

Multiple Jobs

A *freelancer* is the most likely to be pursuing work at more than one venue, and today probably in multiple fields. As one designer respondent to a survey said in the article "Design and the Bottom Line," by Marjorie Bradley Kellogg (*American Theatre*, November 2001):

> *I work as an art director now, and although I am often creatively bored, I no longer go to bed with the worry that I'm going to end up as an old [person] with a tin cup in my hand and a bunch of* Playbills *and glowing reviews in my pocket. (34)*

Although this person is lamenting being bored with design work outside of theatre, I think that is the exception. Most designers revel in the opportunity to work with realistic budgets, new materials, and the professional crews we find on many nontheatrical productions—elements that seldom happen in theatre. In November 2001, *Entertainment Design* magazine ran an article by Ted Ferreira called "Western Philosophy" that was a transcript of a roundtable discussion involving seven West Coast lighting designers. Peter Maradudin summed up his feelings about working in media other than theatre by saying:

> *I don't think we're doing more than just theatre to survive financially. But also to survive intellectually. If I were just doing theatre alone, I probably wouldn't still be doing theatre at all. (32)*

The quote above is preceded by a comment from another designer, Anne Militello:

I'm just saying that because a lot of us have diversified into ar-
chitecture or theme parks and such because of survival. Well, not
only survival, because some of the other stuff is downright fun,
too. (32)

I personally feel that I grow in my craft from the resources, new tricks,
and ideas I gain when I work outside theatre. Plus, I definitely enjoy the financial rewards. Let's be honest, not many of us would agree with the comment attributed to the artistic director of a not-for-profit theatre in the article "Design
and the Bottom Line." Kellogg writes that when the designer complained about
her low fee, the following exchange occurred:

One artistic director told me this was okay (not receiving a living
wage) as I received psychic remuneration. I replied that my land-
lord did not accept psychic remuneration.(34)

Higher Pay

It is a generally held principle that a freelancer is paid more than a staff person
would get for the same design. That is because the employer is not paying for
insurance, health, and welfare, or contributing to a retirement plan on top of
the daily or weekly salary, as she would when paying a full-time employee.
Paying people on a freelance basis reduces the company's cash flow problems,
and the financial analysts can assign exact expenses to each project, thereby
forming a much clearer picture as to which projects made money and which
did not. It is true that if the freelancer is working with the USA contract, the
employer will pay health and welfare and taxes, but there are still some benefits to the employer.

What Are You Worth?

So let's be clear; everyone who is willing to pay the producer for the privilege
of designing his or her show, raise your hand. You say, but they *do* pay me, even
if it isn't much. And I say that you are still paying them. Why? Because when
you work out the actual time and the cost of things you had to purchase to make
the show happen, some of which you were told would be reimbursed (but never
will be), what does it work out to be by the hour? If it is under minimum wage,
then you paid them, pure and simple. If you still feel it is okay, take this book
back to the bookstore and get the cash back, because you need it to go to
Mickey D's for a job.

The rest of us gather closer to the fireplace and let Uncle Jim tell his
tale. I *love* designing lighting. But I also love to eat at nice restaurants; go to

movies; sail; hike; study Southwest American Indian culture; collect Kachina dolls, sand paintings, and Navajo rugs ... did I mention sailing? I couldn't do all these things if I were being paid very well for my creative work. It doesn't matter to me that all my work is not in the confines of the "theatre." I am creating theatrical light where I can be appreciated, both artistically and financially.

We, as a design community, must get over the debilitating notion that we are unworthy of receiving a decent wage for our creative talents. Does that make me, and a growing number of other designers, *bad people* who should be barred from the hallowed halls of theatre? No. Most of us actually enjoy designing so much we have transcended the narrow confines of the three walls of the proscenium stage. Just because you may not have thirty years in the business does not mean you shouldn't be paid a decent wage. The USA union has an uphill battle to keep the pressure on producers who only want to see ledgers that leave a lot of profit for them. We deserve to share in that pie just as much as actors and directors. So, stand up for yourself in negotiations, and if we all demand a living wage, we can get it, individually as well as collectively. And remember: collectively, the unions raise everybody's individual incomes with their efforts to raise the bar.

Profit Center

It is no secret that film studios would be very happy if they had no staff employees. It comes from an accounting premise called "profit center" budgeting. From a fiscal point of view, every department is evaluated as to how it fits into the profitability of the company. Let's say sales bring in 80 percent of the company profit and the other 20 percent is generated by after-market sales and repairs. But what about the accounting department and the maintenance department—how do they contribute to the profit? Actually, they do so by reducing expenses, or making a contribution by saving the company money it had expended in the past. The automobile industry has recognized this for years. What you paid for that new car may be at a "wholesale" cost to the dealer, but he knows that the service department and the parts department will bring big profits even with the lost leader of the actual automobile sale. The accounting department fits the profile because if the paperwork is accurate and well prepared, there will be savings to the dealer from added paperwork. Skillful bookkeepers working with the lending institution can possibly save interest for timely payments on their own loans, and so on.

In recent years, accounting types have introduced the notion that everyone is a mini profit center. What you get in salary and benefits must be weighed against how much the company can, in a sense, charge for your time. In our work, that is pretty simple to compute: we either get a flat fee or a daily rate. Seldom do designers work on an hourly rate.

If I take a design job for a flat fee or a daily fee, I am working as an independent contractor. The fee the client actually pays for my services is the sum of what I wish to take home plus the cost of overhead my design firm needs to stay in business, as well as a profit margin. The client pays what is really a gross amount, say $100 an hour, based on a ten-hour day (freelance is usually based on ten-hour days, plus overtime at time and a half) or, as in my example, a total of $1,000 a day. But I will not take home that amount, because the design company, of which I am an owner and partner, must have money to pay my health, welfare, and taxes, because I am not an employee of the client and therefore they will not be taking tax deductions nor paying into a health plan for me. However, the good news is that the design firm will pay a number of expenses that normally I would pay out of my paycheck if I worked full-time for an employer. Such things as a cell phone, auto lease and gas, life insurance, and some form of a retirement fund can be charged off as a company expense. For that, I give the company a percentage of my fee, say 30 to 40 percent. This is how a *loan*-out company works. Now, if there are assistants, their time can be billed to the client, thus creating another profit center, because the billable rate to the client will cover what the assistant is going to actually receive, plus overhead and profit for the design company. This is why every person is called a *profit* center. Each person is thus evaluated as to how much he or she is contributing to the profit of the firm—and then management looks at a report and says they can't afford janitors because they're not profit centers!

All kidding aside, this is a system that works very well for consultant firms such as attorneys, architects, and, yes, theatre designers. If you are going to freelance, you must consider that your fee not only covers your living expenses, but it must also pay an assistant, a percentage of the electricity and rent, and many other expenses. Have you calculated in a high enough percentage to pay for an office manager or someone to answer your phone? But by this system, those people must be profit centers also. How can they become profit centers? Call them the marketing department and give them bonuses based on the number of clients they contact or follow up on. Since their salary was paid out of a percentage of your design fee, any money they can help to bring in is profit, thus paying for their position. This method will also help in determining if you can afford a full-time assistant or other office personnel.

Now let us look at how we can, as freelance designers, create a career that meets our personal goals. First and foremost, independent designers tell me that they like the freedom it gives them. I once had an opportunity to go to work for a big New York design firm, but I turned it down when I found out I could only do the design work they assigned to me. I knew that meant I couldn't teach now and then, or do a small theatre piece because it would not bring the profit the firm demanded. So, I did not pursue the offer further. To me, that is the key to what I do: I have free choice. I do television or a corporate show because I want to, not because it is assigned to me. Sure, I have the burden of ownership in a company with a dozen employees, offices, equipment leases, and commitments. But we have structured it so all the partners have the freedom to work on the projects they want.

Other freelancers say their goal is to live in smaller communities that are better for their kids and where they can get away from the day-to-day big-city business stuff. Some, quite frankly, "do not play well with others" and would not be comfortable in a staff job. We can even use the ability to choose whom to work for and when to work to allow us to do "charity" theatre work if that is what we want to do. Wouldn't it feel great to know you can do that not-for-profit theatre show simply because you can actually afford to?

And truthfully, even if you don't want to freelance, you may have little choice. Today's market, be it theatre, university, theme entertainment centers, architecture, or any of the others, has fewer and fewer openings for full-time staff and teaching positions.

Freedom

As the Eastern bloc countries have found out, freedom comes with a heavy price. We are truly in charge of our own destiny, and that can be a very frightening thing to face. No one is going to pay your bills. No one is going to make sure you are eating right or getting enough sleep. You are on your own both physically and emotionally. Can you handle the rejection? Can you handle the demands of managing your finances and paying your bills on time? Can you be responsible for the people you hire? Can you keep a hectic schedule that has you running between projects one month and the telephone not ringing the next? Take a big breath. You can do it. It just takes learning some new skills and applying yourself. In the end, you are your own person and able to do what you want, when you want. And to me, that is a great feeling . . . that is freedom!

Academic Positions

If there is one thing that can be said of theatre designers, it is that they have always been on the lower end of the economic scale. Your parents spend thousands of dollars to send you to school and pay for advanced specialty courses.

Today it probably takes four or five years to complete an undergraduate degree with the specter of three more years in a master of fine arts program or a theatre/entertainment gechnology program. Luckily, most design programs mercifully end there. Thank goodness there is little call for a Ph.D. for a theatre design professorship—otherwise your parents would probably tell you to look somewhere else for the money.

Although I could take up one or two more chapters with my views on the educational programs currently available for teaching design and what I think is wrong with them, I do support the need for higher education that is specialized for designers. However, I am a big advocate of design programs that offer a broader prospective, that at least make students aware of the many fields besides theatre into which their skills and creativity can take them.

And, sad to say, take them to higher financial rewards than theatre. However, a sound grounding in basic theatre design theory and techniques will always be the best underpinning to have, no matter what form of entertainment they ultimately pursue. I believe that the educational institutions have a responsibility to present all the career options that may be available to design students.

But right now we are discussing what the opportunities are after graduation for designers as teachers. Being associated with an educational institution can either foster a constricted view of the outside world that says it is better to be safe in a protected shell than to "deal" with all the business of the professional world. But it can also give you the opportunity to think, given a modest but steady salary from teaching, I can now take a chance on designing professionally without starving!

Crossing Over?

I want to quote from the *American Theatre* article "Design and the Bottom Line" again. In it the author and her associates, Susan Tsu and Dawn Chiang, found through surveys that:

> *Today 75% of working scenic designers are also teaching . . . of the two dozen costume designers I spoke to for this survey, over half are or have been teachers and have spent more time training enthusiastic future designers than doing the work that got them hooked on theatre in the first place. (36)*

In an insert, as part of the same magazine article, Susan Tsu wrote:

> *Without undertaking an extensive survey of my own, I feel that it is fair to say that teachers have been able to avoid the sub-standard*

of living by augmenting their albeit, low, teaching salaries with commercial work. So the base of operation at an academic institution can have many benefits. (36)

Chris Parry, who teaches lighting at the University of California at San Diego, has very successfully combined teaching with regional and Broadway assignments. I would be hard pressed to think of a regional LORT show I have done that did not have at least one member of the design team, and most likely the director, attached to some college or university program.

Cloistered in the Tower

Even if we keep ourselves inside the proverbial ivory tower, the fact is that the system itself requires teachers to show continuing advancement in their knowledge of their field. Up until the 1970s that meant getting published. Starting about then some schools began accepting creative work experience from professors in the art, music, and theatre departments as a substitute for written publication. Creative work, both within the school and outside, are often put forth to show high professional standing as part of consideration for tenure.

Early on, I saw what I thought was an abuse of the system by some educators, who took over the design of university shows that previously would have offered design opportunities for students. But over the years, the need to use their universities' shows has lessened because of the reward that can be gained when the teacher works outside of the institution and is paid additionally for that work. Actually, the teacher then gains benefits in two ways: receiving both academic credit and financial reward. An added bonus is the teacher who brings back the latest "real world" techniques and methods to their students.

When we talk about the lower end of the economic ladder in the United States, teachers are always singled out as being underpaid. But for theatrical designers, I believe there is a strong case to be made that a balance can be reached that augments a teaching salary with outside consultant and design work. Recent surveys of teachers produced a picture that tells me that scenic designers can do on average two to three shows outside of their school with an added income of $9,000 to $13,000. Based on an associate professor salary of $50,000, that adds almost 25 percent. Sound designers come in even higher if they can work in live performance music, as well. Although it is difficult to pin down an accurate estimate, most lighting designers who teach actually do more outside work than the scenic people, because the average time involved with the project was fifty-nine days for scenic and only twenty-seven for lighting. Yet the fee per show averages only slightly lower for lighting designers. Costume designers average sixty-two days on a medium size show. (All these statistics come from the November 2001 article, "Design and the Bottom Line" in *American Theatre Magazine.*)

Salary Deduction

This money isn't free; most schools I have spoken with do withhold some salary if the teacher must be replaced during the time she is away on an outside design. But that is a minor issue. And there is the added bonus of being able to involve a graduate student in the project as an unpaid assistant. Both from the standpoint of the teacher/designer needing an assistant and the school viewing this as a great educational opportunity for a graduate student to assist on a project, it becomes a win-win situation. To have the chance to participate in a commercial design project alongside a professor is something many schools tout to prospective students.

Lastly, we cannot overlook an issue that many of us must face: the stability of a teaching position, especially once the first seven years have passed and you have been rewarded with tenure at an institution.

But there is one minor hitch in this seemingly utopian world. If you are on a tenure track at a school, most have a rule that you must make tenure after seven years or you are dropped. Move on, buddy! And if you wish to avoid the cliques and rivalries that play heavily into who gets tenure, you may wish to take a staff position (non-teaching, non–tenure track). I am told you get paid the same and often get raises quicker than if you are faculty, but that "job for life" carrot is not held out there, although retirement and all the other goodies are available. Alas, I have been told that the "staff" is looked down upon by the "academics," but you probably will sleep better.

Health and Retirement Package

The benefits package is a big attraction to teaching. If you work only as a USA designer, it may be difficult to accumulate the days to keep your medical benefits running. At a school, benefits are automatic, and there is also generally a nice retirement package thrown in—something most freelance designer never consider until they are in their late fifties, when they suddenly realize they have not saved a penny! Having benefits is another reason to become a member of and support the theatrical unions, IATSE, IBEW, and USA (even though they are a part of IATSE, they have a separate plan package at this time). They have retirement plans in which you can participate. Of course, the theatrical union's plans probably do not compare to school-backed plans from teacher unions and educational institutions. If someone is a freelancer who also teaches, she should consider her participation in a teacher's union or institutional-sponsored plan as a key to future financial security. In many ways, this is the best reason to add teaching to a full-time design career.

For those designers who wish to have a family and who are looking for a way to stay creative yet have a consistent base income, not many other theatre-related creative employment opportunities can compare to teaching. Even with the legendary bickering and in-fighting of academia, the job can be the most challenging and creative you will ever undertake. The opportunities in today's theatre programs to be creative, both educationally and professionally, are out-standing. And the salary scales are also slowly rising overall. New hires are re-porting increases due to institutions' attempts to keep up with a minimum cost of living increase and, in some cases, their realization that to attract the best people, they need to offer a more attractive financial package.

But be warned, starting as an instructor or assistant professor is equal in salary to working as a manager at Sears. (My recent un-scientific survey showed that salaries for designers and TDs ranged from $50,000 to $70,000 at a major East Coast university and $40,000 to $64,000 at a city college on the West Coast.) And you will probably need to be open to changing schools to move up the aca-demic ladder—not unlike most corporate managers who must start their job in the branch office while they are building their reputation and dream of moving to the corporate headquarters. After you get that first teaching job, I suggest you pick up a copy of USITT's *Theatre Design and Technology Journal*. The fall 2001 issue had a wonderful article by James G. Cunningham called "Some Tips for the New College TD/Designer." It doesn't deal with any pre-hire issues, but it sure does ad-dress being "da new guy," as he calls it. As he says, being the new designer in the department is often traumatic, because that position will influence almost every show the department does that season. I particularly liked one of his comments: "Some people will want things to stay the way they were—even those who are glad to see your predecessor gone"(26). But you'll have to read the full article to get the benefit of what he has so cleverly communicated.

If you choose this road, there are pitfalls, and it could be a long strug-gle to secure the right position. The fact is that there are not that many openings in colleges for designers each year. A current count in *ArtSearch* for teaching positions, at all levels, yielded:

9 - Technical Directors
3 - Costume Designers
4- Scenic Designers
2 - Lighting Designers
7 - Scenic/Lighting Designers

3 - Technology

2 - Production Managers

And if we divide those numbers into the number of higher educational institutions, there are not many openings in any given year. But for those who are looking for stability and a sound financial picture, educational employment can be very attractive.

Staff Positions

The business world has nothing like tenure or a job for life, but a staff position is the next best thing. Of course, educational positions do not have the "golden parachute" clause that almost invites corporate executives to fail so they can get their contracts bought out. Just kidding...I think.

What a staff position entails is a much broader definition than some would expect. In the narrowest context, it means that you are a permanent full-time employee of a business. And in most states, that means that you will not only make at least minimum wage but receive workers' compensation insurance and possibly a health plan. Health plans are often split between the employer, who makes a fixed percentage contribution, and the employee, who pays the difference. Medical bills are one of the biggest reasons for people declaring bankruptcy, so obtaining coverage is very important to most Americans. Most employers require a minimum of three to six months' employment before the plan kicks in. But there is a federal system, called "COBRA," that has been in place since 1986 that allows you to continue your previous plan coverage even after your employment ends. That way you are not missing coverage while you are between jobs and waiting for the new plan to take over. However, this plan is very expensive, especially when you no longer have the employer paying for part of the fees, and there is a time limit.

Full-Time Employee—Or Maybe Not?

The term "full-time" is misleading because the conditions of employment may only be for a specific number of weeks or months, such as a summer festival, or a seasonal production, such as a TV series or a film. Staff positions working directly for the film and television studios are rare when it comes to designers. Most of the studios only employ electricians, carpenters, and other technical positions on a full-time staffing basis, and then, as few as possible. You are hired either directly by the production company or through an outside contract service (employee leasing company) and then assigned to a show.

There is also a trend at the studios to force staff people out before the full twenty years or before they would have qualified for the company retirement program. There have been cases where there was allegedly a systematic purging of the staff within a year or two of retirement so that the company could avoid paying the retirement benefits. Some have been sued in court, and the cases have been won by the workers, but it is extremely hard to prove that there is a direct relationship between the firing and the desire to avoid such payments. I do not have any direct knowledge of cases going to trial in our industry; some might have been settled out of court.

The line "creative differences" appears in the *Hollywood Reporter* on an almost daily basis. It is the stock line used when a production decides to end its relationship with a director or actor. But it can be, and is, used when someone in the production's management team wants to release a designer. And the fact is, the courts are reluctant to rule against the employer, believing that they must give fairly wide latitude so the producer can retain creative control.

Outside Contractors

There is also the "staff" position that is in fact a seasonal contract or weekly agreement of employment and nothing else. It is very common for the studio to hire a person through an outside "contractor" (such as a design firm) or an employee leasing company. So, what is the actual status of this "staff" person? Is there any basis to believe he has a secured position? No. The employer is free to simply not make a *callback* for the next week without explanation. In rare cases, employers will give a "season agreement," but there are so many loopholes that if they want to remove you they can pretty much do so at will. Technically, you have not been fired, so there is no way to collect severance pay or other benefits from the producer. State unemployment benefits may apply, but the employer has avoided any contract-related forced settlement. I don't know of any "pay or play" clause, such as we hear about with actors who get paid even if their part is cut from the series or film. For those of you outside the film business, the term is used in a contractual sense to mean that a person is hired for the run of the show or a season, and that they will be paid full salary even if not used. These agreements usually do contain a restriction as to the actor working in another series or film while collecting the fee, but the person may ask for a waiver to take another project or simply sit back on the beach in Malibu and take in the sun. This is not an option I expect to see for a designer any time soon.

Regional Theatre

Staff positions for designers in a regional theatre are on the decline. Community theatres will hire a combination designer responsible for at least scenic and costume and/or lighting, but the pay is low and usually the position is not covered by a union contract. The downside is that your tenure is often tied to the artistic director's stay. When there is a change in artistic directors, often the design team is also let go. Because the new artistic director will bring in his or her own "team," you may be out no matter how good your work. In short, there may not be the longevity normally associated with a teaching position. However, there is encouraging news now that USA/LORT have finally signed a new agreement. More theatres will now be hiring union designers on contractually set rates and benefit packages. This is very good news.

Architecture

I do not want to leave out another staff position that is a relatively new one, associated with interior design or architectural firms. A few lighting designers have been given an opportunity to be on the staff of a firm that caters to the design and construction or refurbishment of facilities, theatres, arenas, office complexes, and municipal buildings. It isn't that architects don't get training in lighting, but there appears to be a growing interest being voiced by clients for a "theatrical" twist to the lighting, particularly for the outside of the structure. Also, the inclusion of public art, especially statues and fountains, can use the theatrical eye. So, architectural firms are testing the waters, and I certainly hope this trend continues. I know a few theatre lighting designers who have signed up for basic architectural courses so that they are better qualified for these positions—a very wise move. Most of the firms realize if you have no experience in anything other than theatre design. They mostly look for young designers with excellent CAD skills, whom they can teach their specialty work on the job. A good national firm will have a very competitive wage package with benefits, and you can probably continue to do theatre at night.

There is also the teleconference market for major corporations that need a lighting professional to design a system for their videoconferencing. Although there are a limited number of these firms, and most are in major cities such as New York, Atlanta, Chicago, Dallas, San Francisco, and Los Angeles, the opportunity for full-time employment that leaves time to do some theatre design at night and weekends is great.

Summer Stock and Festivals

Staff positions at summer stock theatres or festivals can be an adjunct to a teaching position. There are several cases I am aware of where teachers do their nine months of teaching and then go off each year to the same festival as a resident designer. This adds to the stability of their income, with a guaranteed second job that fills out their calendar. But this is also a testing ground for younger professionals and an opportunity to be re-employed for many summers to come. The pay is not great, but it does allow you to hone your skills and get design credits beyond college productions. However, few are full-time and the fees, although possibly at LORT rates, are at the low end of the scale.

Dance Staff

A survey of staff design positions for year-round employment, although often not truly full-time, showed that many were with dance companies. Many dance companies do travel extensively, which adds an element to the mix that may not be compatible with family commitments, so make sure you are willing to do this before applying. But to others this is a bonus; the thrill of travel can be both challenging and exhilarating. However, many lighting designers report that they often must serve as board operator and even production manager since they are often the only "techie" on the road with the company. As to pay scale, sorry, but most dance companies can hardly make it from month to month, so don't expect to be highly paid.

Pitfalls

What are the pitfalls of a staff position? As with other jobs there are many. Some people would say that the very benefit I talked about of working with the same people is in fact a minus. You are stuck working time and time again with the constraints not only of the facility but of the staff. The budget and resources will probably be quite limited. And though that can be a plus for exerting your creative juices, it can also be very trying. You have to be prepared to face staff members year after year who may no longer put out their best creative efforts. And you may run into someone with whom you don't see eye-to-eye and feel that the "team spirit" is lost. On the summer stock and festival circuit, you are often set up in smaller communities where the housing is minimal and you are isolated for two or three months in an area that does not have the amenities you would prefer. Even at a regional theatre, the community may be small and your contact with the major theatre markets restricted due to the schedule of your theatre.

Staff positions are often paid at a much lower rate than the USA contract because you are on a salary rather than a fee-per-project basis. The USA and the IA try to keep the numbers at least equal, but they have been known to negotiate special deals with the theatres that allow their members some latitude to agree to what might be less than the scale for a single show design. But remember, you are not a slave, and you can turn down the position.

I find that many designers, especially lighting and sound designers, find this type of situation ultimately boring, because they are working with the same equipment and the same physical layout and the same dimming, circuit, and patch system. Some are such that the design only allows for a repertory plot with a few specials for each show.

In the end, however, it is up to the designer to make the most of the situation and be as creative as she can be under the circumstances. So, does the steady paycheck outweigh the other problems? You decide.

CHAPTER 17
Setting Your Salary and Fees

Setting salary and fees is truly one of the worst parts of our business. Very few of us like to negotiate salary or fees. In an ideal world, clients would understand how brilliant we are and just throw money at us. Okay, that was fun; now for something a little more realistic.

What to charge for a single project as a freelance designer? How much should I make if I take a staff position, or what is fair for a teaching position? How much can I add to my teaching salary if I freelance in the summer and whenever the school will allow me to leave campus? These are the issues before us.

Mark Gray, a director of photography in Hollywood, says, "Your daily rate should be the highest number you can say without laughing out loud." I wish that were true for all of us. Yes, I have gotten fees I felt very fortunate to receive, and a few clients offered more than I was prepared to ask for, but in most of those cases, the workload more than made up for the extra money. I am sure the producer knew it and wanted to avoid a confrontation later.

As a freelance designer you must not only be your own salesperson, but your own business manager and company finance officer, as well. Most students just finishing a design school program admit that they will take about anything that is offered. They feel that the employer sets the fees and that is that. And yes they do—for those who do not challenge them.

The worst thing that can happen to you as a new designer is to go into a meeting and be asked what you would want if you were offered this job. What do you say? The guideline should be the union contract scale. However, the unfortunate part is that the unions—USA, IA, IBEW, Actors' Equity, and others—do not cover all the potential work we can do as designers and production managers. Stage managers are a little more likely to be covered by an Equity union contract because of the strong unity they maintain. But for the rest of us, it is a struggle to figure out the street rate or some other watermark, and then build our own salary and fee schedule for different types of work.

Union Wages
Whether you are a union member or not, I believe that you must set your own watermark for your fees. Now, if you have been able to join USA, the union publishes fee schedules based on negotiations it has had with individual pro-

duction companies, theatre production organizations such as LORT, and the League of American Theatres and Producers. In film and television, the IATSE national leadership conducts collective bargaining talks on behalf of the some fifty-five locals in Hollywood every couple of years. These talks are held with the Alliance of Motion Picture and Television Producers, which is made up of the major studios and big independent producers. Normally, the small studios and independent filmmakers who want the union's crews then go along with the contract as negotiated, possibly asking for a few minor concessions. Even with such a major power base, that still leaves hundreds of producers and companies in the Hollywood area that do not sign the union agreement.

Freelance designers are then still faced with negotiating fees for some projects even when they are union members. For me, the pay schedule is not the major reason to back the unions, anyway; it is the form contracts and benefits package they offer. The minimum fee schedules the unions negotiate are of more concern to the stagehands and other hourly workers than to designers. The directors of photography, costume designers, art directors, and special effects experts, it is safe to say, all negotiate higher fees or they are not working on the major films and shows in Hollywood. That is not a putdown; it is actually what allows them to demand and get higher fees. Without the watermark of the contract, they would have no point of reference to start from. And they are secure in the knowledge that they can't get any less. So, what do they have to lose by asking for more?

The nice thing is, the unions have set your walk-away position for you, so you are not under any pressure. The only thing you can do is make the producer mad, so keep the meeting going using the interpersonal relationship and win-win negotiating skills discussed in chapter 11. Use the rate schedule as your watermark for measuring yourself against. Do an honest evaluation of your experience and skill and what you can bring to the plate for a producer, and go for it!

Personal Worth

That evaluation starts by looking at your personal lifestyle and situation. Are you willing to work out of town for short periods or even on a six-month world tour? How about a film in Singapore or a commercial in the Arctic Circle? (Could you even believe these were possibilities when you were in school?) What about a theatre company in Anchorage, Alaska, São Paulo, Brazil, or Mattoon, Illinois; does that interest you? Do you have the responsibility of a family? Are you willing to relocate for two years during the build-out of an entertainment theme park overseas? Consider the effect of travel on your loved ones and your personal responsibilities. These are the deal-breaker considerations you must make before beginning to negotiate for a project.

A lot of people say that they will wait and cross that bridge when they get to it. But that is like sticking your head in the sand. Situations will arise, and there may not be adequate time for you to consult your family and think about it. The pressure will be on for you to make a "go" or "no go" decision. The producer is standing over the table saying, are you going or not? That is not the time to make a decision that affects not only you but also your family and your commitments to other clients without due consideration.

So, I suggest, just as you have done with setting out your fee schedule, that you do some thinking about asking conditions and locations: will you leave town, maximum time away, and all other considerations. Make a list or chart and then paste it on your wall. The two, fees and working conditions, go hand in hand.

Build Scenarios

I believe you should sit down and write out scenarios in which all your options are listed. Talk to your family, talk to others that have gone on tour (especially if they have worked out of the country), consider all the possibilities, and give yourself a chance to reason out your potential answers to the scenarios. Now that you have done all the "What ifs" you can imagine, revisit them on a regular basis, say yearly. See if your situation or your goals have changed, allowing for some options you had not considered before. Such planning must be kept a very fluid thing; don't just lock yourself into a small square you have drawn around a five-mile area and say, that's it. And lastly, understand that the truth is the actual proposition will never match any scenario you have envisioned. But that is all right, doing these scenarios has allowed you to clearly think through possibilities, and now you can more easily narrow down what you will or will not do.

Now that we have the physical limits of your world, how about the financial picture? Next, do an analysis of your monthly expenses, budget, and long-term financial commitments. Do another wall chart, or use a computer program, such as Microsoft's Excel 2000 spreadsheet program, or a money management program, such as was discussed in chapter 4, Accounting for Small Businesses. What is the minimum you can afford to take on a project that will at least keep you from digging into your savings, assuming you have been wise enough to start saving. How you build this financial picture is to take into consideration your fixed monthly payments: auto, rent, utilities, cable TV, and phone. Then make another list of the bills that are not fixed, such as credit cards, and average or place a maximum figure in this column. Then there are the bills that are due yearly, such as insurance and some taxes. My CPA told me a long time ago to take all of these, add in a percentage for food, clothing, and entertainment, and then add 10 to 20 percent as a contingency factor. With these figures added together you will have a pretty good idea of how much a month and a year you need for minimal survival—no spur-of-the-moment purchases, no looking at a new car, or anything else.

In his book, *The Contract and Fee-Setting Guide for Consultants and Professionals*, Howard Shenson refers to a professional poll of 7,003 consulting firms conducted in 1988. The median daily billing rate was $929 per day (after business expenses), with an income average of $91,102 a year. Although theatrical design was not a category, Arts and Culture, Recreation, Broadcast, and Industrial Design were. They came in at $611, $644, $743, and $788 respectively. If you divide the median number by a ten-hour day, it works out to between $60 and $92 per hour for the effort. Though theatre designers would be hard-pressed to ever think of such fees, these figures are very much in line with television, film, and corporate work. So, take this as just another watermark to employ in a long list that is useful in making your own personal fee schedule.

At this point, you are ready to entertain a freelance position, a staff position, or that teaching position. Which one you take is a matter of all the factors you have brought to the table: family considerations, living conditions, location, salary or income level, and your own understanding of your self-worth.

Freelance

If you choose to be a freelance designer, you now need to add to the game, "What could I possibly make this year?" How many weeks do you think you will be able to work for the year? Twenty, thirty, or more weeks of work must be divided into your yearly expense budget to arrive at a minimum fee for the week or a daily rate. Then when that producer puts you on the spot and says, I need your answer right now or it goes to someone else, you can use the information you have already gathered to make up your mind as to what you will say next.

The only problem is, will you actually get that twenty or thirty weeks of work a year you guessed at to create your budget? But let's assume you have done this for a couple of years and have been able to hit your target income and hold to your projected budget so that you come through without a lot of red ink. What to do with that extra money burning a hole in your pocket is a topic for another book, such as Tad Crawford's *The Money Mentor* (see chapter 4) and the good advice of a professional business manager or CPA.

And don't forget to use the watermarks supplied by the unions. Then you have to decide if you are worth more or at least think you deserve more than the minimum fees agreed to by the union for your category of work. And let me make a point here. Many of the studios and producers will try and make you believe that that is the only fee structure they pay. But believe me, if they want you bad enough, they'll pay more than scale. It is up to you to create the atmosphere wherein they are convinced you are worth more! So, over scale is not always a deal-breaker for them. If you have done your marketing and have created an image as a designer who will be worth whatever you ask, then don't hesitate to demand it. Of course, you must also be just as ready to be turned down, and then you have to walk away—or, as the win-win negotiator says, find a way for both sides to win. I have found that there is admittedly less negotiating room in regional theatre agreements than in some other entertainment design areas. But if that is the case, you must be prepared and know what those fees are before you waste time pursuing an assignment that you know will not meet your minimal financial needs.

The hardest area for fee setting is in concert and corporate design. Since there is very little union influence in the design end of these businesses, it is up to you to negotiate your best fee. How you arrive at what you feel the client can or should pay may be based on what you hear other designers are making. I must warn you: we all lie when it comes to admitting what we make. Egos have no more fertile ground than when it comes to fee discussions among peers. That is why I have not provided any fee matrix or schedules in this book. In addition, they vary so greatly due to size of production, the region, the area of entertainment, and other factors that they would be of little help. But you can create your own chart by talking to technical directors (they know everyone's salary/fees) and other designers.

Listen in at parties when someone says they heard so-and-so got $5,000 for that little show last week. Take it all with a grain of salt, and discount the figure a good 15 to 25 percent, and you may be able to build a picture of what you can use to set your own fees.

Another way of assisting your search for a fee is to find out what staff designers are making, then divide that by fifty-two and add 45 percent (that covers their health and welfare and other employer contributions) plus taxes, and divide by your twenty or thirty weeks a year. That will give you a fee range that similar employers are probably already paying. You can even use that for justification in your negotiations.

The one thing that you must do is stick with it. If you start discounting the fees you have asked for, it will be difficult to rise above the lower figure ever again with that client. If it means walking away from a fee that would have paid your bills that month, but was way below the fee you got for your last show, my advice is to turn it down. Now, look again at the win-win method and see if there isn't a way to salvage the project by some creative negotiating. That is not only acceptable, it is encouraged.

I must admit that I have run into situations where there was no time to develop a schedule or find out what others were paid for similar design work before going to the meeting. Two methods can be used here. One that I have used as a lighting designer in small Equity Waiver theatres is to say, I'll take half or two-thirds of what the set designer is being paid. Yes, I am taking a chance that the set designer made a good deal, but when you have nothing else to go on, it is at least a watermark that will not embarrass you when you find out that you shouldn't have taken sympathy on the producer—the same producer who said she had no money, then you later discover she paid the set designer four times what she paid you for the project! My advice: never, never take pity on a producer. If she really doesn't have the money, then why is she trying to produce the show in the first place? That is just bad business. Remember, too, that you don't want to end up shelling out for expendables knowing you'll never get reimbursement.

Business Fee Setting

If you work as a single designer, setting your fee should be directly related to your personal financial needs. It isn't hard to figure out the cost of your rent, food, car, gas, utilities, and telephone.

But let us take it to the next step. You want to open an office and pursue clients in other media, which requires a business presence. Maybe you feel the need for a full-time assistant or associate designers to help with the workload or do the research and paperwork. What do you need in fees to cover these additional costs? We refer to them as the "cost of doing business." There are a few books available that deal with fee setting for consultants. Mostly they were written for architectural firms, but we can use them as a model. You understand that your fees must cover what you wish to take home to pay your personal bills, as well as the salary of an employee. But there is also the rent, telephones, business machines, and other expenses to pay for; how do you handle that?

Three things comprise the calculation needed to come up with a daily fee, according to Howard L. Shenson in his book *The Successful Consultant's Guide to Fee Setting*. He says you need to look at fee setting as a three-step process:

1. A charge for the value of the labor of the practitioner—the daily labor rate

2. A charge for the expense of being in business—overhead

3. A charge for the risk taking, for being in the consulting business—profit

When you are self-employed, the first thing you must do is determine the value of your labor. You compute that from what you know your peers make, or use the union's negotiated scales, or just decide what you want to make (but be realistic). As I mentioned earlier, one friend says he charges whatever he can without breaking out laughing. Now, remember that you will not be working every day as is done in a full-time employment position. So you must start by making an educated guess of how many days a year clients are likely to hire you. But be conservative. Divide your personal living expenses by this figure to come up with the first of the three numbers needed to calculate your fee.

Then do a calculation of the overhead costs. That may be very simple if you have no office, but if you do have one, you will need to add up the expenses that are directly related to that space: rent, telephone, machines, employees, and so on. Take that figure and, calculating it as a yearly expenditure, divide it by the same number of days you used in figuring how often a client will hire you. Don't forget semiannual or yearly charges, such as insurance and business license costs and taxes. Two down, one to go. Lastly, profit. Many people overlook this one. They erroneously conclude that since they are charging for their labor, it is not proper to charge an additional amount on top—that is, profit. But you are a business, and businesses take risks, so they need profit to survive.

If you look at profit as the return on your investment for taking the risk of being in business, it is more understandable. You may think you had very little to invest in starting your business, so the figure should be small. But consider the fact that you want to grow and maybe get a more powerful computer or a nice printer. You need to save the money to purchase these items. You hope that such purchases will not eat up all the profit, because you need to keep some in reserve for slow periods. You may need very little to eat, but the landlord wants the rent for the office whether you are working or not.

Your accountant or CPA will be able to help you with the tangible figures, and he will have numbers of other business profit margins to show you as a comparison. But you must also sit down privately with your business and even your domestic partner and think seriously about what you want to be able to take home to support your lifestyle and family, not only today, but also in the foreseeable future. Only then can you make an intelligent calculation of your fee.

After having agonized over these figures, you will arrive at what you consider a fair number. Then you walk into a meeting and tell the producer what your rate is for the project and, laughing, he throws you out on your ear. Can it happen? Yes. You have just found out that there is another figure out there—the going street rate for the type of work you do. Who set that rate? Where did it come from? What truck hit me? You forgot the reality check. After you come up with your figure, you also need to take into consideration information about what other people charge.

Street Rate

Each area of entertainment design and management has an unwritten, unseen glass ceiling. But the ceiling floats. (By the way, I have never found a "gender" glass ceiling in entertainment.) Discovering what each market will bear for your work is very, very difficult. That is why you will tell one producer your rate and she will jump at it. Later you think to yourself, that was too easy; I must not have asked for enough. But you may have just stumbled on the exact figure she had in mind. Other times it isn't exactly the raw number, it was how it "appeared" to add up to the producer. That is when you get into the win-win negotiating techniques to discover what the boundaries are and how you can fit yourself into the box without being crushed.

Lastly, use the unions' rate sheets as a guide. Just remember that they are low, and that there is room for greater fees *if* you have what the producer believes the production needs and no one else can supply it. That is where marketing comes in. You have to make the client believe you are a steal at that rate. So, go back and study chapter 7 again.

I believe it is fair to say that freelance designers gain in three ways:

* Freedom to pursue creative work when and where they want;
* Potential for greater financial reward;
* Freedom to work as often or as little as they like.

We can use the ability to choose whom to work for and when to work to allow us to do "charity" theatre work if that is what we want to do. Wouldn't it feel great to know you could do that not-for-profit theatre show simply because you can actually afford to?

The Last Man Method

Another way of setting a freelance fee, or even a salary for a staff position, is to ask how long the last designer was with the production and when he got his last raise, if any. Then say you want 2.5 to 5 percent more for every year since that designer last got a raise. And when the producer asks how you arrived at that, I would say that since the last designer's fee hadn't been raised in a while, this would cover the increase in the cost of living that has taken place in the interim. Thus, technically, you are not asking for any more money.

Here are a couple of scenarios that may seem like dreams come true: as a designer, you become attached to a hit show that stays on the air for years, or find employment with a corporate client, which retains you every year for ten or more years in a row for annual product release shows. The problem is that year after year, the fee will most likely not be raised. It is easily possible for you to go for years working for the same company and never receive the full-time employee benefits package of other workers. The fee you started at is still the fee you are paid, even when staff people get a small yearly raise, which eventually brings them up to your income level, plus they have paid benefits.

In theatre, if a show continues beyond the scheduled run, there are provisions in the union contract that provide for additional fees. But if you are working in television, you are probably not an employee of the production company or the show. Often the company does not want to pay you as staff but keeps you on the series for years. This also happens at theme parks that have you design one attraction for a flat fee. Then they start you on another attraction, assuming you'll do it for the same fee. Try to build into your agreement some language that covers a cost of living increase tied to what the staff gets or the national average. If you are lucky enough to be working under a signed union contract, there is still a possible pitfall.

Union contracts usually have a cost of living clause written into them, so you are assured of getting something each year. But if you are hired at a salary or flat daily fee that is higher than the minimum scale, the employer is not required to give you the cost of living increases built into the contracts. So, although you start at 20 percent above the minimum, in as little as four years the minimum fee has been raised to the point where you are now only equal to the minimum scale and the next year could be paid less than others. So, you have not kept pace with the economy.

Review Clause

If you think the project has potential to become a long-term job, you should try and get a review clause that sets an anniversary date for an increase in fees or termination. I even had a clause put in one contract that said they had to fire me! The idea that I asked for a clause in my agreement that said they had to fire me if they didn't give me a raise before each season floored the producer. He said, I could just not agree to come back, but I wanted to put the ball in his court. He had to make the conscious decision not to have me return. I was not allowing him to be passive. Did it work? Yes, for fourteen years, and then his replacement did not renew the agreement. But I had gotten out of it a firm commitment that was based on a mutual understanding that if my work was not meeting his expectations we would confront it and not sweep it under the rug. I was satisfied knowing that I would get a raise without making demands or fighting for consideration, and he got the control that he, as the producer, wanted.

Adjunct to the review clause idea is a hint from a friend who worked for a theme park developer. He says that it is not unusual for the scope of your responsibility to grow after you sign the original agreement. Now you have to wonder if the client didn't know this would happen before you signed. In any event, do not hesitate to build into your agreement a clause concerning this possibility. And by the way, if the client says, no, that won't happen, you don't need the clause; say, so I'll leave it there since it isn't a problem, is it? Use any increase in the scope of your responsibility as a window of opportunity for renegotiating your deal and earning more. Especially if you are out of the country, it will cost them more to replace you than to give you a raise to cover the added duties. So you could be in the catbird seat.

Teaching Positions

If you start your search in one of the higher educational journals that list teaching positions all over the world, you will find that many say that salary is "commensurate with experience." If you have been out of graduate school a short while, that may mean an entry-level position as lecturer, or perhaps assistant professor. The salary is mostly based on a nine-month commitment with the summers off, or an opportunity to teach the summer semester for an additional salary. And the fact is that the salary will be less than you could make if you worked professionally, but more in line with a staff position in a regional theatre.

But consider the advantages. First, many teaching positions can lead to tenure after seven years. A job for life is a pretty nice thing to have in any economic climate. Second, you will get a retirement plan, health care, and other benefits that cover the full year, not just the teaching year. Now add to that the fact that most design teachers I know do professional design work during the summer break, even during the school year. Many run companies that design year-round at theme parks, corporate shows, and consult on architectural projects.

The big change in the past decade has been that most colleges and universities encourage this practice of outside design work. Viewing outside design jobs as advancing the professional competence of the educator in place of the old standby of publishing is now a well-established practice. This has allowed educators to raise their economic base considerably. But make sure that the institution you are applying to for a teaching position does allow this practice, and find out what the limitations and tradeoffs are.

I have to admit that I have made a complete about-face in my understanding of the educational system as it applies to theatre design and management staff in the past five years. Not only do I believe strongly that most design teachers give a tremendous amount of their energy to advancing their students' knowledge and understanding of design, but with their professional design work outside of the school, they bring a clearer picture to their students of the real world.

A recent trend has been to rely more and more on outside professionals to come in and teach the advanced design courses. They are paid, usually, at the instructor or lecturer rate, but not as full-time employees. The school arrives at a per-course fee by determining the class load of a full-time lecturer and dividing that by the number of classes, then paying the adjunct lecturer only that portion of the salary. In my experience, that can be as low as $3,500 for two one-hour classes a week, times fifteen weeks, or about $166 a class. And if drive time to and from school, lesson planning, and submission of papers to grade and report are accounted for, the pay is probably about $50 an hour or less. The school also saves on medical and retirement benefits, and often adjuncts have to pay their own parking fees!

Although I am a big booster of professionals on campus, I believe the schools are taking unfair advantage, quite possibly only to protect their small faculty from being challenged by better designers vying for their full-time positions. Teaching a little often satisfies many designers' need to give back, and they don't push for full-time positions, thus keeping the inner sanctum of the academician.

Loan-Outs

Staffing has become a word that producers hate to hear in many areas of entertainment. The film and television studios have even gone to the extent of using outside, or partially owned, employment firms to actually be the employer of record. You are then "loaned out" to the actual show you are working on. This insulates the studio from employee lawsuits and makes it easier to avoid the legal issues of employee/employer responsibility, such as retirement.

There are also the payroll service companies that are hired by a production company to handle the entire payroll, taxes, insurance and health, and welfare issues. The producer pays an additional fee based on the gross payroll, but that is all. In essence, these companies perform accounting services. There are employee leasing services that do take the full responsibility of the employer/employee relationship off the back of the producer. One thing that can be a plus is that these firms are there for the long haul, while the production company is formed and dissolved around a single production. You are more likely to get paid what is due you, and you can deal with the leasing service long-term for any settlement without worrying that they will be closed the next day.

I know that the legality of all this has been argued over for hours and hours by the unions, but it is still hard for me to understand how the studios gets away with it. For example, I meet with a producer of a specific show, talk about only that show, and he says I will get a specific fee or salary. Yet I get my checks from another firm, which informs me that it is my employer of record and that it has the right to fire me. It is all wrapped up in the financial and legal systems that allow studios to keep multiple books, as witnessed by a lawsuit centering around the1988 film *Coming to America*, involving Eddie Murphy, Paramount Pictures, and humor columnist Art Buchwald. Buchwald had first sued Murphy for not giving him proper credit for his role in developing the story. In the process of the court's determining the dollar amount entailed in the jury award of 19 percent of the film's profits, it was revealed that the studio had kept complicated "double books."

Nevertheless, it is a fact of doing business in the film and television industry, and, to some extent, in the corporate entertainment businesses. However, if you keep in mind the win-win negotiating strategy, there are ways you can make it work for you. First, you can be on the production company's payroll, have taxes taken out, and avoid personal bookkeeping costs. Or you can "loan-out" yourself if you have met the business requirements for being such a company. In many places, such as in Hollywood, you will be required to have an incorporated business to work as a "loan-out." A d.b.a. or partnership status will not allow you to work for many of the Hollywood studios or television networks in any other but an employee relationship. But this is a unique system probably only used in Hollywood.

Review the material on independent contracts in chapter 6. That will move you a long way toward deciding if you want to have your fees paid in the gross amount so you can deal with the taxes and insurance issues in a way most beneficial to your total financial picture. Or you can combine salaried work and work for fees, which is perfectly legal.

Regional Theatre

When it comes to regional theatre, the staff positions for designers, especially in scenic design, have dramatically dwindled over the past decade. Many theatres tout the creative advantages of having diversity by hiring a different designer for each show. They can also pay a flat fee that makes their bookwork easier. Staff costume and lighting designers are also viewed as costly liabilities and are to be avoided when possible. The exception to this for all designers is usually a summer festival situation where the constraints of time make it more economically advantageous to keep the same team together for the three or four productions that will be mounted that season.

I find that the main issue is salary level. Designers working in theatre staff positions, even with a union such as USA setting compensation, on average, receive far less than theatrical designers who receive flat fees, even when health and welfare is taken into consideration. But the staff position has its advantages.

If the theatre where you are interviewing is not a union house, you should come armed with the knowledge of what the fees would be in a comparable union house. That knowledge will provide you with a good watermark to use in negotiating.

If you have a family and do not wish to travel away from your spouse or partner, the same theatre can also hire him or her. The two salaries can mean a more comfortable and stable life for a family.

No matter what road you choose, it need not be a lonely road. Many people work at least two of these roads at once in today's entertainment market. So, if you teach, you still can have opportunities for professional design and the additional income it can bring. And I should point out that the reverse is true, as well: many professional designers can be found on college campuses acting as visiting professors for a semester or as "Artists-in-Residence." If you are on staff at a facility, it is also not that uncommon to be allowed a leave of absence to work on a special project.

In today's entertainment marketplace, the wide range of design opportunities available to designers who started with theatrical backgrounds is, I think, very exciting and finally offers designers the best chance in our history for a decent income. Designers now may have a settled life, if they so choose, or a hectic life of travel all over the world, if that is what they enjoy—but either from an economic base that is equal to other professionals.

Remember, in the end, only you can determine your ideal income level. No union or producer should have that right. I do not mean to imply the unions have held us back financially. On the contrary; remember, they must deal from a position of mean low salary as best they can when negotiating with a group of producers whose only goal is to get the workers as cheaply as possible.

The unions will always stand as my watermark for fees, and you should judge yourself against it also. When people slam the unions for the low scales, they forget that they alone hold the key to receiving a higher fee, not the unions. Nothing in any union contract I have ever seen said the producer could not pay you more than the minimum!

If you cannot meet membership requirements, work in a field of entertainment that has no collective bargaining agreement with the unions, or simply do not wish to belong, that is your choice Many states have a "right to work" clause that allows you to work. There are no closed union shops in those states; you do not need to belong to the union. Just remember that you are receiving the benefits of thousands of hours union organizers have worked to get their people the fees of which you now take advantage.

Even when a production company touts that it has a better deal than the union, do you honestly think it would be offering more if the unions had not raised the bar?

Per Diem

Per diem literally means "per day" and is used in agreements to refer to an allowance paid, usually in cash, to a worker when outside of his or her normal work/living area. See *The Performing Arts Business Encyclopedia* for a more complete definition of this term and what its place is in contractual terms. The Hollywood film industry, with a touch of nostalgia, considers whether payment of per diem is required by taking a fifty-mile radius from the corner of Hollywood and Vine in Hollywood, California, and not the actual studio's physical location (none are actually in Hollywood) as the mark for determining where "away" payment starts. They also refer to this as part of "Distance Location Fees."

For years, the touring concert market used a somewhat arbitrary figure of $45 per day. But now the amount can be negotiated up to around $55 a day. However, most production companies now use the U.S. Department of State's annually published schedules both for domestic and foreign travel. The schedule has three columns, a column for a Per Diem amount, which is to cover food and incidents, a Hotel column, which is the amount allowed for accommodations, and a Maximum column that combines the two figures. The rates are very flexible and can radically change from city to city within a country.

Open Accounts

There are companies that will pay all expenses as receipted to them, but these are rare or at least limited to the upper management of the firm. But understand that the company will not be able to take all of the receipts from such a generous deal as business expenses because the IRS will limit the amount to the State Department standards. Also, some items will not be allowed, such as alcohol.

The three-martini lunch is history. Such expenses will raise a red flag with the IRS, so some of this money will not be written off and will come out of the company's profits for the year. But as a perk for executives and other key people, expense accounts are still allowed, and they are a negotiated issue. There is one other consideration: if you are given more than the U.S. State Department schedule, it is possible that the company will indicate the difference on your tax forms, W-2 or 1099, at the end of the year as "income." That is how the IRS wants it treated. So, it is not what some people consider "free money."

Hotel and Travel
The most usual plan is that the production company makes travel arrangements in advance and pays your hotel and airfare. You only need to present a credit card to cover room service, restaurant, long-distance telephone, pay-per-view TV, and laundry charges, and possibly health club fees that are above the contracted room rate. There are still theatre road companies and touring dance groups that do not pay for hotels. Since you will probably be in the same city for three to six weeks or longer, there is a set housing rate, and it is up to the crew to actually pay for whatever housing arrangements they make. This allows them to have roommates to decrease their individual cost, stay with friends, or use other less expensive methods. But remember, the IRS may consider anything you cannot show valid receipts for additional income.

I have never found this arrangement acceptable, as my schedule does not allow me the time to make such complicated arrangements. But there is certainly an argument in favor of the producer who does not want to put out cash in advance for a large number of hotel rooms. On your first tour, you probably will have no choice but to go along with the majority of the crew's or the producer's desires. Then later you can decide what works best for you and try for such a deal next time.

Make sure the employer is very clear. Of course, it is best to get in writing exactly what the per diem covers, what the employer is going to pay in advance, such as hotel room and travel, and what will be reimbursed from valid receipted expense.

If you are asked to come to a meeting in another city for a potential position, it is sometimes easier for you to make your own arrangements and bill the client. But, obviously, do this only if you have a prior working relationship and are sure the client will repay you for the expense.

Remember, your checking account or credit card carries this burden until it is repaid; can you afford it? Some designers have found a way to make a little money by requesting the employer to agree to a fixed airfare amount that they will bill for, and then they use their airline mileage program credits for the actual purchase of the ticket. Again, I must caution you: the IRS will then view the money as income, not a deductible expense, and since deductions will not have been made, you will probably owe the IRS money at the end of the year. Often on one of these short survey trips, the producer will not restrict you to a set per diem, but will agree to pay actual receipts attached to a formal expense report.

What is to be included in the amount the producer will reimburse you in direct expenses is pretty open. For example, some will agree to pay for one long distance telephone call home per day. Some will cut the per diem rate on the days they will provide a hot dinner for you on the show site. Others have agreed to let employees drive to a distant location and pay mileage per other federal guidelines. However, this is a liability issue for the employer, and many Hollywood film studios will not allow this practice. If there is a highway accident, are you technically an employee of the company while driving to the location? The likelihood that the production company could be sued is great. Also, it is an issue of the crew arriving on time, so many companies insist that everyone meet at the studio and travel by chartered bus or plane together.

Federal Guide
The federal guidelines can be purchased from the U.S. Government Printing Office, P.O. Box 371954, Pittsburgh, PA 15250-7954, or go to their Web site at *http://bookstore.gpo.gov*. Get publication 1542 for per diem rates within the continental United States. In the U.S., if a rate is not specified for a city, there is currently a maximum rate of $85, which is broken down into $55 for lodging and $30 for meals and incidental expenses. Individual cities have rates as high as $46 for meals in larger metropolitan areas.

There are additional federal guidelines for foreign travel, including Alaska, Hawaii, Puerto Rico, and the Northern Mariana Islands. This is actually part of the document entitled *Federal Travel Regulations*, Chapter 301-7. There are fifty pages of these figures that cover not only countries, but also specific cities within a country. For example, Australia has six cities listed with individual rates, and then another rate for the rest of the country, and Brazil has twenty-three cities, plus the rest of the country, listed with various rates. Japan has sixty-three cities listed, but the United Kingdom only has twenty-six. The striking feature is the wide range of rates within a given country. In Brazil, for example, São Paulo has a high of $164 for lodging and $82 for meals, but Campo Grande has a low of $57 for lodging and $48 for meals. Tokyo allows a combined $280 per day, while Kyoto is $253 combined. Working in London will get you $85 for meals, but in Cambridge, you have only $64. The point is that there are very large fluctuations even within a country, so do not accept a single per diem rate when traveling to multiple cities, especially overseas. Assuming you are not working directly for the U.S. government or a contracting agency, these are not restrictive legal limits for commercial or charitable employers. So, you do have the right to negotiate a higher figure. However, the IRS may tax you on the excess as personal income.

Self-Employed

If you are acting as a self-employed, independent contractor/designer, and traveling as part of your business, then what expenses can be written off is a matter to be very thoroughly discussed with your CPA and tax attorney. An auto rental on a location, for example, that was not approved by the client might be deductible under your company expenses if it gives you more flexibility while away from home, so you can see other clients. Some designers ask for an all-encompassing expense account that is not only their per diem but their estimated office incidental expenses, as well—though mostly without breaking anything out into line items. In this method you compute an average figure for office expenses, such as blueprints, long-distance calls, FedEx packages, and other costs, and add it to your fee as estimated expenses. This way, the client doesn't have to worry about bills showing up after the job. Many employers like the fact that they can budget a fixed amount for incidentals and fees, and possibly only prepay the travel and hotel costs, so there are no hidden costs or bills trickling in months after the production.

Any way you wish to work the per diem issue, be prepared for employers to say they already have set guidelines. Then, if they are acceptable, go with their normal system to avoid conflict with them, as well as the rest of the crew. But, if you still feel the numbers are low, you may be able to factor additional money into your fee to cover your personal needs.

CHAPTER 18

Equipment and Service as a Side Business

The notion of a side business may seem a little out of place in this book, but there are opportunities for additional income for designers who provide physical services to the theatre and entertainment community. Rentals of sound and lighting systems can obviously benefit sound and lighting designers, but rentals can also offer some very interesting potential for costumers and scenic designers, as well. And understand, this does not necessarily mean you have to become a rental house or construction shop to take advantage of such additional income.

There are two primary reasons to get involved in a side business while keeping your design career as the number one priority:

1. It can increase your contacts with the theatre/entertainment community
2. It can bring in additional income

This first point goes back to the marketing discussed in chapter 7. Since you are already making contacts with potential clients in your design or management careers, why not use the same mailer or your opportunities to meet with a client to get even more out of the meeting?

I know there is a fear that the client will start to think of you as a salesperson for a rental house. But you can create a separation simply by using two different company names. You can design under the business name of Billy Bean Designs Inc., for instance, and also present a card for All Nations Costume Shop when you are marketing or doing sales for your employer. The odds are probably against you getting the first show after you meet new clients. But there is a much better chance that they will allow All Nations Costume Shop to bid on their costume construction or rental needs. Now you have the opening to meet with the client again and build your personal worth with good, honest business dealings that will flow through to a feeling that you must also be reliable as a designer. I realize this sounds strange, but I have seen it work time and again. Funny how seemingly bright management people can be fooled into seeing two when there is one. Maybe it goes back to their wanting twice as much for their dollars—they just naturally think double!

Let's start at the beginning. First, you need to establish yourself as a designer, as a business, by following the advice in the first six chapters of this book. Assuming you have done that and are legally doing your design work under a business name, even if it is Billy Bean Designs Inc., you already know what to do, and starting another business to provide additional services will be easy. You don't need to separate the businesses if you don't want to, but some people fear that they will not receive personal recognition if clients only see the business name.

But it isn't just about selling or leasing equipment. By combining your design abilities and expanding yourself into niche markets, you can increase your income. The reality is that there are only so many hours in the day. So figure it out: Ten hours times seven days a week means you can only bring in a finite income. And you can't be in three places at once (very often). So, your potential is limited when it comes to what you can personally expect to earn, even with a big design fee. One of the ways to deal with this and the marketing issue at the same time is to join forces with another designer, or another person who would be willing to run the rental side of a business, possibly a set or costume construction shop, to which you will only attach your name or expertise. Do I even need to say that if you do this, make sure you have a partnership agreement?

My Business Story

I myself avoided using my own name as part of the company name for the first twenty years of my career. Only then did I feel comfortable about including my last name in the title. The first company was Sundance Lighting, later changed to Sundance Lighting Corp., when I learned more about liability and insurance issues. I subrented all the equipment and never even had a warehouse. I worked out of a home office and toured with the biggest artists of the day. Not only did I supply my design services but the equipment and road crews, as well. As the business grew, the need for specialized designs for transporting the equipment to make setup easier grew accordingly, and a new term was born: "roadability." We got tired of opening the truck doors to find screws and bolts all over the floor every day. The manufacturers just didn't understand our problem; they built most of the equipment to sit in a theatre, not bounce thousands of miles every day. The need to modify and reinforce equipment prompted the move to a real office and warehouse. My financing had been out-of-pocket up until that point. But the couple of years of touring had added enough money to my bank account that I could pay for the offices and start purchasing some equipment. I applied for an SBA (Small Business Administration) loan and used it to buy more equipment and build my own special road dimmer racks and transport cases. Not wanting to sit behind a desk, I continued to design and tour for over ten years.

I told people that the day I had to become a "businessman," I'd sell out. And that was just what I did: I sold all the equipment to another firm. That sale allowed me to broaden my personal design world from just concerts into film and television design, yet I was still able to keep my theatre contacts and do some designing in regional theatre. Since I didn't want to finance an additional buildup of specialized equipment that would be needed in those markets, I got out of the rental business.

I moved to a smaller office and changed the name of my company back to simply Sundance. I worked with just one assistant on staff for several years until a mutual friend suggested that another designer, Jeff Ravitz, would be a good fit as a partner. Jeff had built a great reputation as a concert designer, but I knew he was also a theatre school graduate like myself. We decided to join forces, and since he didn't feel comfortable continuing under my company name, I finally agreed to Moody Ravitz Design Partners Inc.

We did not own any equipment, but continued to sub-rent when the opportunity was right. Eventually, we built the firm into other areas of design, especially themed entertainment and some architectural work, to supplement the concert and television work, which was about 80 percent of our activity. Theatre and film made up the other 20 percent of the design work. Corporate shows had fallen off for us, but there were still some clients even in that area. The staff had grown to six people, and we had outgrown our second set of offices. Then Jeff introduced me to Dawn Hollingsworth, an old friend of his from Chicago.

Dawn not only was very active in the themed and architectural lighting design market but she also had an M.B.A. in business management from Pepperdine University. Her added design skills and clients, plus the bonus of her business knowledge, led to our combining with her firm and extending the name to Moody Ravitz Hollingsworth Lighting Design Partners, Inc., which we referred to as M/R/H on a day-to-day basis.

Then in early 2000 Dawn brought another designer to us whom she had worked with and knew well. Lisa Passamonte-Green had been designing mostly in the themed area since graduation from San Diego State University ten years before, working for Disney Imagineering, as well as freelancing. She eventually opened her own design studio. But trying to design and be on remote construction sites had taken its toll, and Lisa wanted the support we could offer, so we joined her firm with ours. We decided that simply adding another name to the business title would sound too much like a law firm, so we struggled to find a name. In 2001, we came up with Visual Terrain Inc.

Now there we have four principal designers working actively in virtually every area of lighting design—theatre, concert, television, corporate, themed, and architectural. Recently, we have begun to provide production management and site management services, as well. The staff now consists of six associate designers and one office manager who is also a Web master and computer draftsperson. We also usually have an intern from an accredited design program on site. The offices are 2,700 square feet in an industrial park, a size that we feel is right. Taking on too much space and staff can be the downfall of a consulting business in design, just as it is for architects. So, consider how big to grow, and base it on sound financial advice.

A testament to Dawn's managerial leadership is that in 2001 the U.S. Chamber of Commerce awarded M/R/H Lighting Design Inc. their Blue Chip Enterprise Award for excellence in business. The award was based on growth and market penetration.

What to Offer

Deciding what services or equipment to provide is where imagination comes in, so start with a good look around your own community. Get out the phone book and look under theatrical services; what do you find? Depending on your area of expertise and the community you live in, it could be a very short list. The tried and true sidelines can work; however, let's sidestep the obvious, such as lighting, sound, and costumes, or even a construction shop for sets or props, and think instead of possible "niche" markets that are potentially easier to start and less costly to run

For lighting, you might think about who is the color media supplier in the area—is there one? Could you do a little business out of the garage by selling color media to local community theatre, high school, and church groups? As a sound designer, could you market yourself as a system design person for high-end home entertainment? If you are a costumer, you could hook up with a party planner who does themed parties and become a coordinator for parties and events. A scenic designer could well have skills as a mural artist, or market such talents to businesses as a coordinator of public art. Many communities and states have plans that give tax breaks to firms owning and displaying public art; it is a big business. Most of these services take no cash outlay for stock, but they do have the potential for a nice cash flow to supplement your design income.

Obviously I have not given all the possibilities. You have to come up with your own to make it a unique service that people will want. I know some will say, but I don't want it to overpower my real desire to design theatre. I fully understand, but I can only offer myself as an example. For thirty-two years now, I have run businesses such as these, yet maintained an international reputation as a designer.

Profit

Just because you have started a business doesn't mean there is going to be profit. And this may come as a surprise; maybe you don't want any. If you are using the side business as pocket money to buy your "toys," there is no need to show excess profit that could then just go out the window in taxes. Look for legitimate ways to reduce your tax liability with your CPA. Why go to all the work of a side business if all that happens is your hard work only pays for taxes? Now, as was discussed in chapter 8, Making Contacts, the side business can work as a marketing tool for your design business, but keep everything in perspective and you can make the most of your efforts. I have to say that the tax laws state that you must make a profit for two out of five years to receive the tax and deduction benefits of being a business. But there is a very low minimum profit figure attached to these laws, so $100 shown as profit could easily meet the legal requirement. Check with your tax attorney.

First, there is something not immediately apparent in saying there was no profit after you deducted all your expenses from a fee. Your CPA will go over what items can be written off on your taxes, but they normally include the office rent, office supplies, computers, postage, hired worker's salary or subcontractor payments, advertising costs, transportation costs, and so on. These things are considered the cost of doing business. If your business brings in enough to cover these costs and more, then there is probably profit—profit that you can reinvest in the business or take out of the business as your salary. Again, consult a tax attorney or your CPA about all the ways this works. The point is that profit can legally be minimized to keep your tax liability low. Yet it can also pay for a lot of needs you have, such as publicity, a business phone, a bigger computer, and other necessities. Yes, you may be able to do this as an individual and write off these items on your personal income tax, but it is much harder.

Loss-Leader

The term *loss-leader* most commonly refers to items that businesses advertise and sell at cost or below just to attract customers. It's fairly common to see an electronics store, for example, advertise a toaster or small camera at an unbelievable savings. We, as designers, can learn from this concept. I use the term to mean a project I do where the fee barely covers my out-of-pocket expenses.

Is there another way we can use the *loss-leader* technique? Networking. Providing equipment for a benefit show can not only be a tax write-off but a great way to meet potential clients you might otherwise be unable to come in contact with in your position. You can expand your base of people who can potentially use your primary design services or will put you in touch with someone who will. It may not be necessary that your side business do more than pay business expenses out of the gross profits to be of benefit to you. All of these possibilities are open to you. You have imagination and creativity . . . use it.

CHAPTER 19
Non-Union Shows and Other Productions

Let's be realistic. First, as I stated in chapter 12, the theatrical unions have not blanketed all of the new entertainment fields. There are a lot of reasons for this, and I leave it up to the union representatives to defend their position on this issue. The practical fact is that we, as designers and production managers, now have a wide range of opportunities to use our training for gainful employment, and I, while trying to be a loyal union member, do not choose to limit my creative work to only those union-controlled areas of the business. Let us take a look at some of the major areas that are not traditionally union controlled. High on the list must be concerts, followed by theme parks, corporate television, party production, and architectural, with television, film, and theatre being their strong markets.

Negotiating Your Own Fees

When it comes to figuring out what you feel you are (a) worth, (b) the client will pay, and (c) what you have guts enough to ask for, I admit I am not the greatest at this game. I, like most of you, was brainwashed into believing that we did this for the love of the art. But that's pure bull. We give and give of our time and resources. How many of you have used your own furniture to dress a set or reused patterns from previous shows to help a show that cried poor? Now it is payback time. But remember, there isn't a free lunch in other entertainment media; they are businesspeople out to get you as cheap as they can. The difference is that they are starting from a financial base that is above the poverty level, unlike most theatres.

Concerts

The IA has, to my knowledge, never tried to organize this area for designers other than the work I did with national representative Al Di Tolla years ago. Though many concert tours do have IA members as part of their road crews, it is my understanding that they are doing so with special permission and not under the Yellow Card contract. A check with several of the largest concert lighting suppliers has confirmed that none have been approached in recent years by the IA to organize their workers. Or if they have, it has never come to a vote by the workers for or against unionization. This covers the electricians, carpenters, props, and sound crews—but not the designers, I might add.

As for the designers, the USA position on this issue is less clear. Since the union also does not have signed agreements with the major concert promoters or artists management companies, it has asked that members use the "Individual Artists Agreement" or the "Project Only Agreement." Your fee structure cannot be less than the agreement applicable to the member category states—that is, scenic designer, single set or multiple set, and the rest. But concert design pays double, even triple, what theatre does, even at the midlevel tours, so it's not a problem. Getting the artist's management to agree to sign this agreement has not always been easy, because it obligates management to make health and welfare contributions. And it forms a legal relationship and a chain of responsibility that many do not wish to have with anyone, not only unions. But you need a contract, union or not, so why not take advantage of the union's preproduced forms and receive health and welfare benefits?

Another issue is a reuse clause. Can the concert artist reuse your design without your permission and payment of additional fees? This is a burning issue. I have practically never had a concert promoter (or artist's manager) ask me to use someone else's design. And even if the tour lighting supplier is the same as before I joined the tour, there has been no question of my being able to make changes if I stay within the budget. Corporate theatre is the same. Both areas are more concerned in presenting a new, shinier, brighter show each time, so that issue has never come up.

But there is a related issue where a problem does arise, especially when working with concert artists, in which a show is being broadcast live, taped, or shot for direct sale on DVD. If you have designed the tour and nothing will be changed (which is probably not true for lighting, but could be true for costumes and sets), you should have a clause in your agreement allowing for some payment and screen credit. However, I have always had to fight for this. Management doesn't want anything that will impede their negotiations with a network or distributor for its artist's services under these conditions. The best I have been able to do is have a clause that says management will negotiate a fee. In the case where we are brought in specifically to punch up such an event, the fee will be a flat one. I have never, never seen an agreement that gave a designer "points" in the sale of the tape or DVD. Good luck; maybe you are a better negotiator than I am, and if so, I bow to your negotiating skill.

USA does have a clause for payment if the theatre production is shot for anything other than "record" purposes. That is generally held to mean one camera in a fixed position. But I just heard of a case where the producer shot with multiple cameras and paid the actors without even contacting the set or costume designer. The designers only found out because one of the actors called one of them after the fact. The producer obviously didn't intend to tell them, thinking that they would not learn about it and payment could therefore be avoided, or that they were just ignorant of the clause in the agreement they had signed. In any case, now the designers will have to get the union to try to enforce the provisions of the agreement and collect, which is far better than if they had to use personal funds to defend themselves.

Computing fees for some of the concert tours can be very difficult because you cannot be sure how much time and travel you may be getting yourself into. So, again, be very clear in your agreement about how you are to be paid. Yes, you will miss on some situations that just could not be foreseen, but learn from these, and you will do even better next time. And remember Mark Gray's line, quoted in chapter 17: don't be afraid to ask for a rate that makes you almost want to laugh. Management can only say no, and oddly enough, once in a while, they'll say yes.

Corporate Shows

A number of the key producers of corporate shows are signatories to the USA agreement. The "Individual Artists Agreement" would probably be appropriate. In fact, the words "Industrial Productions" are actually in the USA Constitution, but nothing is directly said about concerts or themed design work. The theatre fee schedules are quite representative of what you can expect for the smaller regional corporate shows. The bigger multinational firms will pay much higher rates, but you will have to work your way up the food chain to get in with these producers, who only work with seasoned designers. Many do use Broadway veterans, both for their skill and as a marketing tool with clients. Just remember: these shows are probably the most intense work you will ever do, especially for stage managers and lighting designers who are working the actual live production. Any slip could cost your client the contract with the corporation. A lot of money is at stake, so be prepared for long days and a highly charged atmosphere.

From a creative point of view, I have always found these the most interesting shows because I meld my experience in theatre, dance, TV, and concerts . . . all in the same production. And, like any show, they are all unique and can be extremely rewarding, both financially and creatively.

Television/Film

In most markets, the designers will be covered by an IATSE or IBEW local. This area is well organized by the unions, except in the very small local television markets and independent producers. Thus you will most likely have to be a member to work for them. Consult with the local for the specific rules about joining. When it comes to film or some video production companies, there is a grayer line. If the company has been formed specifically to produce a single project, which is often the case, there may not have been time for the union to organize the workers. In that case, the union will often give permission for you to work—*if* you are paid the going union contract rates. The film and TV locals do not have any form contracts like what the USA has for designers' use. Mostly the studios and production companies will use the "deal memo" form. In most cases, they will have their own, and you will be asked to just fill in the blanks. It is up to you to negotiate your best rate. But if you are a USA member, you might be able to use the USA "Independent Artist's Agreement" for the protection it affords and the contribution to your health and welfare funds.

Remember, the major studios and TV networks are part of the Hollywood Collective Bargaining Agreement that says you must work a specific amount of days for a company that is a signatory of the agreement to get on the roster to be allowed to work for the producer. The old "Catch-22 Syndrome" is definitely at work here. Working for one of these producers does not automatically give you union membership. They are two separate issues, because the agreement says that the producer cannot hire a person who is not already on the roster. But to get on the roster, a person has to, among other qualifications, have worked for a producer who *is* a signatory to the agreement. Therefore, it is conceivable that you already hold IA membership, but are not on the roster. The one practical way, whether you are already in the union or not—and remember, you have to be on the roster to work at the major studios, and union membership is not the sole criterion for making it onto the roster—is to get the producer to ask for a waiver to hire you because of "special skills," such as your ability to climb mountains while operating a camera, design and light underwater productions, program computer lighting, or construct period costumes. Another more common way is to be on a non-union crew that votes to join the IA. Then you will be grandfathered into the union and the roster.

Does this cover work for entry-level designers and technicians? Probably not. There are hundreds of independent producers in Hollywood, and there are a large number of cable networks that are not signatories to a union collective bargaining agreement. Any of these can be your starting point, both to get work experience and to get what is most coveted in Hollywood—a *reel* of material that shows your design work. In Hollywood, a reel is your best sales tool. And don't be surprised if the producer says, "Send me your reel," not your resume. So, start collecting tapes of your work from the producer or even off-air copies—any way you can to get to tape a show.

Now I guess I am obliged to answer the question myself. No, I do not have a reel anymore. I have done them, but for the past twenty-plus years I have had a program on the air virtually six days a week to which I can refer a potential client. Currently, my focus is not on TV, so I would be hard pressed to get a reel together quickly. They are very time-consuming and expensive to produce. And they are out-of-date after your next project. So, if you wish to take the path from lighting designer to director of photography, consider that you will incur this as a cost of doing business.

Themed Entertainment

If you are to work for an independent company that designs rides or parks as its prime business, then there may be a union contract in place that covers your designer work. However, such coverage is spotty. There are only a few companies that fall under the USA agreement. Again, using the "Individual Artists Agreement" would be the correct procedure here if you were a union member. Then there is a layer of builder-owned parks, such as Sea World, that do not, to my knowledge, have an agreement for their designers. The park employees who run the rides and maintain the equipment are also rarely unionized, and designers are not kept on staff. So it is a moot point. If you are hired to make changes to an existing project, try and use the "Project Only Agreement," or at least try and become an actual employee so you can get the health and welfare benefits during the time you are working on the project. As for fees, the parks have been doing this a long time now, and they will have their own fee schedule already worked out. Can you get more? You should always try to raise the bar; there is nothing to lose.

When it comes to working for the major theme park builders and owners, Universal or Disney, there are very specific employee plans that probably will not allow for negotiation. And, as I told one of my younger employees who had been offered a design spot on the team that was to build Universal's Japanese park, *do it for the experience and the travel, but I think you will hate the corporate culture and politics.* He's now back with us and says I hit the nail on the head. Don't get me wrong; many people have worked for these companies for years, with excellent relations. Our newest partner worked for Disney's Imagineering for several years. It is a wonderful way to build up a contact base and valuable experience. But such companies know that, so don't be shocked by what they offer. Make the best of it, learn as much as you can, and then choose what to do next. But you probably should approach the work more for the knowledge and experience to be gained than the financial rewards—although they will still be, I believe, well above regional theatre rates.

Before closing this section, I must advise you that there is a new term being used in this market: *location-based entertainment*. Since the architects and owners of theme parks also create restaurants, shopping malls, events such as the attractions connected to the Olympic games, and so much more, the field is growing. There are a lot of opportunities for young designers waiting to be found. Since the unions do not have a complete roster of employers, I suggest contacting TEA (Themed Entertainment Association) and possibly joining. TEA also operates an availability list of people that can be accessed by potential employers and that you can take advantage of as part of your search for work.

Architectural

As far as I know, the IA does not have any jurisdiction with architectural firms. Since they are turning more and more to theatrical designers to add that special creative element to their buildings, there is a growing need to have representation. What form that should take is another matter. Since many look very favorably on the certification program run and jointly sponsored by IALD (International Association of Lighting Designers) and AIA (American Institute of Architects) for which a lighting person can get an LC (Lighting Certification), that may be the best route. IA or USA membership cards don't guarantee you work, but they do show experience, so your membership should be listed as a major selling point. Architects see themselves as professionals, like lawyers and doctors, who have never been widely unionized in the United States.

Fees will be structured by the firm based on a very complicated system. You will probably have very little negotiating room if you are seeking permanent employment. As an outside consultant on a per-project basis, know that there are a growing number of design firms that specialize in this area, and they have very competitive pricing. Clients know this and usually ask for bids on projects from these firms. This work is priced on a daily and hourly rate system for associate designers and principals, with breakout costs for drafting. Take a look at a book on architects' fee planning to get a view of the way they structure their fees. You can bid as an individual, of course, but be prepared to spend a lot of time and money preparing a submittal package. It is not easy for an individual to compete for this business, but it is done. And in fact, some architects seek out name designers to add to the prestige of the firm, so there are always possibilities.

Theatre

Now we are at the heart of the theatrical unions' area of influence. However, they do not cover every design opportunity you will encounter. Again, the best approach is to contact the union local that you believe has jurisdiction. See if it will give you a list of the producers who are signatories to its agreement. If the producer doesn't show up on the list, you can ask for permission to work for her, especially if it is at higher than union-scheduled rates. There are a lot of theatre companies that fall under the radar of the unions. Small community theatres are where many young designers will find their initial professional design assignments. Assuming that you do not have enough work experience to qualify for union membership and have not passed the union exam, you are not legally obligated to adhere to the union contract. But I would suggest that, if nothing else, you use the union fee schedule as your watermark, and don't let the producer talk you into working for slave wages.

The big issues are who pays for your insurance and whether there is a re-use clause. By the latter, I mean the re-airing of the show without paying the designer an additional fee, which is generally much smaller than that from the first airing, and so on with successive airings. The situation is easier to resolve because producers in this field are used to such a clause. They still may not want to sign one, but they know it is coming, so there is room to negotiate.

Loan-Out Companies

Are there other ways to protect your health and welfare plan? The solution is to have your own loan-out company and become a signatory to the union agreement. Then any work you do is covered by your union contract. This has some great advantages. First, you will gain access to the union health plan, a retirement fund, and other benefits without setting up your own private fund. These are items that you, as a small company, would pay a much higher rate to obtain. Particularly if you are already paying union dues, why not take advantage of the full plan? There is one small problem: in many situations, the IA will insist that all employees of your company must be covered under some union. If you hire a draftsperson or assistant full-time or even part-time, he or she will need to follow the union rules, and you will be required to pay him or her at the union scheduled rates. Even a general office worker will need to belong to a clerical union. It does make your business paperwork and obligations more involved, but it is something to consider for everyone's benefit. And yes, in most cases, even if the producer you are working for is not a signatory to the IA agreement, you can work because you are working for a company that is a signatory. The only hitch could be if the production were picketed by the union; as a union member, you had better think, should I cross the line, and what are the consequences if I do or don't?

Unions Changing

The situation with the USA locals has undergone a huge change since it separated from the International Painters and aligned with the IATSE a few years ago. There is a lot of work ahead for the union to cement its position. Currently, there is a major push to increase the membership. This is definitely a renewal and reorganization period for USA. And I applaud the union's commitment to bettering the theatrical designer's life. With the added weight of the IATSE behind USA's efforts to solidify its position as the representative of theatrical designers in theatre, as well as other media, I can see the possibility of a brighter future for all designers.

But in the meantime, designers must negotiate their own fees and working conditions for the majority of their work outside of Broadway or at the LORT theatres around the country. I hope that they will turn their organizing efforts to themed and concert design representation very soon.

It is a tough decision for a new entrant into the professional world to turn down any work while trying to build a reputation, let alone feed yourself and possibly your family. But there is a pitfall here. The producers know very well how much you need to work, and they are out to take every advantage they can to keep their costs down. You must look at your financial needs and really consider if the project is going to advance your career. Also, clearly consider that a producer unwilling to be a signatory may be a sleazy one, and you may end up not getting paid. Without the unions, you have no one to defend you in your attempt to collect, except an overpriced attorney who doesn't know anything about the field and will charge you while he learns.

The unions are there for your protection. They have spent a lot of time and money on their members' behalf in working with production companies and individual producers to ensure they are legitimate. I believe you should take a step back from any producers who are unwilling to work with the union contract; there is often a reason for their not being a signatory. And that reason may very well be that they do not live up to their commitments—and you will just become another name in a long list of unpaid designers.

CHAPTER 20
The View from the Producer's Desk

Over the years, I have often done surveys of producers for my articles and books on concert lighting. I have not seen an appreciable change in producers' attitude toward designers and crews in general, except they now know they can play one designer or equipment rental house against another to get the cheapest price. Yet I also don't see it getting any harder to work with them, either. Their view has always been centered on the bottom line, which hasn't changed and probably never will. But they are even less inclined to want to work with the theatrical unions—with the exception of the LORT theatres, who last year signed a collective bargaining agreement with USA after a six-year fight. Establishing a union presence is a battle, but it has seen some softening now that the LORT theatres have come in line. The fight in other media—theme parks, corporate shows, and parties—is still very hard, but some progress has been made.

Without making any assumptions, let us look at what I believe underlies this their position that we are asking for too much, that we should be honored to work with the artist, and so on. First and foremost, as I have said before, the people who run the production companies and serve on the boards of not-for-profit theatres are businesspeople who have been schooled in the belief that the end product is not to make the best car or serve the best food, but to give the shareholders a return on their investment. That is the American system of business. Even if the production is not a publicly traded stock, the paramount concern of the CEO will be how the books look to the owners or backers.

Theatre

Even if a theatre company is a not-for-profit group, the producers quickly realize that if they do not meet their budget and build a reserve (profit by any other name, but since they are tax-exempt groups, they couch it in a different language to go through the legal loophole), they can't keep the theatre going. To accomplish that they believe they must do three things. First, get corporate sponsorship; second, sell tickets; and lastly, find federal grant money. One show that does poorly can pull down three other marginally profitable shows in a season and make the final figures look less than attractive. It turns out that ticket sale grosses are the real variable, and the one they cannot rely on to pay the overhead.

A corporate mentality is at work here. Not-for-profit groups rely on sponsorship to make up any income shortfall. As strange as it sounds, these sponsors want to back a winning horse—not critically, for they don't care about *ART*. But they are not going to associate their name with a theatre that does not do well financially. So, as another old banking adage goes, *you must have money to attract money*. The financially strapped theatre companies who really need the support of corporate sponsors can't get it because they don't have any money.

If you can see that this is true with not-for-profits, you can begin to see the picture that develops for commercial ventures. When it comes to a commercial theatre producer, you find a person educated to think left-brain, probably trained as a lawyer or accountant. He is completely paperwork centered. In recent years, this type of producer is more and more associated with the Broadway shows and national tours. The days of Broadway Danny Rose (A Woody Allen character in the 1984 film by the same name) are over; gone are the days of the old Broadway producer who loved the people, the neon way . . . you get the idea. Then you have the enigma of Disney, which entered the Broadway market by completely refurbishing an old theatre and getting New York politicians to clean up the area around the theatre. Since then, Disney has done the same for two theatres in Los Angeles. So you can expect the corporate Disney mentality to be the same in its theatre venues, the El Capitan and the Pantages theatres in Los Angeles, and in New York, the New Amsterdam Theatre, as it is in its theme parks.

The producing directors at the LORT level of regional theatre and smaller have a more personal stake in the future of their theatres because their continued employment depends on receiving critical acclaim and community support. They spend a lot of time with grant writers and sponsors who can supplement the ticket income. Therefore they often have dual personalities concerning their goals: get cash, and do good theatre. It is unquestionably the toughest producer position in theatre today. They may still be bottom-liners who will do whatever they have to do to keep production costs down. But on the whole they recognize that decent fees must be paid to attract quality designers—or at least barely "living," in their interpretation of the word. That is why the new LORT agreement is so important to all designers.

At the community theatre and Equity waiver production level, the union is not a controlling factor. Since this is often the entry level for a designer, the competition keeps the fees low. And the producer knows she can trade a program credit for a lower fee because the designers at this level are trying to establish themselves. Plus, the fact is that the potential for making money in small 99- to 250-seat theatres is slim to none. Although Equity does require contracts for actors and stage managers that allow for a percentage of non-Equity actors to be in the same production as Equity actors (mostly in minor roles), there is no effort by Equity to insist that USA designers be used, let alone IA stagehands.

The picture for theatre designers will always be cloudy until IA and Equity come together in a united front. But that will probably never happen given the current economic climate in the United States and the history between the two groups. Therefore, the designer who wants to get a credit on a show that will be reviewed needs to take the work he can get. This credit will then go toward building the professional resume that is part of the requirement to get into the union, anyway. Again the Catch-22 problem: you may want to support the union, but you can't get in without professional credits.

And the producers know it. So, understand that these people may say their goal is to just keep the theatre doors open, they are not looking at the paint and lights; more often than not, they are looking at the journal ledger. You will have to use the win-win negotiating technique if you hope to get any money from them.

Corporate

When we move over to corporate shows, the money is a little looser because the producers have probably been involved with big budgets for years. They know all the elements that go into producing a onetime, mega show. A new term that you will hear under this heading is the "change order," also extremely popular in architectural circles. After a pitch has been done and the client agrees to the budget, the creative process is hardly done. Many, many more meetings and creative sessions will happen, and there will be changes suggested either by the client or the producer. In either case, a "change order" is a document that the client is asked to sign that essentially says she will pay X dollars for the script change, casting more dancers, new slides, film, set pieces, and other expenses, over and above the original concept and its proposed budget. It is never taken on word alone that the client will pay for anything new, so the producer does this religiously. How does that affect you? Simple: if you are in a meeting and make a suggestion for a change, never, ever give an estimate of the cost unless asked by the producer—never the client. The show producer will mark up the actual costs, and if you have already said what it will cost, you are really speaking of out-of-pocket or net cost. So, never offer any cost estimate without the producer very clearly asking for it, if you expect to work for the producer again.

Producers who do this work, on the whole, lean more toward an advertising mentality rather than a theatrical one. Here, theatre is the end to the means of selling the product: the show. So, be very clear when you go into a meeting with them that you understand what is expected and how to act. Have a very good portfolio presentation prepared. Make it short and very visual. These producers tend to utilize a same small cadre of designers. If you do well with one, the word will spread to the others. Your stock can be as high or as low as the last show you were involved in, no matter how well you did your part. And lastly, don't take it personally if producers don't use you again right after doing a terrific job on a show. They are susceptible to the same illogical whim as others in advertising. The line, *we just want to go in a different direction*, is often heard at the same time they are saying what a wonderful job you did. Don't take it personally; just move on to the next project. They'll probably be back.

Theme and Location-Based Entertainment

Enter *themed entertainment* and *location-based entertainment*—which is the new term that seems to be coming into vogue to define the difference between theme parks with rides and businesses that use the "themed" idea to attract customers in such places as restaurants, museums, and shopping malls. Disney and Universal are the major players around the world on the park side, but there are other such park groups like Sea World and Six Flags Inc. These companies recruit heavily in colleges for young, fresh (cheap) designers looking to establish themselves and pay back college loans. Unfortunately, they do not have a great reputation for keeping many people long-term. Rather, they hire on a project-to-project basis, except for the core group, and when the project is over, you are out. Then you may be rehired a week or month later for the next project. They view this as cost management, centered wholly around the project without much consideration for the people they displace.

Themed entertainment companies often go outside for creative design services, but there is a corporate mentality that is at work. Even though the division that oversees the design of the park is part of the corporation, the people who will operate it after completion are often left out of the planning and don't get any input prior to opening. Therefore it can be very frustrating to find that the concept of the show does not fit into the physical structure presumably designed to house it.

They also do not want to hear about how cost-effective running the facility will be, or what the lamp life will be, because that is another division's problem. And be prepared for a multiple layer of people that think you are working for them. The executive game is hard at work, and people constantly are jockeying for position. Then, when the project is ready to launch, do not be surprised if you are not even invited to the opening. Again, another division has taken control, and this is about the time you will get a notice that your services are no longer needed. Even if another project is about to start up, you will often need to reapply as if you were never there. That is just the way they work, which is very inefficient from our perspective, but not from the corporate perspective.

The other avenue for work in this field is through outside producers who are contracted by the theme park or location-based client to create and develop a theme from concept to script to storyboards, to design the attraction. The producer will likely subcontract many members of the design team rather than keep a staff of designers who must be paid when there are no projects in-house. In this regard, they are no different than the big theme park employers, but they are much more flexible about their "hired guns" working for other clients at the same time or possibly teaching at a university and moonlighting, so to speak.

These companies will even go to the extent of asking for bids by designers for their services and negotiate back and forth between designers to get the lowest price. Some independent show producers like designers to be part of a company so that they can be assured that the designer is a legal, independent contractor, since independent show producers are in essence subcontractors to the site owners themselves.

Film

Wall Street loves the film industry. Studio and big producers', such as Dream-Works S.K.G.'s, stock is always well received, and although it can fluctuate, the facts are that over the years, the return on investment in entertainment stock has been very consistently in the positive range. A single film can cost hundreds of millions of dollars, and many do not gross more than they cost to make, but there are also after-market sales of DVDs, tie-ins with fast-food concerns, tee-shirts, and other merchandise that can bring in many millions more.

The percentage of profit on a film is much higher than in other categories of venture capital offerings, so the prospects are excellent that there will be a return on the investment, which attracts investors. The producers, director, and stars can take a huge chunk of the budget for themselves, although it is quite normal to defer the majority of it until after the film is released. Very often, these same people get "loans" from the studio against the film's future earnings, thus avoiding some tax issues and making it seem that they are sometimes working for "scale." Yet the "back-end" money (the money deferred prior to filming) after the film has been released can amount to millions of extra dollars.

The producer/star of 1990's *Dances with Wolves* was accused of just such a trick, when he reportedly talked the crew into accepting minimum fees to make a "meaningful statement of the plight of the Native Americans" and then reaped enormous residuals after the film was released. He didn't offer to share this windfall with the crew. Case in point: do not be sucked into the "we are doing it for the art" ploy, be it for film or theatre. Believe me, the producer and actors are in it for the money, whether they get it now or in the future.

Producers know that they can hire a crew to actually shoot the film for a fraction of the total cost of making the picture. But there is hope: after a hard struggle, you can reap a big cash reward once you make it to the creative positions of production designer or director of photography. Eventually you have the potential to make a lot of money. But as in the world of the stock market, only the strong survive!

All this means that there is a lot of money changing hands, but it also widens the gap between the haves and the have-nots. Top designers do very, very well, but the working crew members are pigeonholed and categorized into their union classification and will be hard-pressed to beat the "street rate" for any nondesign position they get on a film. If you are interested in production design, there is no way to get there but to work for an established designer as an assistant. You must work your way up the food chain. Expect financial rewards to be in the middle to low end at the beginning of that climb up the mountain. However, the fact is that most gaffers (master electricians) can make six-figure incomes. On par with theatre, there is virtually no comparison in pay.

Concerts

Touring is a wide-open game. Mostly an artist's management company will hire you if you are the lighting, sound, or scenic designer. Then the equipment and crew will probably be contracted separately from a major touring supplier, or a major scenic construction shop will build the set.

When it comes to negotiating with the artist's managers, remember that you are a necessary evil to them. They would be very happy to have their artist go on stage in a single spotlight. The only reason a production is built around most singers is the artist's desire to present a show. Do not try to appeal to managers in creative terms, they are only interested in what they can do that will keep the artist happy and cost as little as possible. That doesn't mean that a designer cannot make a lot of money in this field, but the hours are long and the travel constant, so be prepared.

In a very few cases, management will have had the artist's own road designer stay on payroll, but the actual big tour design is given to a "name" designer. That name designer then turns the design over to the artist's person to operate on the road. Management sees this as a cost issue. A top designer, although managers want that level of creativity, is too expensive on a daily fee basis, so they would rather use someone who is loyal (and cheap) and knows the artist.

Scenic and costume designers rarely go on the road with a concert tour, and they may be able to get management to sign an agreement using the USA "Individual Artist Agreement." Sound engineers that tour are a different breed than studio engineers. Although some crossover is possible, it is rare for the studio engineer to be the tour sound mixer. I am told it takes a different ear, and the sound reinforcement equipment and techniques used on tour are vastly different than studio gear. Management, but only at the insistence of the artist, will sometimes keep the recording engineer on retainer when the band is not touring—which shows how closely they work with and how important they are to the artist for his or her individual sound. It is very, very rare for a lighting designer, even when one has been with the same artist for fifteen or twenty years, to get a retainer. I only know a couple, including U2's designer, Willie Williams, who doubles as the show concept designer with the band.

Financing the Production

I must tell you that I have rarely come across a producer in any entertainment field who doesn't cry about how much he has to pay for design services and stage crews, how he doesn't have the budget to pay, and that the unions are killing him with their demands. It must be a mantra they are taught in business school.

Luckily, theatre producers are not on the top of my list of producers I do not trust. Frankly, I find corporate producers to be the most up front—although very business-oriented—of any I negotiate with. You always know what their goals are, and if they like what you present, you will probably get the job without a big battle over costs.

Now I need to vent a little. I will make the disclaimer that not all producers are like the following examples, but do be on guard. My experience with producers time after time leaves me shaking my head. The same person who has the gall to sit behind a $5,000 mahogany desk in a thirty-story office tower tells me he doesn't have the budget to pay what I am asking—and then, with a straight face, tells me he needs to hire a road masseuse. That makes me seriously consider buying a bookstore in a small town. I can almost guarantee you this is the same producer who later will not hesitate to spend production money to fly his girlfriend out to the location and charge it off to the production. Or—and I have direct experience with this one—have the carpenters come to his home and do a remodeling job while they are on the production payroll.

To me, the funniest thing is when a production manager has his neat little budget spread out and tells me the lighting equipment budget won't handle the bids he has received from the suppliers. What makes this really hard to comprehend is that the budget was probably developed without any knowledge on the part of the people creating it as to the specifics of the production. In other words, the director and production designers haven't met. And when I ask what another line item is costing, because I know it is under budget and the funds could easily be transferred to the lighting, I get a look like I must be totally crazy. No one knows what the specific needs are going to be, yet you will be hard-pressed to shift any funds between line items, even if you are not asking to review the total budget.

Another wrinkle is a line producer whose deal is that, as an incentive bonus, she gets to keep whatever she can save on the production budget. This is unbelievable to me, but I have been involved on TV specials where this was the reported case. If this is what you think is happening to you, know that you will never get enough money, so don't waste your time trying.

The Promoter

It may appear that the job of a promoter isn't any different than that of a producer. And it is true that often the producer and the promoter are one in the same. The distinction I make is that a promoter is not the person or entity that developed the show. Promoters do not have any say in the content of the show. They do, however, have a voice in the physical requirements, such as crew, safety of the facility, and security issues connected with the show. While the producer sees the production from concept to opening, the promoter sees it from show date to load-out and then moves on to the next show.

Promoters are often attached to the facility, either by a negotiated exclusive contract, or in a staff capacity. They can also be large national promoters who will book all or regional sections of a tour. The national promoter fronts money for the rehearsal time, possibly tour staging and lighting equipment, and national promotional materials. He will then bring in local promoters who are more attuned to their markets and facilities to provide on-site assistance. This way, the artist and the production staff have one source to go to for their needs, and there is more consistency in execution of the preproduction planning. For all this, the national promoter takes on a major financial commitment, believing that the artist will sell well enough to pay back all his costs and then some, which is the gamble. But you will have time to learn all about them, as it will take a while before you reach this heady country. Many colleges promote shows via an entity they have formed either within the administration of the school or a local private promoter. Some radio stations use their in-house promotions department to book shows. They have the contacts to work closely with the newspapers and local radio stations because they are heavy media buyers. The key is they are usually the ones who know the local markets and what audiences want to see. In fact, they are basing their whole business on it, literally. All in all, promoters come in a very wide range of experience, expertise, and financial backing (deep pockets).

So why would a designer need to know about this person? Often a local promoter is the business entry point for lighting designers and sound engineers. Though they are not strictly producers, they may have control of a local club or small venue at which they produce younger artists. Also, there is work for a lighting designer with a local promoter when a big headliner plays his venue because the opening act may not have its own designer, and the promoter either provides one or suggests a local person—who can be you.

For the scenic artist, a local promoter could produce a festival or a summer concert series that will require design elements. Often we see the front of the sound towers covered with a theme design or even a full proscenium with a design. There is no reason that a theatre-trained designer cannot do this work easily. Other promoters regularly do fairs or antique shows and car shows that may need a designer to do floor plans, site allocation arrangements, and signage.

From an employment standpoint, the best opportunity is for a production manager. This is often a great way for someone interested in management to become involved in professional production. Promoters and artist management companies hire people in this position to look out for their interests. Though the title probably will be "promoter's representative," the job encompasses all the work the production manager has been trained to do, plus some.

There is usually the added responsibility of settling up the box office receipts at the end of the night. This is where the box office manager, the artist's representative (most often the road manager or tour accountant), and the promoter's representative look over the ticket sales. They subtract the total by seats sold, paper (free tickets given as part of a marketing promotion), and, finally, a count of the "dead wood" (the unused tickets). All this is tallied against the seating chart so the appropriate split of the profit, less expenses (rent, local crew, security, advertising, etc.), can be calculated. Many artists get a percentage of sales over a set figure, banking on their name as a draw. This helps lessen the promoter's exposure to loss. Now is when the chapter on accounting will come in handy.

When a dance company or legitimate play tours, they also deal with a group other than the producer. This is often called the booking agency. But even with a concert artist there can be a booking agency. So, unless the producer has a national organization to handle promotion and ticket sales, there probably will be many local promoters involved. Sometimes the local promoter is actually a group that promotes a "season" at a theatre or summer venue. Some of the productions may be designed and mounted in-house, while others are booked as a package production from outside sources. All these offer work to the designer and production mangers, especially when starting out.

Will time change the way management, producers, and promoters treat the designers and crews? I doubt it; not as long as M.B.A.s are in charge. But there are exceptions, such as producers who love theatre and know what it takes to put on a great production, and promoters who simply love music. Let me know when you meet them, please!

CHAPTER 21
The Designer's Perspective

When I tried to conduct a survey among a diverse group of designers using a specific set of questions, I failed to get the results that could be translated into meaningful comments for this book. There was no way to construct a statistical set of charts to show trends. The problem is that every designer I interviewed had taken a different road, which includes an infinite number of roads to the work they are currently doing. But I knew that this had to be addressed. And though I know it would be foolish to think that any one person can speak for a whole industry, there needed to be some recap of the issues repeatedly raised by the designers I spoke with, even when voiced in many different ways. I feel that the comments I make in this chapter relate to them and are as valid as any I could have quoted.

Most of the comments are given as generalities that cross the broadest spectrum of entertainment design, but I did allow a couple of people to speak directly about their perspective of the business. Paul Dexter is a lighting designer for museum projects, concerts, and corporate shows, as well as a columnist for two trade publications. He has also been a friend for most of both our careers. I will leave it to him to speak in his own voice. Speaking for the young professional is Matt Levesque, a 1997 graduate of Boston College. Matt has now experienced several levels on his journey up the ladder to big-time designer status, first as an intern, then as an associate designer. He enjoyed a stint as a site production manager during the construction of a new theme park, and is now a freelance designer.

To begin with, I hope this book has not left you with the impression that I believe that schools have failed you as a design student. I am encouraged to discover, when I visit universities to speak to students and faculty alike, that they are more aware than ever of the larger design industry out there, and that any constraint in providing more information on the business of design will be helped by this book. I sincerely hope that this volume will be the mortar that fills in the cracks in your design education.

In the end, the solid foundation you receive in your formal education will be what gives you strength to challenge your creative abilities. The schools can't teach you to be creative, but they can give you some of the tools it will take to awaken within you the ability to focus what creativity you possess.

Whether you already have some of the business skills I believe you need to be financially self-sufficient, or you believe you can continue to rely on someone else, is another issue. That will partially determine what path you take in your career and how much you are willing to take chances. You should never put yourself into a situation for which you do not have the coping tools. It is how you choose to use those tools that makes the difference between success in entertainment design and the need to start thinking about making a career change.

There are two areas I want to address in these closing remarks that were themes that came up again and again with designers. Although specific areas of entertainment have their unique problems for the designer, these transcend all media and are essential to your career.

Intellectual Property and Ownership

The issues of intellectual property and ownership concern costumers and scenic designers more than lighting and sound designers, because it is difficult to protect a light plot or sound levels and microphone placement from venue to venue. When producers hand you a contract, you are virtually assured they have written into the agreement that the design work you are doing is a "work made for hire." Copyright law says works of authorship, such as any type of written work, artwork, graphics, photograph, sculpture, video, music, and architectural plans and designs, are automatically protected by copyright the moment they are created. But if the work is a "work made for hire," the employer owns all rights to the material. In that case, all the copyrights flow to the employer, not you as the creator of the work. Now, there can be partial assignment of rights, such as the right to reproduce under specific circumstances or for consideration of a fee. All that is very flexible and can be agreed to among the parties. Thus if the show is a hit and moves to another theatre or city, you may or may not be involved, but it could still be your design that is used. USA is very watchful of this issue in its contracts.

In California, an employer who hires you as part of the design team can be considered the employer and therefore must pay workers' compensation, unemployment, and disability insurance under CAL Labor Code 3351.5 (c). California is the only state with such a law. Therefore you are an employee and the producer owns the copyright on your work, unless the producer or owner of the show specifically agrees to your retaining ownership of the intellectual property. That is a very strong reason for being an independent contractor, as we have discussed before.

There are way too many stories of producers not informing the original designer of further use of her work. Unless you have made provisions to retain your ownership, they own it to do with it what they like. They are under no obligation to even give you credit for the work. Recently, a designer I know had to pull a submission for an award, because the theme park for which he had designed the attraction held all copyright to the material, and would only let the designer submit the project if the theme park's owner, rather than the designer, were listed as the creator. And all because the designer was an employee under California law.

So, be prepared to defend your ownership rights. You can agree to relinquish specific rights while retaining others, such as retaining "credit" even if not receiving future payments. Or you can allow the producer to use the set at one other venue before further payment. Whatever you can negotiate—and that is the key word: *negotiate* your rights, don't simply give all your rights to the producer. We get very little for our work monetarily; to lose the credit for the work, is, to me, the ultimate slap in the face.

Be a Problem-Solver

One of the most important nondesign, nonbusiness skills you need to attain is the ability to be a problem-solver. Don't underestimate how much time problem-solving will take up for you. Remember, what we do is participate as part of a "team." My belief is that much of my work is actually done after the light plot is completed. All the other issues—actors' movement, scenic problems, costume colors, space limitations, power concerns, on-time delivery of components, and crew—are then dumped in my lap. I have my road map, but I can't predict what detours I will face or how I will navigate around them. As a sailor, I must constantly check the approaching weather and be on the lookout for other ships to keep my vessel on a safe and steady course. At air traffic control school, we were taught to constantly consider the real possibility of problems so that we could quickly make a decision that could save lives. People could die if we let emotion interfere with judgment. I am not advocating that we should be dispassionate. We are by nature right-brained people. Logic doesn't always come easily to designers. Now, if you are thinking of becoming a production or stage manager, you should more appropriately fit into the left-brained, logic-minded group.

Many people say they support the position that balance in your skills of creative and logical interpretation of an issue will move a career forward faster. A design is not even half finished when the plans are completed. I am sure that the sound designers feel the same way, because whatever has been recorded will sound different in the actual environment of the theatre, with or without an audience. Costumers need to have the costume on an actual actor to make the costumes come alive. Color renderings of sets often fall far short of the actual painting because of inexperienced scene painters.

In all we do, we must combine creativity with logic, business acumen, and a respect for the needs of the rest of the design team. With these approaches, you will be successful.

Paul Dexter's Advice

Selling yourself is as important as selling your design. You can be extremely talented, but if you lack social skills or the ability to sensibly integrate yourself and your ideas with the production, chances are good that your phone will soon stop ringing with offers of work—providing that you had already started to get work in the first place.

It is a big playground. You have to prove that you can adapt to any situation and play nicely with the other kids! This shouldn't cause any alarm. One of the side benefits of the backstage business is that it attracts like-minded people. There are exceptions, of course, because you cannot control others' personalities, but for the most part, those who are in it are there primarily for the same reasons that you are: they love it, too! Once you are accepted into the privileged culture of design—because integration with all of the other professionals involved is key—your address book will directly expand with names of people from every area needed in a production team. The subsequent camaraderie will develop, in some instances, lifelong friendships. This will become your biggest resource.

Although you may close this book with a clearer understanding of the business of design, it will not be of great consequence until you put it into practice. Understanding is one thing—practicing your newfound knowledge is another.

Knowledge will enhance your ability to recognize the physical or social elements required in the entire creative process, but practice and the painful lessons of your mistakes (and by the way, it doesn't end) are the ingredients for experience. Once experience leaves its indelible mark on your memory, that's when your confidence enters. The caveat is, use your confidence to benefit the production and your design decisions, and to add comfort to those around you without becoming haughty or condescending. Kenneth Bancroft Clark, an American educator and psychologist, said, "Pride, like humility, is destroyed by one's insistence that he possesses it."

Matt Levesque's Advice

I agree with Jim, in that I wish now that school had taught me more about the business end of my craft. My challenges have come not from not knowing how to illuminate an object but how to budget my time and myself or knowing how to handle a tough political situation. Success as a working designer is dependent on your attitude. I have to admit, even though I have been in the industry for a relatively short time now, I have never been hired for a job for my lighting skills alone. I always get the job for three reasons:

1. I am easy to work with and enjoy what I do.
2. I always come through on my promises.
3. I am always willing to say, "I don't know, but I will find out."

These are the elements that will make you successful. Very few will notice the subtlety of your lighting. Nobody will ever know how hard it was for you. But people remember how simple you made the work and how enjoyable you were to work with. This industry is a relatively small world, and your reputation, good or bad, will precede you. That's not to say you are allowed to be a lousy designer, but we are only as good as the energy we project on ideas and work relationships. So be the best person you can be, and you will succeed.

While my two contributors are both in the lighting field, I believe they speak for us all. And I have to feel that my inability to elicit comments on business from scenic and costume designers is due to a far wider gulf between these designers and a business mind-set. No matter what you read here, the approach of each of us will be influenced by our own experiences and the roads we choose to travel.

CHAPTER 22
The Future of the Business

This is the hardest chapter to write, because I do not believe anyone can predict the future. And it is folly even to say it is an "educated" guess. But why should I be any different from the "experts" who make a very good living telling us what our lives will be like ten to twenty years from now? So, I have asked several of my colleagues to give their thoughts on the subject. The views expressed have value if for no other reason than to open dialogue and encourage reflective thought, which is what you need to do to build your "business plan" for your career ahead. Many of the speakers are from the lighting side of the business. Please do not think less of their comments because you are in another design or management area. It is because of the explosion in lighting technology that I believe lighting designers as a group are simply more aware of the business issues than others, which all the more emphasizes the need for this book.

I will start with Paul Dexter again. Paul has had a varied career that pushes well outside of theatre. He has toured for years with concert artists, has designed corporate shows, and is currently heavily involved with a world-class painter and sculptor who uses lighting as part of his huge installation artwork. Paul also writes columns for commercial lighting magazines that are peppered with wit and insightfulness. Yet Paul is self-taught; he started his career as a "roadie" and learned on the go.

Paul's Thoughts

The advantage that we have as a business is that people will always need light. Lighting is a principal commodity. Owing to that, I believe that as an industry, we are going to remain in good shape. For new lighting designers, I say: diversify your knowledge into understanding how business works—this is essential! If you have to ask why, go back and read the preceding sentence again.

Liz Stillwell is a lighting designer working primarily in dance and musical theatre and is a trustee to the national executive board of the United Scenic Artists local USA-829.

Liz's Thoughts

I think the state of the business and the state of the art play off one another. The art has been getting more technical and spectacle oriented. This trend has allowed the business to become more commercial, which has demanded more high-tech, high-budget spectacle. This environment supports designers who are more businesslike and further discourages bohemian designers that are in it for the enlightenment and satisfaction of the art. I see less artistic collaboration between designers and more box-office-driven design. In this context, designers will be treated as hired guns rather than artistic partners. They will need to vigilantly protect their own rights and interests. This pattern will eventually run its course, and a new generation of collaborative designers and directors will rise from the ashes. I hope I'm still around to participate when the pendulum comes back to the art I was educated to believe in.

Jeffrey Ravitz is one of my partners. He and I have been in business together for over ten years. Jeff was raised in New Jersey, went to Northwestern University outside Chicago, and then moved to California after becoming involved in concert lighting. He still does theatre, but the majority of his work is in concert design, with a growing following for his services in television and DVD production. His success in crossing over was witnessed recently with the 2001 Primetime Emmy for television lighting design.

Jeff's Thoughts

The future will see an increasing respect for the enormous task the lighting designer has to carry out. Most shows require at least a programmer in addition to the designer. Some have two or more programmers. The amount of documentation necessary to keep track of the cue data will necessitate more personnel. The lighting design team will continue to grow in proportion to the quantity of choices to be made for each instrument.

The lighting designer will evolve into a lighting producer, leading a team of designers, programmers, project managers, assistants, and technicians through the complexities of the creative and organizational process.

All in all, the business will continue to grow more complicated. In the concert business, there still is no show director on most projects. The lighting designer remains the sole visual consultant on the majority of shows. Most still balk at the hiring of a scenic designer, thus pressuring the lighting designer to suggest and execute those elements. The result is that the lighting designer still must work to educate clients as to what the lighting is accomplishing for them. Lighting will continue to be evaluated by performers from their onstage point-of-view, making the lighting designer's job that much more difficult.

> *D. Martyn Bookwalter carries the hyphenated title you hear about only in L.A.: he is a scenic/lighting designer-art director. After moving west and struggling to make ends meet doing up to fifteen theatre projects a year, he now splits his time between being the art director on the syndicated television series* MADtv *and an average of four theatre designs a year. He has designed more than 300 productions for theatres around the country, including the Mark Taper Forum, the Geffen Playhouse, and Pasadena Playhouse, among others. He received the Angstrom Award for career achievement in lighting last year from the Los Angeles Critics Circle, and he has received two Emmy nominations for his set design work on* MADtv.

Martyn's Thoughts

I can't say it enough: build your contacts and attach yourself to working designers. This is a business based on relationships. Building solid relationships with directors, producers, and other designers will be the key to constant work. Assist as much as you can when starting out or when you want to cross over into other media. I have designed all my professional life, but it wasn't until I worked in TV that I had the freedom to pick the theatre projects and the people with whom I wished to work. I have tried to branch out as much as possible, such as taking on consulting work, teaching, and learning new skills so that I remain versatile, employable, current, and motivated.

> *Joseph Tawil has been my employer (I went to work for him right after I got out of college), mentor, and friend for over thirty years. He graduated from Carnegie Tech (now Carnegie-Mellon University) in Pittsburgh with classmate Jules Fisher, but turned the corner onto the road of marketing and sales. He founded and is the owner and president of the Great American Market, a company in Hollywood, California, that manufactures and markets color media, lighting products, and acces-*

sories. A fellow of the USITT and a person with a great love of theatre, Joe has collaborated with the world's designers to create tools to help them create their designs.

Joe's Thoughts

Looking back can help you determine where you are going. The trend in lighting equipment has been automation, compression in size, expansion of efficiency, and even widening choices. So, what does that predict for the future? It seems that we will have a lot more toys to pick from as we go forward, and more options than ever before. It doesn't make it easy for the designer or technician to learn all he or she needs to know about the business, but it does make it more interesting. So, at the top of my list of where we're going in the future is that we have more choices, more innovative lighting sources, and new optical systems—and probably a complete lack of standards so that nothing will be interchangeable.

There was a time not too long ago when, if you had 200 conventional lights on a Broadway show, you had an enormous amount of equipment. Now if it is only 200 moving lights, you can probably get by if you have to. But moving lights require many channels of control. We will need boards that do more and interface easily with the operator. The multiple channels of control required to direct robotic equipment is too time-consuming and too tedious. We need a way to just touch or point at the light board to tell it where to go and it goes there, at the same time changing the color, beam size, shape, and whatever else we can think of that needs changing. I make these projections fully aware that somebody might read this twenty years from now (or sooner) and get quite a laugh. But I have been betting on the future of the industry all my life, and I'm not going to stop now.

Mike Zinman, another young designer and one who has taken the idea of a side business seriously, is the creator of Auto-BLOCK 2000, a lighting program compatible with CAD for creating lighting plots and the paperwork. Mike is also an active theatre and corporate show designer in Southern California who has had no formal training.

Mike's Thoughts

In the not-so-distant future, technology will play a much larger role in the creative world than today. With software to aid vision and hardware to execute it, the lighting designer only needs to be imaginative. He or she must understand

and utilize the technology available. Great tools are out there to be used. However, we must not let the technology overshadow our creativity.

As the mighty beam projector of the past has been replaced with the oversaturation of moving lights, and pen and ink exchanged for the mouse, will it get better?

The overuse of technology may not be a plus. Will it smother the creativity so necessary to create a perfect design? Will technology merely enable us to quickly overload a stage with too much superfluous equipment that creates chaos and not art?

I guess we'll have to see.

Craig Wolf, professor of theatre at San Diego State University, is an active designer in his own right. Craig is also the coauthor, with W. Oren Parker, of Scene Design and Stage Lighting, *the eighth edition of which will be out in late 2002. As a dedicated educator and professional designer, Craig has actively brought his insight to students and professionals alike with his writings and participation in many committees of the USITT.*

Craig's Thoughts

Although it has been a fairly quiet shift, the manner in which educational institutions view the requirement for teaching theatrical design has changed a great deal over the past twenty years. Due in part to the proliferation of M.F.A. graduate design programs, it is no longer possible for a student to graduate and move directly into a teaching position at a major institution. Theatre departments now demand that new faculty have some degree of professional experience, and larger programs additionally require teaching experience. Combined with requiring more experience of their new faculty, foresighted institutions are looking to hire lighting designers with additional experience in fields other than theatre. Graduate training of young lighting designers has shifted from the previous narrow concern with legitimate theatre to design for a variety of entertainment fields, industry, and architecture. The most desirable lighting faculty member of the future will be a proven theatrical designer, but will also possess interest and experience in related fields. Major training programs across the nation currently have in place healthy exchanges with fields such as television and film, themed entertainment, and architecture, which enhance the education of their students. This trend will continue as theatre education adjusts to the marketplace and maintains its place as the appropriate training ground for lighting design.

Dawn Hollingsworth has a unique perspective on the issues concerning the future of the business, as she was trained at the University of Oklahoma in theatre and migrated to Chicago to start her career. After moving to Los Angeles, she went to work for an architectural lighting manufacturer in marketing, sales, applications, and management, obtaining her M.B.A. from Pepperdine University before joining my company, which then became Visual Terrain, as the managing partner several years ago. She still actively designs corporate shows, and most of her work focuses on architecture. Her most visible projects to date are the towers at LAX Gateway.

Dawn's Thoughts

The future will be nothing less than amazing. Theatrical designers from all disciplines are expanding beyond the fourth wall to participate in the creation of experiences. Many of these opportunities may be from nontraditional producers or new media ventures. It is incumbent upon all of us, especially the educators, to accept and encourage the opening of these doors as being as legitimate as the theatre from which they sprang.

My Thoughts

I believe we see the future in the past, so I will base my observations on history, a history that I have been a part of for more than half a lifetime—and not just half of my own life, but also half of the life of the field of lighting design. What does all this have to do with the future of the entertainment design business? A lot, because you will create the future and it will become the history. You create the past every day. So your future is up to you. But without trying to foretell the future, I can make some predictions.

Predictions are not pronouncements, which would be useless to make. Even large corporations, which pay millions of dollars a year to research firms, know how little they can accurately forecast the future. A top executive at Universal Studios once told me that he hated sitting in on these "assessment of market share and projections" meetings. He said he always feels like the whole thing was a giant waste of resources. But the studio heads have to protect their stockholders' investment; they have to do strategic planning. Yet in the end, it is anybody's guess as to what is actually going to happen. All they can do is imagine possible scenarios, and then not be too shocked when they don't come true.

The entertainment design business is much like that. We shouldn't be shocked when a prediction doesn't come true. You may think you have your careers strategically planned from the time you entered college. Be a theatre designer, go to Broadway, and knock the critics on their ears with your brilliant designs. You will become the toast of Broadway and live the good life happily ever after. But what are the chances the plan will follow a straight line to that dreamed of conclusion? I can tell you about all the different media that use the skills you learn in theatre school. I can help direct you to resources that could be helpful to you for getting clients and employment in your field. But what I can't do, nor can your teachers, is force you to keep your mind's eye wide open to the possibilities around you.

If you are so narrowly focused that you refuse to see anything else but a straight-line path to Broadway, fine, go for it! Maybe some of the things I have shown you will help accelerate your meteoric rise. Use the marketing and interpersonal skills we have discussed. Create yourself a sound financial base to sustain that climb to Broadway.

But here is a thought: Broadway is NOT the single Holy Grail. There are other mountains to climb, other creative challenges that can fulfill the needs of your creative right brains while making your lives exciting and rewarding. What is so wonderful is that in today's business climate you can now climb several mountains at the same time while keeping a spyglass trained on that one radiant pinnacle of design nirvana you long to achieve. And guess what: one day you may wake up and say to yourself, I've done pretty darn well, and I am happy. Be happy with life before anything else—because I don't believe they will ever build statues to a Broadway designer, only composers! Have a great career and a full life.

Epilogue

I feel very strongly that we, as designers and production and stage managers, must be aware of the business of theatrical design, as I have presented it in the book. But I am not advocating we make this a priority in our professional lives. We must balance the business needs with the fun and joy of our creative work. Never lose the "child" in the designer, nor the "master" in the manager. We can combine both to make our lives more fulfilled and free.

BIBLIOGRAPHY

ACCOUNTING

Accounting Edge, Version 2.0. Rockaway, N.J.: MYOB Technology Ltd., 2001.

Dixon, L. Robert, and Harold E. Arnett. *The McGraw-Hill 36-Hour Accounting Course.* New York: McGraw-Hill, 1979.

Federal Travel Regulations, Chapter 301-7. Washington, D.C.: Government Printing Office, 2001.

Minbiole, Elizabeth A. *Accounting Principles I.* Lincoln, Nebr.: Cliffs Notes Inc., 1998.

Peachtree Accounting 2002. Norcross, Ga.: Peachtree Software, Inc., 2002.

QuickBooks. Mountain View, Calif.: Intuit, Inc., 2002.

BUSINESS

Abrams, Rhonda. *The Successful Business Plan: Secrets and Strategies.* Palo Alto, Calif.: Running 'R' Media Publishing, 2000.

California Business Adviser. Tiburon, Calif.: Employer Resource Institute Inc., 1998.

Crawford, Tad. *The Money Mentor: A Tale of Finding Financial Freedom.* New York: Allworth Press, 2001.

DuBoff, Leonard. *The Performing Arts Business Encyclopedia.* New York: Allworth Press, 1996.

Grant, Daniel. *The Business of Being an Artist.* New York: Allworth Press, 2000.

Stasiowski, Frank A. *Starting a New Design Firm, or Risking It All.* New York: John Wiley & Sons, Inc., 1994.

LAW

Black, Henry Campbell. *Black's Law Dictionary.* St. Paul, Minn.: West Publishing Inc., 1968.

Fishman, Stephen. *Consultant and Independent Contractor Agreements.* Berkeley, Calif.: Nolo, 2000.

Fishman, Stephen. *Hiring Independent Contractors: the Employer's Legal Guide.* Third edition. Berkeley, Calif.: Nolo, 2001.

Holtz, Herman. *Consulting Contracts.* Chicago: Upstart Publishing Company, 1997.

White, James L., and Robert S. Summers. *Handbook of the Law under the Uniform Commercial Code.* St. Paul, Minn.: West Publishing Company, 1972.

MARKETING

Ball, Frederich, and Barbara Ball. *Killer Interviews*. New York: McGraw-Hill, 1996.

Beckwith, Harry. *Selling the Invisible*. New York: Warner Bros., 1997.

Bly, Robert W. *Selling Your Services*. New York: Henry Holt and Company, LLC, 1991.

Hiebinger, Roman G., Jr., and Scott W. Cooper. *The Successful Marketing Plan*. Lincolnwood, Ill.: NTC Business Books, 1997.

Kozicki, Stephen. *Creative Negotiating*. Holbrook, Mass.: Adams Media Corporation,1998.

Maiman, William. "Tell Someone!" *Protocol,* Fall 2001: 38-39.

McGaulley, Michael T. *Selling 101*. Holbrook, Mass.: Adams Media Corporation, 1995.

Qubein, Nido R. *How to Be a Great Communicator.* New York: John Wiley & Sons, Inc., 1997.

Reck, Ross R., and Brian G. Long. *The WIN-WIN Negotiator.* New York: Pocket Books, 1987.

Shenson, Howard L. *The Contract and Fee-Setting Guide for Consultants and Professionals.* New York: John Wiley & Sons, Inc., 1990.

Shenson, Howard L. *The Successful Consultant's Guide to Fee Setting*. Washington, D.C.: Bermont Books, Inc., 1980.

Ury, William. *Getting Past NO*. New York: Penguin Books, 1991.

Ury, William and Roger Fisher. *Getting to YES*. New York: Penguin Books, 1998.

PSYCHOLOGY

Argyle, Michael. *The Psychology of Interpersonal Behavior.* Baltimore, Md.: Pelican Publications, 1967.

Bolton, Robert. *People Skills*. Englewood Cliffs, N.J.: Prentice Hall Inc., 1987.

Nierenberg, Gerold I., and Henry H. Calero. *How to Read a Person Like a Book*. New York: Pocket Books, 1971.

THEATRE

Cunningham, James G. "Some Tips for the New College TD/Designer." *Theatre Design & Technology,* Fall 2001: 26-33.

Designer's Resource Booklet. New York: United Scenic Artists, USA-829, 2001.

Dexter, Paul. "Is There Life after Rock'N'Roll Touring?" *Pro Lights & Staging News,* August 2000: 40.

Dexter, Paul A. "Laughter and Common Sense" *Pro Lights & Staging News,* November 2001: 48.

Ferreira, Ted. "Western Philosophy." *Entertainment Design Magazine,* November 2000: 28-33.

Kellogg, Marjorie Bradley. "Design and the Bottom Line." *American Theatre Magazine,* November 2001: 34-37.

Literkort, Ingrid, ed. *Theatre Words*. Amsterdam: OISTAT, 1995.

Moody, James L. *Concert Lighting: Technique, Art, and Business*. Second edition. Boston: Focal Press, 1998.

Parker, W. Oren, and R. Craig Wolf. *Scene Design and Stage Lighting*. Seventh edition. Fort Worth, Tex.: Harcourt Brace College Publishers, 1996.

APPENDIX

The preceding bibliography has all the books that were quoted in this book, and the following five appendixes will be an additional useful reference. The list of associations and organizations was compiled with the generous assistance of the USITT. For up-to-date accuracy, check the contact information for listings, as they occasionally move or disband. The current list contains over sixty groups, and I am confident there are many more.

A list of many of the theatrical unions, guilds, and associations follows. Since the IA has over five hundred locals alone, this list is limited to some of the locals that are most germane to the search for specific craft, design specialty, or technical skills that are covered in this text.

Next is a list of magazines and periodicals that are commercial in nature and not believed to be associated with any of the nonprofit organizations I listed in chapter 13. Due to the very nature of business publishing, this can never be a complete list; periodicals come and go. Many of these are published by firms who also publish annuals and resource books, either under the name of the magazine or another title. Write or go online to the publisher's Web site to get a full list of what may be available. I am not as knowledgeable as I would like to be about non-English language publications. You will need to find those on your own by reading other publications, articles, and books that make reference to them, or in ads in other publications.

Lastly, I have separated the list of book publishers that currently produce books of interest to theatre design and the technical community, and another for business book publishers. There are a lot of universities that have their own publishing operations, and I do not have room to list them all; for that, I apologize. I trust that these will be useful in your continuing education, a process that is never complete! Good luck.

Associations and Organizations

Academy of Motion Picture Arts and Sciences
8949 Wilshire Boulevard
Beverly Hills, CA 90211-1972
Tel 310-247-3000
Fax 310-859-9619
Web *www.oscars.org*

Academy of Television Arts and Sciences
5220 Lankershim Boulevard
North Hollywood, CA 91601-3109
Tel 818-754-2800
Fax 818-761-2827
Web *www.emmys.tv*

Alliance of Resident Theatres
131 Varick Street, Room 904
New York, NY 10013
Tel 212-989-5257

Alliance of Special Effects and Pyrotechnic Operators
12522 Moorpark Street, Suite 111
Studio City, CA 91604
Tel 818-506-8173
Fax 818-769-9438

American Alliance for Theatre and Education
Theatre Department
Arizona State University
P.O. Box 872002
Tempe, AZ 85287-2002
Tel 602-965-6064

American Arts Alliance
805 15th Street NW, Suite 500
Washington, DC 20005
Web *www.artswire.com*

American Association of Community Theatres
8402 Briarwood Circle
Lago Vista, TX 78645
Tel 512-267-0711
Web *www.aact.org*

American Association of Producers
15030 Ventura Boulevard, Suite 675
Sherman Oaks, CA 91403
Tel 818-503-6102
Web *www.tvproducers.net*

American College Theatre Festival
Kennedy Center
2700 F Street, NW
Washington, DC 20566
Tel 202-416-8857
Fax 202-416-8802

American Film Institute
2021 N. Western Avenue
Los Angeles, CA 90027
Tel 323-856-7600
Fax 323-467-4578
Web *www.afi.com*

The American Society of Cinematography
5700 Wilshire Boulevard, Suite 600
Los Angeles, CA 90038
Tel 323-634-3400
Fax 323-634-3550
Web *www.cinematographer.com*

The American Society of Theatre Consultants
Theatre Projects Consultants, Inc.
6600 Manor Hill Court
Chapel Hill, NC 27516

American Society for Theatre Research
Web *www.music.uiuc/theatre/astr*

Americans for the Arts
1000 Vermont Avenue NW, 12th Floor
Washington, DC 20005
Tel 202-371-2830
Web *www.artsusa.org*

American Women in Radio and Television
1595 Spring Hill Road, Suite 330
Vienna, VA 22182
Tel 703-506-3290
Fax 703-506-3266
Web *www.awrt.org*

Arts and Science Collaboration Inc.
P.O. Box 358
Staten Island, NY 10301-3225
Tel 718-816-9796
Web *www.asci.org*

Arts International
809 United Nations Plaza
New York, NY 10017
Tel 212-984-5370
Web *www.iie.org/ai*

Association of Arts Administration Educators
Box 78
525 W. 120th Street
Dept. of Arts and Humanities
Teachers College
Columbia University
New York, NY 10027
Tel 212-678-3271
E-mail jj64@columbia.edu

The Association of British Theatre Technicians
47 Bermondsey Street
London SE1 3XT
United Kingdom
Tel 020-7403-3778
Fax 020-7378-6170
Web *www.abtt.org.uk*

Association of Lighting Designers
P.O. Box 89
Welwyn Garden City AL7 1DG
United Kingdom
Tel 01-707-891848
Fax 01-707-891848
Web *www.ald.org.uk*

Association of Local Television Stations
1320 19th Street NW
Washington, DC 20036
Tel 202-887-1970
Fax 202-887-0950
Web *www.altv.com*

Association of Performing Arts Presenters
1112 16th Street NW, Suite 400
Washington, DC 20036
Tel 202-833-2787
Web *www.artspresenters.org*

Association of Theatres in Higher Education
P.O. Box 4537
Boulder, CO 80306-4537
Tel 888-284-3737
Web *www.hawaii.edu/athe*

Association of Theatrical Artists and Craftspeople
225 West 70th Street, Suite 6C
New York, NY 10023-4374
Tel 212-591-1626
Web *www.theatreweb.com/atac*

Audio Engineering Society
60 East 42nd Street, Room 2520
New York, NY 10165-2520
Tel 212-661-8528
Fax 212-682-0477
Web *www.aes.org*

Black Theatre Network
3705 Holly Vista Drive
Highland, CA 92346
Tel 909-880-5893
Web *www.btnet.org*

Canadian Institute for Theatre Technology
132 St. Clements Avenue
Toronto, ON M4R 1H2
Canada
Tel 416-485-4435
Fax 416-485-5228
Web *www.culturenet.ca.citt*

Central Florida Theatre Alliance
398 W. Amelia Street
Orlando, FL 32801
Tel 407-872-2382
Web *www.OrlandoTheatre.com*

Cinema Audio Society
12414 Huston Street
Valley Village, CA 91607
Tel 818-752-8624
Fax 818-752-8624
Web *www.ideabuzz.com/cas*

Conference of Personal Managers
12358 Ventura Boulevard, Suite 611
Studio City, CA 91604
Tel 310-275-2456
Fax 818-765-2903
Web *www.personalmanagers.org*

The Costume Society of America
55 Edgewater Drive
P.O. Box 73
Earleville, MD 21919
Tel 800-272-9447
Fax 410-275-8936
Web *www.costumesocietyamerica.com*

The Costume Society of Great Britain
56 Wareham Road
Lytchett Matavers Pool
Dorset BH16 6DS
England
Web *www.costumesociety.org.uk*

Educational Theatre Association
2343 Auburn Avenue
Cincinnati, OH 45219-2819
Tel 513-421-3900
Web *www.etassoc.org*

Entertainment Services and Technology Association
875 Sixth Avenue, Suite 2302
New York, NY 10001
Tel 212-244-1505
Fax 212-244-1502
Web *www.esta.org*

Illuminating Engineering Society of North America
120 Wall Street, Floor 17
New York, NY 10005
Tel 212-248-5000
Fax 212-248-5017/18
Web *www.iesna.org*

The Institute of Outdoor Drama
1700 Airport Road, CB #3240
UNC-Chapel Hill
Chapel Hill, NC 26599-3240
Tel 919-962-1328
Web *www.unc.edu/depts/outdoor/*

International Association for the Leisure and Entertainment Industry
33 Henniker Street
Hillsboro, NH 03244
Tel 888-464-6498
Web *www.ialei.org*

International Association of Amusement Parks and Attractions
1448 Duke Street
Alexandria, VA 22314
Tel 703-836-4800
Web *www.iaapa.org*

International Association of Assembly Managers
635 Fritz Drive
Coppell, TX 75019
Tel 800-935-4226
Web *www.iaam.org*

International Association of Lighting Designers
The Merchandise Mart, Suite 9-104
200 World Trade Center
Chicago, IL 60654
Tel 312-527-3677
Fax 312-527-3680
Web *www.iald.org*

The International Costumers' Guild
7348 Milwood Avenue, #1
Canoga Park, CA 91303-3426
Web *www.costume.org*

International Organization of Scenographers, Theatre Architects, and Technicians
P.O. Box 15172
1001 MD
Amsterdam
The Netherlands
Tel 31-74-2525095
Fax 31-26-4457235
Web *www.oistat.nl*

International Society of Ticket Vendors
250 West 57th Street, Suite 722
New York, NY 10107
Tel 212-572-0600
Web *www.intix.org*

League of American Theatre Producers
226 West 47th Street
New York, NY 10036
Tel 212-764-1122
Web *www.broadway.org/league*

League of Historic American Theatres
34 Market Place, Suite 320
Baltimore, MD 21202
Tel 410-659-9533
Web *www.ihat.org*

Music Video Production Association
940 N. Orange Drive #104
Hollywood, CA 90038
Tel 323-660-9311
Fax 323-660-9357
Web *www.mvpa.com*

National Association of Broadcasters
1771 N. Street, NW
Washington, DC 20036
Tel 800-342-2460
Fax 202-429-3922
Web *www.nab.org*

New England Theatre Conference
c/o Department of Theatre
Northeastern University
360 Huntington Avenue
Boston, MA 02115
Tel 617-424-9275

New York Women in Film and Television
Tel 212-679-0870
Fax 212-679-0899
Web *www.nywift.org*

Opera America
1156 15th Street NW, Suite 810
Washington, DC 20005
Tel 202-293-4466
Web *www.operaam.org*

Production Equipment Rental Association
P.O. Box 55515
Sherman Oaks, CA 91413
Tel 818-806-2467
Web *www.productionequipment.com*

Set Decorators Society of America
8687 Melrose Avenue, Suite MB28
Los Angeles, CA 90069
Tel 310-289-1959
Fax 310-289-1076

The Stage Managers' Association
P.O. Box 2234
Times Square Station
New York, NY 10108-2020
Tel 212-543-9567
Web *www.stagemanagers.org*

The Society of British Theatre Designers
47 Bermondsey Street
London SE1 3XT
United Kingdom
Tel 020-7403-3778
Fax 020-7378-6170
Web *www.theatredesign.org.uk*

Society of Stage Directors and Choreographers
1501 Broadway, Suite 1701
New York, NY 10036-5653
Tel 212-391-1070
Web *www.ssdc.org*

Southeastern Theatre Conference
P.O. Box 9868
Greensboro, NC 27429-0868
Tel 336-272-3645
Web *www.setc.org*

Southwest Theatre Association
3000 General Pershing Boulevard
Oklahoma City, OK 73107-6202
Tel 405-946-9380
E-mail swtajimmyv@theshop.net

Texas Educational Theatre Association
Box 15990 NE Station
Austin, TX 78761
Web *www.tetatx.com*

Theatre Communications Group
355 Lexington Avenue
New York, NY 10017
Tel 212-697-5230
Web *www.tcg.org*

Theatre Historical Society of America
152 North York Road, Suite 200
Elmhurst, IL 60126
Tel 630-782-1800

The Themed Entertainment Association
P.O. Box 11148
Burbank, CA 91510-1148
Tel 818-843-8497
Fax 818-843-8477
Web *www.themeit.com*

United States Institute for Theatre Technology
6443 Ridings Road
Syracuse, NY 13206-1111
Tel 315-463-6525
Fax 315-463-6463
Web *www.usitt.org*

University/Resident Theatre Association
1560 Broadway, Suite 414
New York, NY 10036
Tel 212-221-1130
Fax 212-869-2752
Web *www.urta.com*

Western States Arts Foundation
1543 Champa Street, Suite 220
Denver, CO 80202
Tel 303-629-1166
Fax 303-629-9717
Web *www.westaf.org*

World Waterpark Association
P.O. Box 14826
Lenexa, KS 66285
Tel 913-599-0300
Fax 913-599-0520
Web *www.waterparks.com*

Theatrical Unions, Guilds, and Associations

Actors' Equity Association (Los Angeles)
5757 Wilshire Boulevard, Suite 1
Los Angeles, CA 90036
Tel 323-634-1750
Fax 323-634-1777
Web *www.actorsequity.org*

Actors' Equity Association (New York)
165 W. 46th Street
New York, NY 10036
Tel 212-869-8530
Fax 212-719-9815

Costume Designers Guild
13949 Ventura Boulevard, Suite 309
Sherman Oaks, CA 905-1560
Tel 818-905-1557
Fax 818-905-1560
E-mail cdgia@msn.com

Equity (Great Britain)
Guild House
Upper St. Martins Lane
London WC2H 9EG
England
Tel 020-7379-6000
Fax 020-7379-7001
Web *www.equity.org.uk*

I.A.T.S.E. (International Alliance of Theatrical Stage Employees, Moving Picture Technicians, Artists and Allied Crafts of the United States, Its Territories and Canada, AFL-CIO, CLC)
International Offices
1430 Broadway, 20th Floor
New York, NY 10018
Tel 212-730-1770
Fax 212-730-7809
Web *www.iatse.lm.com*

I.A.T.S.E. Local #1 (New York Area)
320 West 46th Street
New York, NY 10036-8399
Tel 212-333-2500
Fax 212-586-2437
Web *www.iatse-licat1.org*

I.A.T.S.E. Local #33 (Los Angeles Area)
1720 West Magnolia Boulevard
Burbank, CA 91505-1871
Tel 818-841-9233
Fax 818-567-1138
Web *www.ia33.org*

I.A.T.S.E. Local #705 (Motion Picture Costumers)
1427 N. La Brea Avenue
Hollywood, CA 90028
Tel 323-851-0220
Fax 323-851-9062

I.A.T.S.E. Local #768 (Theatrical Wardrobe Union)
13245 Riverside Drive, Suite 300
Sherman Oaks, CA 91423
Tel 818-789-8735
Fax 818-789-1928

I.A.T.S.E. Local #816 (Scenic Artists)
11969 Ventura Boulevard, Suite 204
Studio City, CA 91604-8161
Tel 818-487-8161
Fax 818-487-8161
Web *www.artist816.org*

I.A.T.S.E. Local #876 (Art Directors)
11969 Ventura Boulevard, Suite 200
Studio City, CA 91604
Tel 818-762-9995
Fax 818-762-9997

I.A.T.S.E. local #892 (Costume Designers Guild)
4730 Woodman Avenue, Suite 430
Sherman Oaks, CA 91423
Tel 818-905-1557
Fax 818-905-1560

I.B.E.W. (International Brotherhood of Electrical Workers)
Local #45 (Western States)
6255 Sunset Boulevard
Hollywood, CA 90028
Tel 323-851-5515
Fax 323-466-1793
Web *www.ibew45.org*

International Photographers Guild
I.A. Local #600 (National Camera Local)—Los Angeles
National Office
7715 Sunset Boulevard, Suite 300
Hollywood, CA 90046
Tel 323-876-0160
Fax 323-876-6383
Web *www.cameraguild.com*

I.A. Local #600—New York
Regional Office
16 West 61st Street
New York, NY 10023
Tel 212-581-0300
Fax 212-977-0211

I.A. Local #600—Chicago
Regional Office
203 N. Wabash, Suite 1210
Chicago, IL 60601
Tel 312-857-0829
Fax 312-857-0819

I.A. Local #600—Miami
Regional Office
10459 S.W. 78th Street
Miami, FL 33173
Tel 305-596-4772
Fax 305-596-6095

I.A. Local #600—Boston
Regional Office
304 Newberry Street, Box 380
Boston, MA 02111
Tel 401-351-9294
Fax 401-351-9294

National Association of Broadcast Employees and Technicians (NABET-CWA)
501 Third Street, N.W.
Washington, D.C. 20001
Web *http://union.nabetcaw.org*

NABET-CWA Local 43
20833 Southfield Road
Southfield, MI 48075
Tel 248-557-0735
Fax 248-424-8585
Web *www.nabet-cwa43.org*

NABET-CWA Local 57
3210 West Burbank Boulevard, Suite D
Burbank, CA 91505
Tel 818-567-9935
Fax 818-567-9965
Web *www.nabet57.com*

U.S.A. (United Scenic Artists) I.A. Local USA-829
National Office
16 West 61st Street
New York, NY 10023
Tel 212-581-0300
Fax 212-977-2011
Web *www.usa829.org*

U.S.A. Local USA-829—Chicago
Regional Office
203 N. Wabash, Suite 1210
Chicago, IL 60601
Tel 312-857-0829
Fax 312-857-0819

U.S.A. Local USA-829—Los Angeles
Regional Office
5225 Wilshire Boulevard, Suite 506
Los Angeles, CA 90036
Tel 323-965-0957
Fax 323-965-0958

U.S.A. Local USA-829—Miami
Regional Office
10459 S.W. 78th Street
Miami, FL 33173
Tel 305-596-4772
Fax 305-596-6095

U.S.A. Local USA-829—New England
Regional Office
304 Newbury Street, Box 380
Boston, MA 02111
Tel 401-351-9294
Fax 401-351-9294

Commercial Publications: Magazines, Periodicals, and Resource Publications

Amusement Business
P.O. Box 24970
Nashville, TN 37202
Tel 800-407-6874
Web *www.amusementbusiness.com*

Archi*Tech
P.O. Box 10915
Portland, ME 04104
Tel 207-761-2177
Web *www.architechmag.com*

Architectural Digest
6300 Wilshire Boulevard
Los Angeles, CA 90048
Published by
The Condé Nast Publications Inc.
4 Times Square
New York, NY 10036
Web *www.archdigest.com*

Audience
Miracle Publishing Ltd.
1 York Street
London W1U 6PA
United Kingdom
Tel 44(0)-207486-8008
Fax 44(0)-207486-2002
Web *www.audience.uk.com*

Backstage and *BackstageWest*
5055 Wilshire Boulevard.
Los Angeles, CA 90036
Tel 323-525-2225
Web *www.backstage.com*

Billboard
770 Broadway
New York, NY 10003
Web *www.billboard.com*

The Blue-Book Directory
5055 Wilshire Boulevard
Los Angeles, CA 90036
Tel 323-536-2000

Business Resource Book
Hollywood Chamber of Commerce
7018 Hollywood Boulevard
Hollywood, CA 90028
Tel 213-469-8311

Church Production
P.O. Box 66
Benton Harbor, MI 49023
Web *www.churchproduction.com*

Contract
One Penn Plaza
New York, NY 19119
Tel 212-714-1300

Creative Industry Handbook
3518 Cahuenga Boulevard West, Suite 203
Los Angeles, CA 90068
Published by GMM Inc.
Tel 323-874-1600
Web *www.creativehandbook.com*

Digital Cinema
Published by
Entertainment Technology Network
460 Park Avenue S., 9th Floor
New York, NY 10016
Tel 212-378-0400
Web *www.digitalcinemamag.com*

Display & Design Ideas
1115 Northmeadow Parkway
Roswell, GA 30076
Tel 800-241-9034
Fax 770-777-8828
Web *www.ddimagazine.com*

Entertainment Design
Published by
INTERTEC Publishing
32 West 18th Street
New York, NY 10011-4612
Tel 212-229-2965
Web *www.entertainmentdesignmag.com*

Event Solutions
5440 S. Lakeshore Drive, Suite 101
Tempe, AZ 85283
Tel 480-831-5100
Web *www.event-solutions.com*

HL&A Contract Lighting
1011 Clifton Avenue
Clifton, NJ 07013
Published by
Doctorow Communications Inc.
P.O. Box 2147
Clifton, NJ 07015
Tel 973-779-1600
Web *www.contractlighting.com*

The Hollywood Reporter
5055 Wilshire Boulevard
Los Angeles, CA 90036-4396
Tel 323-526-2000
Web *www.hollywoodreporter.com*

Interiors
770 Broadway
New York, NY 10003
Published by
Bill Communications
Tel 646-654-5786

Interiors & Sources
Published by
L.C. Clark Publishing Co.
840 U.S. Hwy. One, Suite 330
North Palm Beach, FL 33408-3834

LA Architect
Balcony Press
512 E. Wilson, Suite 306
Glendale, CA 91206
Tel 818-956-5313
E-mail danette@balconypress.com

Landscape Architect
14771 Plaza Drive, Suite M
Tustin, CA 92780
Web *www.landscapeonline.com*

Latin Heat
146 North San Fernando Boulevard, Suite 201
Burbank, CA 91502
Tel 818-846-9258
Web *www.latinheat.com*

LA Stage
644 S. Figueroa Street
Los Angeles, CA 90017
Tel 213-614-0556
Web *www.theatreLA.org*

Lighting Dimensions
32 West 18th Street
New York, NY 10011-4612
Tel 212-229-2965
Web *www.lightingdimensions.com*

Location Update
7021 Havenhurst, Suite 205
Van Nuys, CA 91406-3802
Tel 818-785-6362
Fax 818-785-8092
Web *www.cineweb.com*

Makeup Artists Magazine
P.O. Box 4316
Sun Valley, CA 91041-4316
Tel 818-504-6770
Web *www.makeupmag.com*

Millimeter
P.O. Box 1170
Skokie, IL 60076-8170
Fax 847-647-7543
Web *www.millimeter.com*

MIX Magazine
P.O. Box 1939
Marion, OH 43306
Tel 800-532-8190
Fax 740-382-3322
Web *www.mixm@kable.com*

OnStage Magazine
32 W. 18th Street
New York, NY 1001
Tel 800-441-0294
Web *www.onstagemag.com*

Pacific Coast Studio Directory
P.O. Box V
Pine Mountain, CA 93222-0022
Tel 661-242-2722
Fax 661-242-2724
Web *www.studio-directory.com*

Performance Magazine
1101 University, Suite 108
Ft. Worth, TX 76107-4272
Web *www.performancemagazine.com*

Pollstar
4697 W. Jacquelyn
Fresno, CA 93722
Web *www.pollstar.com*

Production on Location
7021 Havenhurst, Suite 205
Van Nuys, CA 91406-3802
Tel 818-785-6362
Fax 818-785-8092
Web *www.cineweb.com*

Professional Lighting
23 Hannover Drive, #7
St. Catharines
Ontario L2W 1A3
Canada
Tel 905-641-3471
Published by
Norris-Whitney Communications Inc.
Web *www.professional-lighting.com*

Pro Lights & Staging News
18425 Burbank Boulevard, Suite 813
Tarzana, CA 91356
Published by
Timeless Communications Inc.
Tel 818-654-2474

ShowBiz Digest
34 West 13th Street
New York, NY 10011
Tel 212-656-1568
Web *www.showbizdigest.com*

Stage Directions
Published by
Lifestyle Ventures LLC
250 W. 57th Street, Suite 420
New York, NY 10107
Tel 212-265-8890
Web *www.stagedirections.com*

Television Broadcast
460 Park Avenue South
New York, NY 10016
Tel 212-378-0400
Fax 212-378-2158
Web *www.televisionbroadcast.com*

Total Production
P.O. Box 5435
Southend-on-Sea
SS1 3HW
United Kingdom
Tel 44(0)-170246-7111
Published by
Mondiale Publishing Ltd.
E-mail m.cunningham@mondiale.co.uk

Tour Guide
107 Music City Circle, Suite 305
Nashville, TN 37214
Tel 615-321-4787
Fax 615-321-5975
Web *www.tourguidemag.com*

Variety
5700 Wilshire Boulevard, Suite 120
Los Angeles, CA 90036
Tel 323-965-4476
Web *www.variety.com*

Videography
460 Park Avenue, South
New York, NY 10016
Tel 212-378-0400
Fax 212-378-2158
Web *www.videography.com*

VM+SD
Visual Merchandising and Store Design
407 Gilbert Avenue
Cincinnati, OH 45202
Tel 513-421-2050
Web *www.visualstore.com*

Publishers of Theatre and Entertainment Books

Allworth Press
10 E. 23rd Street, Suite 510
New York, NY 10010
Tel 212-777-8395
Web *www.allworth.com*

Allyn and Bacon Inc.
75 Arlington Street, Suite 300
Boston, MA 02116
Tel 617-848-6000
Web *www.ablongman.com*

Back Stage Books
770 Broadway, 8th Floor
New York, NY 10003
Tel 646-654-5452
Web *www.watsonguptill.com*

Betterway Books
F&W Publishing
1507 Dana Avenue
Cincinnati, OH 45207
Tel 800-289-0963
Web *www.writersdigest.com*

BroadStreet Books
P.O. Box 41075
Philadelphia, PA 19127

Broadway Press
3001 Springcrest Drive
Louisville, KY 40241-2755
Tel 502-426-1211
Web *www.broadwaypress.com*

Broadway Television Network
268 W. 44th Street, 3rd Floor
New York, NY 10036
Tel 212-471-6060
Web *www.broadwayonline.com*

By Design Press
Quite Specific Media Group Ltd.
7 Old Fulton Street
Brooklyn Heights, NY 11201
Tel 718-237-0264

Currency Press
P.O. Box 2287
Strawberry Hills, NSW 2012
Australia
Tel 61-293-195-877
Web *www.currency.com.au*

Drama Book Shop Inc.
723 7th Avenue
New York, NY 10019
Tel 800-322-0595
Web *www.dramabookshop.com*

Drama Book Specialists
150 W. 52nd Street
New York, NY 10019

Entertainment Technology Press Ltd.
1 Kiln House Yard
Baldock Street
Royston
Hertfordshire, SG8 5AY
Web *www.etnow.com*

Focal Press
225 Wildwood Avenue
Woburn, MA 01801
Tel 800-366-2665
Web *www.bh.com*

Globalstage Productions
1210 Union Street
San Francisco, CA 94109
Tel 415-749-6840
Web *www.globalstage.net*

Harcourt Brace College Publishers
6277 Sea Harbor Drive
Orlando, FL 32887-6777
Tel 800-782-4479
Web *www.harcourt.com*

Heinemann
361 Hanover Street
Portsmouth, NH 03801-3912
Tel 800-541-2086
Web *www.heinemann.com*

John Wiley & Sons Inc.
Wiley-Interscience Publishing
605 Third Avenue
New York, NY 10158-0012
Tel 212-850-6000
Web *www.wiley.com*

Little, Brown & Co.
3 Center Plaza
Boston, MA 02108
Tel 67-227-0730
Web *www.littlebrown.co.uk*

Mayfield Publishing Co.
1280 Villa Street
Mountain View, CA 94041
Web *www.mayfieldpub.com*

McGraw-Hill Book Company
P.O. Box 182604
Columbus, OH 43272
Tel 877-833-5524
Web *www.mcgraw-hill.com*

Meriwether Publishing Ltd.
885 Elkton Drive
Colorado Springs, CO 80907
Tel 800-937-5297
Web *www.meriwetherpublishing.com*

Nathan Muchnick, Inc.
1725 Chestnut Street
Philadelphia, PA 19103
Tel 800-373-9873

Northwestern University Press
625 Colfax Street
Evanston, IL 60208
Tel 847-491-2046
Web *www.nupress.northwestern.edu*

Pacific NW Theatre Associates, Inc.
333 Westlake Ave. N.
Seattle, WA 98109
Tel 800-622-7850
Web *www.pnta.com*

Prentice-Hall Inc.
One Lake Street
Upper Saddle River, NJ 07458
Tel 800-282-0693
Web *www.prenhall.com*

Prestel Verlag
Mandlstrasse 36
Munich
Germany 80802
Tel 089-38-1709-0

16 West 22nd Street
New York, NY 10010
Tel 212-627-8199

Quite Specific Media
7 Old Fulton Street
Brooklyn Heights, NY 11201
Tel 718-237-0264
Web *www.quitespecificmedia.com*

R.A.T. (Book Stands) Ltd.
16 Melville Road
London SW13 9RL
United Kingdom
Tel 44(0)-181741-4804
Web *www.ratstands.com*

R.L. Shep Publications
P.O. Box 2706
Fort Bragg, CA 95437
Tel 707-964-8662
Web *www.rlshep.com*

Scarecrow Press
4720 Boston Way
Lanham, MD 20706-4310
Tel 301-459-3366
Web *www.scarecrowpress.com*

SECOA
8650 109th Avenue, N.
Champlin, MN 55316-3789
Tel 800-328-5519
Web *www.secoa.com*

Simon & Schuster Co.
Pocket Books
1230 Avenue of the Americas
New York, NY 10020

Sound Ideas
105 W. Beaver Creek Road, Suite 4
Richmond Hills
Ontario L4B 1C6
Canada
Tel 800-387-3030
Web *www.sound-ideas.com*

Southern Illinois University Press
P.O. Box 3697
Carbondale, IL 62902-3697
Tel 618-453-2281
Fax 618-453-1221
Web *www.siu.edu/-siupress*

Stage and Screen/Bookspan
401 Franklin Avenue
Garden City, NY 11530
Tel 516-490-4700
Web *www.stagenscreen.com*

Theatre Arts Video Library
174 Andrew Avenue
Leucadia, CA 92024
Tel 800-456-8285
Web *www.theatreartsvideo.com*

Theatre Directories
P.O. Box 510
Dorset, VT 05251
Tel 802-867-2223
Web *www.theatredirectories.com*

University of Chicago Press
1427 E. 60th Street
Chicago, IL 60637
Tel 773-702-7700
Web *www.press.uchicago.edu*

University of Michigan Press
839 Green Street
Ann Arbor, MI 48106-1104
Tel 734-764-4388
Web *www.press.umich.edu*

Publishers of Business Books

Adams Media Corp.
260 Center Street
Holbrook, MA 02343
Tel 800-872-5627
Web *www.adamsmedia.com*

Bermont Books, Inc.
815 15th Street, NW
Washington, DC 20005

Cliffs Notes Inc.
Hungry Minds
909 Third Avenue
New York, NY 10022
Web *www.cliffsnotes.com*

Henry Holt & Co., LLC
115 West 18th Street
New York, NY 10011

Nolo (Law Books)
950 Parker Street
Berkeley, California 94710-9867

NTC Business Books
4255 West Touhy Avenue
Lincolnwood, IL 60646

Penguin Books USA, Inc.
375 Hudson Street
New York, NY 10014
Web *www.penguinputnam.com*

Random House Inc.
Dell Publishing Group
Bantam Books
1540 Broadway
New York, NY 10036
Tel 212-782-9000
Web *www.randomhouse.com*

Running 'R' Media
555 Bryant Street, Suite 180
Palo Alto, CA 94301
Tel 650-330-1030

Upstart Publishing Company
A Division of Dearborn Publishing Group, Inc.
155 North Wacker Drive
Chicago, IL 60606-1719

INDEX

BOOKS FROM ALLWORTH PRESS

The Stage Producer's Business and Legal Guide
   by Charles Grippo (paperback, 6 x 9, 256 pages, $19.95)

Building the Successful Theater Company
   by Lisa Mulcahy (paperback, 6 x 9, 240 pages, $19.95)

Movement for Actors
   edited by Nicole Potter (paperback, 6 x 9, 288 pages, $19.95)

Producing Your Own Showcase
   by Paul Harris (paperback, 6 x 9, 224 pages, $18.95)

Technical Theater for Nontechnical People
   by Drew Campbell (paperback, 6 x 9, 256 pages, $18.95)

The Health & Safety Guide for Film, TV & Theater
   by Monona Rossol (paperback, 6 x 9, 256 pages, $19.95)

Career Solutions for Creative People
   by Dr. Rhonda Ormont (paperback, 6 x 9, 320 pages, $19.95)

Booking and Tour Management for the Performing Arts, Third Edition
   by Rena Shagan (paperback, 6 x 9, 288 pages, $19.95)

An Actor's Guide—Making It in New York City
   by Glenn Alterman (paperback, 6 x 9, 288 pages, $19.95)

Clues to Acting Shakespeare
   by Wesley Van Tassel (paperback, 6 x 9, 208 pages, $16.95)

Creating Your Own Monologue
   by Glenn Alterman (paperback, 6 x 9, 192 pages, $14.95)

Promoting Your Acting Career
   by Glen Alterman (paperback, 6 x 9, 224 pages, $18.95)

VO: Tales and Techniques of a Voice-Over Actor
   by Harlan Hogan (paperback, 6 x 9, 256 pages, $19.95)

Please write to request our free catalog. To order by credit card, call 1-800-491-2808 or send a check or money order to Allworth Press, 10 East 23rd Street, Suite 510, New York, NY 10010. Include $5 for shipping and handling for the first book ordered and $1 for each additional book. Ten dollars plus $1 for each additional book if ordering from Canada. New York State residents must add sales tax.

To see our complete catalog on the World Wide Web, or to order online, you can find us at www.allworth.com.